Franklin, Thomas Jefferson, John Hancock and many others.

This book makes it clear that the actual signing of the Declaration of Independence was the ratification of a series of events which made the Declaration inevitable, and that many of these acts were done at Washington's initiative and recommendation. For example, he suggested that Congress should make helping the king an act of treason, that Congress should establish a navy of its own, and that the Colonies should act against the Tories. These are only a few of the dozens of actions instigated by Washington which made conciliation impossible. Throughout it all, he understood the necessity of the civilian authority over the military, in order to prevent civil war by the citizenry and factional rivalries within the armed forces.

Professor Nettels's style is fluent and the material exciting. His book will appeal to the general reader of biography and history as well as to historians.

BOOKS BY

CURTIS P. NETTELS

The Roots of American Civilization
The Money Supply of the American Colonies
George Washington and American Independence

GEORGE WASHINGTON
and American Independence

From the Houdon Bust, modeled from life at Mount Vernon in 1785. Here reproduced by permission of the Mount Vernon Ladies' Association of the Union

George Washington
and American Independence

CURTIS P. NETTELS

WITH ILLUSTRATIONS

LITTLE, BROWN AND COMPANY · BOSTON · 1951

FIRST EDITION

Published simultaneously
in Canada by McClelland and Stewart Limited

PRINTED IN THE UNITED STATES OF AMERICA

TO

ELSA NETTELS

IN CONGRESS

We, reposing special trust and confidence in your patriotism, valor, conduct, and fidelity, do by these presents, constitute and appoint you to be General and Commander in chief, of the army of the United Colonies, and of all the forces now raised, or to be raised, by them, and of all others who shall voluntarily offer their service, and join the said Army for the Defense of American liberty, and for repelling every hostile invasion thereof: And you are hereby vested with full power and authority to act as you shall think for the good and welfare of the service.

— COMMISSION OF WASHINGTON AS COMMANDER IN CHIEF, JUNE 17, 1775

Contents

I	England on the Eve	3
II	The Court and the Colonies	24
III	April and May, 1775	47
IV	Washington	60
V	Congress Votes for War	81
VI	Parties in Congress	100
VII	Washington and Congress	121
VIII	The Generals	137
IX	Washington Acts	159
X	More Action	181
XI	A Setback	201
XII	Congress Bestirs Itself	217
XIII	The Militants and the South	235
XIV	Action in the South	244
XV	Action in the Center	262
XVI	The Last Act	280
	Notes	299
	Acknowledgments and Bibliography	313
	Index	325

Illustrations

George Washington — *Frontispiece*
John Wilkes — 10
Samuel Adams — 10
Concord and Lexington — 51
Washington and the West — 79
John Dickinson — 106
Richard Henry Lee — 106
Scene of Operations of the Army in the North — 162

GEORGE WASHINGTON
and American Independence

I. England on the Eve

What is England now? — A sink of Indian wealth, filled by nabobs and emptied by macaronis! A senate sold and despised . . . A gaming, robbing, wrangling, railing nation, without principles, genius, character, or allies.[1]

— HORACE WALPOLE

THE Seven Years' War, with its victories, its profiteering, and its spoils, left in its path in England a course of extravagance and dissipation without parallel in the country's history. A ruling class, imbued with a feeling of superiority that had been nourished by recent triumphs of British arms, pursued its quest for pleasure and intrigue, unrestrained by any strong opposing elements within the state. Lords, gentlemen, and *nouveaux riches,* scornful of the poor and lowly, asserted the right of nobility and wealth to rule, without question, those inferior beings, at home and in the colonies, who did the empire's work. "The unbounded riches of the many" afforded "the means of every species of luxury." "Clerks and factors from the East Indies, loaded with the spoil of plundered provinces; planters, Negro drivers, and hucksters from our American plantations, enriched they know not how; agents, commissaries, and contractors, who have fattened, in two successive wars, on the blood of the nation; usurers, brokers, and jobbers of every kind" had "found themselves suddenly translated into a state of affluence unknown to former ages."[2]

"Gaming," wrote Horace Walpole in 1774, "has exceeded its own outdoings. . . . One is tired of asking every day who has won or lost? And even the portentous sums they lose, cease to make impression."[3] The sensation of the gambling world, Charles James Fox, ran up debts of £140,000. A prominent minister of George III,

Lord Weymouth, often sat at the card table until six o'clock in the morning—and was so worn out the next day that he could not attend to the duties of his office. His life was described as "a long drawn-out debauch."[4] One of the gamblers, said Walpole, "has committed a murder, and intends to repeat it. He betted £1500 that a man could live twelve hours under water; hired a desperate fellow, sunk him in a ship by way of experiment, and both ship and man have not appeared since."[5]

Late in 1765 Lord Chesterfield heard of nothing in London "but the separation of men from their wives."[6] "Chastity is out of fashion," wrote Henry Laurens in 1771, "and women talk another language than that in which modesty was best understood twenty years ago."[7] When Thomas Hutchinson called upon the Lord President of the Privy Council at eleven o'clock one morning, a servant reported that his master was not yet stirring. "This," observed Hutchinson, "is the dissipated way of life of most of our great men at present."[8] Of the Duke of Grafton, the king's chief minister in the late 1760's, we read: "His frequent appearance in public with Nancy Parsons, a well-known courtesan, gave offense even to the laxer age in which he lived. His contemporaries beheld with surprise that woman seated at the head of the ducal table, or handed from the opera house by the first lord of the treasury in the presence of the queen."[9]

The riches of the few offered a tempting prey to numerous highwaymen who infested the roads, so audacious as to strike in the daytime. Bolder spirits among the opulent relied upon personal weapons; more timid souls traveled with armed guards. Even a short journey might turn into an adventure. Mobs that periodically gathered in London added to the excitement and insecurity, for though it was said that they would not attack a man during the day, they were not so restrained at night. In one letter in 1774 Walpole noted three attacks by highwaymen on important people. The prime minister, Lord North, was shot at and his postilion wounded. The ladies of the bedchamber dared "not go to the queen at Kew in an evening."[10]

In the span of six months after November 1774 a series of sensational happenings befell a number of great personages. News from the colonies at this time led Walpole to read such signs of the times as portents of disaster. "There are advices from America that are said to be extremely bad. . . . I fear we neither know how to proceed or retreat! . . . Within this week we have had two deaths out of the common cause." A certain Bradshaw, secretary to the Treasury, had shot himself. "His beginning was very obscure; when he grew more known, it was not to his honor. He has since been a very active minister, of the second or third class, and more trusted, perhaps, than some of a higher class. Instead of making a great fortune, he has spent one, and could not go on a week longer. The Duke of Athol is dead as suddenly; drowned certainly; whether delirious from a fever or from some disappointment, is not clear. Two evenings ago Lord Berkeley shot a highwayman: in short, frenzy is at work from top to bottom, and I doubt we shall not be cool till there has been a good deal of blood let. You and I shall, probably, not see the subsiding of the storm, if the humors do boil over; and can a nation be in a high fever without a crisis?"[11]

Hutchinson recorded in March 1775 that for several weeks the Earl of Chatham had been under doctors' treatment for insanity and had been kept in a strait jacket. From high officials Hutchinson learned soon afterward the story of the death of Lord Clive, famous for his victories over the French in India. "The whole story of laudanum was a fiction. He had been giving directions to his maid about writing a card a few minutes before his death: left her to go into his room, and she soon heard him fall . . . went in, and found him dead; his throat being cut, or terribly hacked with a knife used for erasing writings: and in two or three hours his body was moved out of the county, to avoid the coroner and inquisition."[12]

At the end of 1774 people of fashion in London were talking much about the case of the Duke of Gloucester, brother of George III, who had incurred the sovereign's wrath by marrying outside the circle of European royalty. For many years the duke had lived with a certain Lady Waldegrave, not in wedlock, and yet without provoking the displeasure of the king. When, however, the duke announced the "honest act of matrimony," George III denied him the royal presence and banished him from the court. The estrangement of the royal brothers continued and the duke soon found himself without adequate means of support for his wife and daughters. While the American crisis was deepening in January 1775, the duke canvassed the expediency of seeking from parliament a grant to circumvent the unrelenting king.

Equally mortifying to the king was another royal brother—the Duke of Cumberland. A libertine in "this licentious time," as George III phrased it, the duke involved himself in an amour with the wife of another nobleman, who brought an action for "criminal conversation."[13] The court awarded damages of £10,000. In November 1770 the king besought Lord North, his chief minister, to find at once £13,000 for a speedy settlement, lest further publicity disgrace the royal family. Thus the sovereign who punished one brother for the "honest act of matrimony" bestirred himself to raise a large sum to protect another from the consequences of a sordid intrigue.

ii

The government of England and the nation's politics in 1774 reflected the state of society. Party leaders recognized in theory the supremacy of parliament and managed it in such a way as to keep the control of the machinery of state in their hands. Ostensibly, the House of Commons held the reins of power, for indirectly it designated the king's ministers. George III, in his quest for personal influence, did not defy parliament as two of his predecessors had unwisely attempted. Instead he joined forces with the aristocracy and helped to establish a new oligarchy of rank and wealth.

A seat in the House of Commons was a coveted possession. The honor conferred social prestige and marked one as a pillar of the state. Many a purse would be fattened if a certain bill were enacted into law. The crown, now receiving an immense revenue, had cash to distribute from secret funds. It had honors, titles, and offices to bestow. It could afford to pay well for deciding votes. In 1774, nearly two hundred members held offices under the crown. The fortunate member resembled an honored guest at a sumptuous feast, where many tempting dishes were freely tendered. A meeting with a party manager; a visit to the House; a vote of yes or no — such were the labors enacted in return for the proffered bounty.

Once a parliament had been chosen, the members held their seats for seven years before they were exposed to the ordeal of a new election. Even then, in most instances, the ordeal was not very severe. Only a few among the people had the right to vote. Some electoral districts had so declined in population that they had but two or three electors. Here and there the land comprising a district belonged to one person, and the seat was in effect his property, to be filled as he desired. Six peers owned forty-five seats and controlled as many members. In some towns the electors banded together to sell the seat to the highest bidder, dividing the proceeds among themselves. Elsewhere the few qualified voters were dependents of a local magnate and did his bidding. In districts with more electors, candidates paid £7 or £8 per vote: in one case it was reported that only seventy of four hundred voters refused such bribes.

The new plutocracy, with fortunes made during the wars or acquired in India or the West Indies, paid lavishly for seats, which went at competitive prices. The business flourished as never before in the election of 1761, and the tide of corruption was still running high when the elections of 1768 and 1774 were held. Brokers sold seats as if they were wheat or stocks. The king's managers purchased many for the court. Independent buyers recovered purchase outlays by selling votes on specific measures. One critic of the unsavory business, the Duke of Richmond, wrote in October 1775: "All I can do, is now and then to join with a few to show the nation, that although but a few, yet all are not sold."[14]

If the Earl of Shelburne is to be believed, the proceedings and debates in parliament had become by 1775 a matter of form. In both houses the ruling party commanded large majorities. "Everything," he said, "is considered in the cabinet, and brought into parliament, not for consideration, but for the sanction of the legislature, and the screening of the counsellors of the king." [15] This mode of government required that the managers give much attention to the task of securing votes by backstairs maneuvers. "What does not tend to this, is no more than business by the by." [16]

iii

For a large majority of the people of Britain — servants, tenants, laborers, mechanics, and farm hands — the condition of life was hard and meager. Without privileges, protection, or security, they bowed under the weight of an arrogant aristocracy and its middle-class allies. By reason of the two preceding wars the poverty of the propertyless working people had grown worse. Wartime inflation had caused prices and profits to rise faster than wages. The discontent of the people deepened; their unrest was intensified; frequent outbreaks of mob violence occurred; class hatreds sharpened; and rumblings of revolt foretold the coming of a storm.

One target of such discontent was the government. People other than the ignorant poor deplored the unjust scheme of representation in parliament which deprived them of the right to vote. Merchants, artisans, and manufacturers in newly flourishing towns resented their disfranchisement, their exclusion from public affairs, their inferior lot. Having property and interests to protect, they were without adequate influence in politics. In this respect they were in the same box with the most lowly among the poor. Unable, alone, to overcome the entrenched oligarchy, discontented members of the middle class formed an uneasy alliance with the lower orders. The symbol of this alliance was John Wilkes — a force in the politics of London and Middlesex County and the focus of bitter conflicts over demands for a reform in the scheme of representation in parliament. Wit, agitator, firebrand, and popular idol, Wilkes was blamed by the oligarchy for instigating noisy street demonstrations against the government and its agents. In 1776 he introduced a bill for "a just and equal representation of the people of England in parliament." In his introductory remarks he said: "The meanest mechanic, the poorest peasant and day laborer has important rights respecting his personal liberty . . . his wages, his earnings, the very price and value of a day's hard labor, which are in many trades and manufactures regulated by the power of parliament."[17]

The unrest among the poor burst into flames in 1763. Soldiers and sailors, trained in the arts of wartime violence, and demobilized without means of support, gathered in London. High prices, unemployment, poverty, and hunger kindled the fires of discontent. Without influence in government, the victims of misfortune could not hope for redress from legal channels, for the ruling class had no relief policy and refused to make concessions to the "rabble." The wretched sufferers, poorly organized and without a systematic program, resorted to agitation in the streets. Wilkes served as the match which started the fire. When the government attacked him as a libeler, he displayed extraordinary courage, resourcefulness, and daring in the battle, and thereby won the acclaim of the populace. Great crowds assembled in the streets to cheer him and to encourage him in the fight. But, with the whole weight of the government arrayed against him, he was unequal to the contest. Expelled from his seat in parliament, and subject to trial before a hostile judge (Lord Mansfield), he went to Paris near the end of 1763. He remained abroad until March 1768. The king pronounced a sentence of outlawry against him on November 1, 1764.

The excitements of 1763 were minor compared with the tumults that shook the kingdom in 1767 and 1768. To the ills of low wages, high prices, and unemployment was added a serious food shortage, arising from a bad harvest. Sailors mutinied; watermen, sailors, hatters, and glass workers went out on strike; coal heavers and seamen fought each other in the streets. Weavers who were unemployed or on strike assaulted their fellows who remained at work. The violence, confusion, and street fighting of that time suggest the wildest scenes of the French Revolution. Returning to England in March 1768, Wilkes again became the focus of discontent. He resumed at once his war with the government and the oligarchy, thereby concentrating upon them the wrath of the discontented masses. "Wilkes and liberty," the battle cry of the popular forces, reverberated throughout the country. Turbulent processions and great demonstrations of shouting enthusiasts kept the country in a continual ferment.

iv

The prince who ascended the throne of Britain in 1760 was a positive, opinionated young man, then in his twenty-third year. Fate decreed that George III was to devote the energies of his kingship to one continuing task — that of battling persistently against a series of revolutionary movements — in Britain, in America, and in Europe.

The beginning of his reign inaugurated a new era. In the preceding forty years the kingdom had enjoyed in good measure the blessings of quiet and repose. It had been governed by Whig noblemen in the spirit of the Revolution of 1688. The reigning sovereigns, George I and George II, had been so inactive in British politics as to be ciphers. The country had been spared the menace of despotic government, for the Whig ministers who ruled in the name of the king respected the rights of the subject, as proclaimed in the state papers of the Revolution. A series of wars with Spain and France had periodically unified the country, affording employment and creating prosperity. The progress of the Industrial Revolution had not yet produced severe dislocations of unemployment. The American colonies were not seriously molested in their rights of self-government. They, too, were entitled to the legacy of the Revolution. Since the government had frequently needed their assistance against Spain or France, they had been treated with consideration and indulgence.

John Wilkes.

From a painting by Robert Edge Pine

Saml Adams

From a painting by John Johnston

The accession of George III coincided roughly with the end of the long war with France. The old order of Whig supremacy passed and was superseded by a new dispensation. In the young monarch the postwar oligarchy found a ruler who was suited to its temperament and its needs. To him the times assigned the task of shaping a political party to be dedicated to the defense of the new order — a party of "king's friends" that would provide unity at the top level of society, afford continuity in government, and prevent abrupt, disturbing shifts in the tenure of power.

Both inclination and early training prompted the youthful king to assert his right to rule in fact as well as in name. He affected a patriotic attitude, proclaiming that he gloried in the name of Briton. He cherished his empire, his church, his kingdom, and his court. Boundless was his affection for royalty, nobility, and aristocracy; immeasurable his devotion to rank, authority, and order. He strove to perfect a regime of status in which each person would have an appointed place. From the common people he expected obedience and submission to superiors. Affairs of state were not their business. He had little respect for the civil liberties of the subject when they were asserted in opposition to his will. In his attitude toward the colonies he suggested a dogmatic schoolmaster, devoid of sympathy, understanding, and knowledge, and therefore disposed to employ the rod. Strong in his convictions and ardent in his prejudices, he repaid the loyalty of adherents with steadfast support. Of enemies and critics he spoke with aversion and contempt. In personal relationships he saw only black and white. His perseverance expressed a faith that was untroubled by doubt. His courage in the face of danger bore him dauntlessly through perilous times. Upright in his moral conduct, he lamented that so many of his ministers were dissolute in their private lives.

Narrow in his interests and outlook, he seemed to care little for books, travel, and the arts. Appointments, even to trivial posts, absorbed his attention, and he conferred honors upon faithful servants with evident relish. He fondly followed the news of the courts of Europe and observed punctually the ceremonials of his office. He conferred continually with his advisers on the leading questions of the day and personally directed the political warfare against the opponents of the court.

The government, under his guidance, was not a despotism, a tyranny, a totalitarian regime, a police state, or a reign of terror. It did not resort to torture, executions, concentration camps, or cruel and unusual punishments. It was not a personal dictatorship. It was a plutocracy. Bribes, contracts, offices, pensions and the like were its principal instruments. The king did not profit financially. His court was not lavish in display. Its style of living was modest—even mean. He did not waste the royal substance on splendid palaces, furnishings, and court extravaganzas. The revenues of the state were devoted to the preservation of the *status quo*.

In the face of growing unrest among the people, the attitude of the oligarchy hardened as in a mold. Year after year additional recruits enlisted under the banner of the court. Its rule suggested permanence. Traditions were outwardly observed. One might with complacency accept the innovations of a new power if they were clothed in the garments of custom. The new order saved the devotees of pleasures from the tiring exactions of thought and sacrifice. Most of the articulate men of the kingdom supported the court, accepted its bounty, or submitted to its rule. No opponent in England was capable of grappling successfully with the leviathan. None could arouse the indifferent from their apathy or divert the idlers from their pleasures. The aristocracy did not quarrel with the king's purpose of resisting social change. It was more pleasant to accept the good things of life from the court than to engage in an unequal struggle with so potent an adversary.

The executive branch of the government consisted of two main parts. Its mainspring was the "inner cabinet"—a small group of the chief favorites of the king, plus his principal ministers. The members usually met informally and concerted plans and proposals for the king's consideration. Final agreements were often arrived at in conferences between the chief minister and the king and were then embodied in an executive order or an act of parliament. The inner cabinet represented the oligarchy. It did not dominate the king nor did he dominate it. Each was necessary to the other. Each exercised a veto; each initiated proposals. The two worked together harmoniously, by reason of a similarity of views.

The "exterior cabinet" consisted of the ministers who presided over the well-known departments of the government. In some cases ministers were less important than favorites of the king who occupied minor offices. Each minister managed his department independently. But the ministers were not knit together and did not function as a unit. They could not make initial decisions when the king and the inner cabinet exercised a large and separate power in shaping measures. If a minister did not belong to the inner cabinet, he had to act submissively or risk repudiation if he took an independent course. The system fostered the influence of subordinate officials in departments who had the backing of the king.

v

After 1770 the party of the king's men had a dependable servant in Lord North. Appropriately, he presided over the Treasury, the paying department of the government. He also managed the House of Commons. Though personally honest, and of modest means, he willingly operated the machinery of patronage for the benefit of others. He was a stout, good-natured man who labored faithfully at his duties, confident that in some way things would come out right in the end. Neither vain nor offensively ambitious, he did not incite envy or provoke animosity. He resembled a punching bag in his capacity to absorb abuse. He often dozed in parliament while his enemies berated him. Since he held conventional views and did not originate ideas he had no pride of authorship and was content to effectuate the plans of others. He denied that he was a prime minister, disavowed responsibility for the trend of events, asserted that he served only from a sense of duty, and frequently offered to resign. In 1775 he was in his forty-fourth year — six years older than the king.

It was the office of Lord North to hold together the loosely connected parts of the government. He served as conveyer of plans, proposals, and information — as negotiator, mediator, manager of parliament, and shock absorber. He moved from the palace to informal meetings of members of the inner cabinet and conferred with ministers and leaders of parliament — all in the business of arriving at agreements and compromises. In this he was assisted by one of his chief lieutenants, Charles Jenkinson, an active politician and manager, now in 1775 in his forty-seventh year. Jenkinson held only minor offices, such as vice-treasurer of Ireland and master of the mint. He had been attached to the court party for nearly fifteen years. He had grown to political maturity in the favor of George III, at the center of power, so that he probably knew as much as anyone about the springs and wheels of the government and the impulses which set them in motion. He regarded England as nobly unselfish: to charge her with ambition, he said, "must appear so absurd . . . that it ought to be treated rather as calumny than accusation."[18] He had pressed urgently for the Stamp Act and opposed its repeal. In 1774 he professed to be "astonished at the unanimity of the nation" in opposition to the colonies.[19]

To Horace Walpole, Jenkinson appeared to be "able, shrewd, timid, cautious, and dark; and much fitter to suggest and digest measures than to execute them. His appearance was abject; his countenance betrayed a consciousness of secret guile; and though his ambition and rapacity were insatiate, his demeanor exhibited such a want of spirit that had he stood forth as prime minister, which he really was, his very look would have encouraged opposition; for who can revere authority which seems to confess itself improperly placed and ashamed of its own awkwardly assumed importance."[20]

Holding minor offices, Jenkinson could devote more time to the maneuvers of politics than could a second major figure of the inner cabinet — William Murray, Baron Mansfield. Seventy years of age in 1775, Lord Mansfield was the premier elder statesman of the court party. His duties as chief justice of the King's Bench precluded his taking an active part in the details of political manipulation. His was the higher function of offering advice on weighty matters of policy — for which role he was equipped by more than thirty years of experience at the bar, in parliament, and in important executive offices. He served the court party now as its leader in the House of Lords.

Born at Scone in Perthshire, he left Scotland when he was but fourteen years old. "He never returned to his own country; he never saw his parents again; he never seemed to care to revisit the home of his boyhood."[21] Under the spur of ambition he obtained the best education the times afforded. He began the practice of law in 1730. Being of a "cold and placid" heart, he married, when he was thirty-three, a lady of quality whose father was a member of the cabinet. Few of his legal maxims survive; one is a bit of advice to a colleague: "No case, abuse the plaintiff's attorney." His critics asserted that "he was without moral courage, a sun worshiper who frankly loved the easy path and the sweet things of life."[22]

His antidemocratic views and his long service to the aristocracy did not endear him to the masses. In 1780 his carriage, en route to the House of Lords, was attacked and his gown and wig were almost torn to shreds. Later, "the mob attacked his house in Bloomsbury Square. . . . When the rioters battered at his door he escaped with his wife by a back passage. . . . Books, pictures, and furniture were burned in a bonfire on the pavement; the cellars were pillaged, and the miscreants grew drunk on the chief justice's claret; soon the flames reached the house, and in the morning nothing remained but a blackened shell."[23]

In America Mansfield was one of the most detested of the king's men. His widely circulated speech in defense of the Stamp Act had not flattered the colonists. "Madness," he said, "is catching in all popular assemblies." He declared that he understood the Americans, and he ventured to say that "their heat will soon be over, when they come to feel the consequences of their opposition to the legislature."

The rule of England had conferred many benefits on the colonies; if it should cease, a host of evils would befall them. They were really incapable of governing themselves. He resorted to threats. "If the offspring are grown too big and too resolute to obey the parent, you must try which is the strongest, and exert all the powers of the mother country to decide the contest."[24]

Mansfield explained frankly why the government must reject the American slogan of "No taxation without representation." In Britain millions of people were taxed who could not vote. If the Americans were conceded the right to consent to their taxes, the same right would have to be granted to millions of unprivileged Englishmen. That would revolutionize the British government. It would destroy the power of the oligarchy. In rejecting the claims of the colonists, Mansfield was above all rejecting the demand for reform at home. He was insisting that the *status quo* be safeguarded by retaining all the deformities that made the parliament of his day a mockery of representation.

In 1770 Mansfield used his judicial office in an effort to stifle published criticism of officials and to debase the members of juries sitting in trials of persons accused of seditious libel. The repressive attitude of the government drove opposition writers to sign fictitious names to printed attacks on the court. In such cases the king's agents could identify only the printers among the persons responsible for an abusive publication. Mansfield undertook to deprive printers of the benefit of a real trial by jury and to put them, unprotected, at the mercy of the judges, who were then instruments of the crown. He asserted, in charges to juries, the doctrine that, in a case of an alleged libel against public officials, the jury should render a verdict of guilty or not guilty, but that it should consider only whether a printer had published the statements complained of. It was not, he insisted, the function of a jury to interpret the statements or to determine whether the official had been libeled. The judges would do that. Yet he asked the jurors to find a man guilty of the alleged crime, although they were supposed to consider merely the simple fact of publication — not whether the publication was illegal and criminal. He demanded that the jurors should pronounce a man guilty of a crime without examining the evidence pertaining to the crime.

vi

Another careerist from Scotland served the court with energy and diligence. Alexander Wedderburn, the king's solicitor general, had come to England as a young man to study law. Through the patronage of Lord Bute he obtained a seat in parliament in 1761. When thirty-four he married an heiress. A Tory in 1767, he supported the radical Wilkes in 1768, re-entered parliament as a Whig in 1770, and joined the king's friends in 1771. His desertion to the court party branded him as an outstanding turncoat in British politics. Now, in 1775, in his forty-third year, he was an aggressive servant of the oligarchy. A ready speaker in debate and a master of invective, he was the ministry's oratorical "hatchet man" or "ferocious dog." Early in 1775 he deplored that the "mobs" in America had not been dispersed by troops and that the leaders of the Continental Congress had not been seized. He added that "the people of Scotland were better humored ever since the bloodshed in the Rebellion" of 1745.[25]

In high circles Wedderburn was a much-talked-of man in 1774. Early in that year he inflicted on Benjamin Franklin a tongue-lashing so fierce as to afford unbounded delight to the king's friends. Franklin appeared before a committee of the Privy Council, to present for the assembly of Massachusetts a petition requesting the king to remove from office the governor of the province, Thomas Hutchinson, and the lieutenant governor, Andrew Oliver. The petition had sprung from an action of Franklin's. He had sent to the speaker of the assembly in Boston certain letters written by Hutchinson and Oliver, in which they had suggested that the liberties of the colonists should be curtailed. Franklin did not explain how he got the letters, which had mysteriously disappeared from the papers of the man who had received them in England. Wedderburn, by prearrangement with the leaders of the court party, attacked Franklin in a vicious manner. The American, he said, had used the presumably purloined letters in such a way as to embarrass the king's most worthy servants in Massachusetts and to foment opposition in the province. The attack was made before a large assembly of privy councilors. "Nothing," Wedderburn is reported to have said, "will acquit Dr. Franklin of the charge of obtaining them [the letters] by the most fraudulent or corrupt means for the most malignant of purposes, unless he stole them from the person who stole them. . . . Into what country will the fabricator of this inquiry hereafter go with unembarrassed face? Men will . . . hide their papers from him and lock up their escritoires. Having hitherto aspired after fame by his writings, he will henceforth esteem it a libel to be called a man of letters."[26]

The great men present interrupted Wedderburn with shouts of approval and rewarded him with an ovation at the end of his tirade. The incident occurred at an exciting time, when feelings were inflamed and bitter. The news of the destruction of the tea at Boston had barely been received. The Privy Council committee branded the Massachusetts petition as "groundless, vexatious, and scandalous," as "calculated only for the seditious purposes of keeping up a spirit of clamor and discontent in the said province."[27] At the end of Franklin's ordeal, the king's friends clustered about Wedderburn to congratulate him, while the humiliated victim walked away silently, alone.

Wedderburn's coarseness reflected the vulgarity of his superior, the attorney general, Edward Thurlow. Next to Lord Mansfield, Thurlow was the most imposing dignitary of the court party. He was a tall man of impressive bearing, whose dark complexion was accented by penetrating black eyes that glared beneath heavy eyebrows. He had been so obnoxious as a boy that he was sent to a school noted for its strict discipline. There he was expelled as "incorrigibly bad." At Cambridge University his indolence and insolence led to his dismissal for misconduct. He studied law and found a patron who put him into parliament, where he busied himself with attacks on the enemies of the court. Freedom of elections, freedom of the press, trial by jury, and legal safeguards for accused persons were targets of his blows.

A persistent enemy of America, he upheld the Stamp Act, favored a type of colonial government that dispensed with the elected assembly, argued that colonial governors were authorized to use troops against the colonists, and recommended the pillory for English defenders of the insurgents. He conducted the most celebrated trial of his day with "bad taste and cruelty." He remained unmarried, but his mistress bore him several children. He dabbled in trivial scholarship; his conversation bristled with profanity; and his speeches resounded with invective and abuse. Secure in the power of the court, he indulged in the luxury of indolence, employing experts to supply him with arguments and information. "In politics he seems to have had no principles beyond a high view of the prerogative and an aversion to change."[28] His loyalty to the king turned into treachery during the latter's illness. His career is epitomized by his defense of the slave trade, at a time when public opinion, in both England and America, condemned the nefarious traffic. He expressed his contempt of the colonists when he sought to extend slavery among them—an institution deemed too iniquitous to exist in England.

vii

In the upper category, with North, Mansfield, and Thurlow, was the master of the British Navy, the First Lord of the Admiralty, the Earl of Sandwich. In the fifty-seven years of his life before 1775 he had accomplished little worthy of remembrance. Ignorant, arrogant, corrupt, and sensual in his pleasures, he bore himself as a man entitled to power for which he was accountable to only a few superiors. A onetime companion in dissipation with John Wilkes, he had turned against him in politics, getting thereby the nickname

"Jemmy Twitcher" from a line in the *Beggar's Opera.* When he once said that Wilkes would die on the gallows or of venereal disease, the latter replied: "That depends, my lord, on whether I embrace your principles or your mistress." To Horace Walpole, he was a "notorious coward," who had "a predilection to guilt if he could couple it with artifice and treachery."[29]

> Too infamous to have a friend,
> Too bad for bad men to commend.

Although industrious and attentive to business, Sandwich proved to be a poor administrator. In his effort to form a coterie of followers he put incompetent dependents in office. While he was in charge of the navy, its administration sank to its lowest point of inefficiency and corruption. In 1775 he offered to pay £2000 for a member of parliament (for five years' service) on condition that the member should vote as he dictated on American questions. In the colonies he became notorious and detested for a harangue he made in the House of Lords in March 1775. Anticipating war he declaimed: "Suppose the colonies do abound in men, what does that signify? They are raw, undisciplined, cowardly men. I wish instead of forty or fifty thousand of these brave fellows, they would produce in the field at least two hundred thousand; the more the better; the easier would be the conquest. If they did not run away, they would starve themselves into compliance with our measures. . . . Believe me, my lords, the very sound of a cannon would carry them off . . . as fast as their feet could carry them."[30]

One of the most active of the ministers was a commoner, Lord George Sackville, now known as Lord George Germain. In 1775 he replaced the pious, ineffective Earl of Dartmouth as secretary of state for the colonies. Sackville received his first training in public service in Britain's hard school of oppression in Ireland. In 1758 he was a lieutenant general and commander in chief of British forces in Germany, serving under the supreme command of Prince Ferdinand of Brunswick. At a critical point in the battle of Minden his disobedience to repeated orders was thought to have cost the

British a decisive victory. Found guilty by a court-martial (1760) he was ousted from the army and condemned as "unfit to serve his majesty in any military capacity whatsoever." Ten years later he changed his name to Germain.

Slowly he retrieved himself under the new sovereign. Early in the American contest he had foreseen that the colonists could be overcome only by military force. When the court decided in favor of vigorous coercion it placed him in the colonial office as chief director of the war. In his sixtieth year in 1775, he was a tall, impressive man, cold in manner, quick in action, sharp and forceful in debate. He was an aggressive egoist, heedless of critics and given to outbursts of temper — a "second Duke of Alva," who would treat the colonies with "Roman severity." His limited knowledge and his distaste for study disqualified him for his office. His chief weakness was his notion that the majority of the colonists were loyal to the king. In 1779 he said: "Our utmost efforts will fail of their effect if we cannot find means to encourage the people of America in support of a cause which is equally their own and ours." [31] Unhappily for him, a large majority of the active, fighting men in the colonies were attached to the American cause. The upsurge of British Empire loyalism on which he counted did not materialize.

The secretary at war was an administrative officer who looked after the details of recruiting and army supply. In view of the popular unrest in England, the control of the army was of the utmost importance to the court. This may account in part for the unique record of the man who headed the war department in 1775 — Viscount Barrington, a self-seeking placeman devoted to the king. His public career began in 1740, when he married an heiress. Thereafter he held many important executive offices. His distinction in 1775 arose from the fact that he had served as secretary at war for ten consecutive years in five successive ministries, having been given the post at the insistence of the king. When asked the secret of his holding onto high office so long, "when everybody else had gone out," he replied, as we are told, that "he could compare the state to a great plum-pudding, which he was so fond of that he would never quarrel with it, but should be taking a slice as long as there was any left."[32]

More precisely, Barrington derived his good fortune from the royal favor. Shortly before he took charge of the war ministry he assured George III that he owed allegiance solely to him and would serve only because his majesty had selected him. He said that "the crown has an undoubted right to choose its ministers, and that it was the duty of subjects to support them," adding that if he should leave office his conduct would "be exactly the same when I am only your subject as if I continued your faithful servant."[33]

George III had an abiding aversion to public meetings, which, he thought, were prone to end in riots. In May 1768 occurred the affair of St. George's Fields. A multitude congregated to greet John Wilkes upon his expected release from prison. Soldiers of the regular army fired into the crowd. A score of citizens were shot, including one who had not taken part in the demonstration. On the following day Barrington wrote to an officer of the troops, conveying the personal approval of the king, assuring that "every possible regard" would be shown to the officers and men, and promising that should any "disagreeable circumstance" befall them, they would "have every protection that the law can authorize and this office can give."[34]

Barrington did not have faith in the policy of coercing the colonies with troops, and yet he was persuaded to continue as secretary at war for three years after 1775. Is it surprising that British arms did not triumph when the army was in the care of a minister who held his post for the spoils of office and openly expressed his lack of faith in the policies he was supposed to carry out?

Less experienced than Barrington was the Earl of Suffolk, secretary of state for the northern department — the official in charge of British diplomacy in northern Europe. An ambitious, pushing young man of thirty-five (already afflicted with the gout) and a rival of Lord North, Suffolk was useful to the ministry for his high rank, his extensive family connections, and his venomous tongue, which he used freely in the House of Lords to chastise the colonists. He prided himself on his consistent opposition to the Americans: "All our misfortunes," he said, "were owing to the unsteadiness of government when they repealed the Stamp Act."[35] He thought that "it would be a work of difficulty to restore the friendship which had subsisted between the kingdom and the colonies, and it could be done in no other way than settling the authority over them, which, for himself . . . he thought must be done at all events."[36] One scheme in which he was implicated failed dismally — that of obtaining mercenary soldiers from Russia. In September 1775 he supervised negotiations at Moscow for the hiring of twenty thousand troops. For a moment it seemed that the effort might succeed. But it was thwarted by the empress, Catherine the Great.

II. The Court and the Colonies

I have therefore also looked forward to a time of war.[1]

—GEORGE III TO LORD NORTH, AUGUST 9, 1772

ON November 18, 1774, George III sent a note to Lord North. It read: "The New England governments are in a state of rebellion. Blows must decide whether they are to be subject to this country or independent."[2]

This brief notice ended a period of dissension and hesitation preparatory to a showdown with the colonies. It announced that the government had decided to use military force and was soon to act. It marked a high point in a trend toward a new order that, setting in with the accession of George III, had moved ahead relentlessly during the fourteen years that followed.

The political strife of the time revolved around the financial needs of the government. The late war had boosted the national debt to the then enormous sum of £140,000,000. The interest charge alone amounted to £4,500,000 a year. Canada and Florida, newly added to the empire, required further outlays for their government and defense. A costly Indian war, growing out of Pontiac's Conspiracy, revealed that the acquisitions of 1763 were not unalloyed gain.

Within England, the transition from war to peace had had a dislocating effect. Peacetime trade did not revive quickly enough to take up the slack caused by the tapering off of military spending. A serious depression resulted. Yet the apparatus of the government had grown and the king's faithful servants needed continuing employment. Officers in the armed services were entitled to pensions or other rewards. Wartime inflation and profiteering had increased the costs of government — a disagreeable handicap to a king who used the national revenues to improve his political fortunes.

Although the financial needs of the crown were great, no group within the kingdom was disposed to pay. The profits of war had dwindled; trade was dull. The landowners writhed under heavy taxes. Merchants dreaded new levies on trade. Each group wished to shift the larger share of the tax burden onto the shoulders of the other. An intense conflict between the two ran through the political warfare of the time. By reason of high prices the poor protested vehemently against proposals for taxing the necessities of life.

In this unhappy situation the American colonies promised some relief. As dependencies of Britain they were subject to the authority of king and parliament. Most of the king's advisers believed that they should help to pay for the war and that they ought to contribute to the costs of their government and defense. Moreover, it was now deemed essential to enforce the old laws which aimed to give Britain a near monopoly of the American trade. More money would be needed for that. And so the ministry turned willingly to the expedient of parliamentary taxation of the colonies.

ii

An early expression of the coalition between George III and the postwar oligarchy was the Stamp Act of 1765. It was endorsed by the king and approved overwhelmingly by both houses of parliament. Its repeal in 1766 did not signify a change of heart at court. It had provoked in America an opposition so fierce and general as to convince the ministry that it could be enforced only by a war. The king's friends did not like the prospect — so soon after the end of the struggle with France. A critic of the court party, Lord Rockingham, was permitted to put through the repeal of the act. George III agreed to the repeal and at the same time disapproved of it. Thus he continued to assert the principle of taxing the colonies — a stand that was highly popular in England. The odium of surrender fell upon the king's enemies. Immediately after Rockingham had rescued the court from its dilemma, he was forced out of office by the king, in July 1766.

The resistance to the Stamp Act, together with its repeal, left a legacy of extreme bitterness in England. To most of the nation's leaders it seemed an outrage that the colonies had been able to defy, successfully and without punishment, an urgently needed law that had been enacted with almost no opposition. Such defiance could not go unrebuked. In this mood parliament in 1767 passed the Townshend Revenue Act. It imposed on the colonies taxes comparable, in effect, to those of the Stamp Act. Another storm of indignation and resistance swept over America. Again the alternatives of war or forced acquiescence in the nullification of a British law haunted the government. Unwilling to go to war at this time, or to give way, the ministry hesitated and delayed.

In the meantime, the agitation in the colonies for popular government and the rights of man was stimulated by a parallel agitation in England. Outbreaks of street violence in London and other English towns preceded the Stamp Act disturbances in America. George Grenville, prime minister when the Stamp Act was passed, believed that it could have been enforced "without any difficulty, if America had not received such encouragement to oppose it from hence."[3] Reversely, the successful resistance in America spurred on the English insurgents, who demonstrated in the streets. Grenville remarked that "the populace of London have a better right to give the law to the king and the government of Great Britain than the populace of Boston."[4] He could not believe that ministers who trembled before the Bostonians would dare to encounter the people of London.

It may be difficult to prove that the court leaders met the double menace of unrest at home and resistance in the colonies by a deliberate strategy. But we know what happened. Decisive action in America was deferred while the court party concentrated on the task of repressing the popular unrest in England. An acute observer reported in 1769: "Since it was apparent that they could not intimidate the colonies by violence, nor deceive them by finesse, the ministry seemed disposed to give way to them; not indeed upon principle, but from conviction that it would be impossible to carry their point while things were in such disorder at home."[5] Moreover, the ministers, having been incensed by the colonial resistance, hoped that it would "awake the indignation of all parties, and unite them against the Americans."[6]

Late in 1767 the king's friends, for the first time, secured a firm grip on the government. Until then, they had not dominated the ministry, despite both their influence in parliament and their power derived from the king's determined use of the appointing power. The pre-1760 tradition of dominance of the king by great Whig leaders did not die without a struggle. In the early 1760's a number of Whig chieftains sought to preserve the old order, each seeking to succeed, like Sir Robert Walpole, in controlling parliament and treating the king like a puppet. But the Whig chiefs were no longer united. The party had split into numerous factions—one headed by the Duke of Bedford, one by George Grenville, one by Lord Rockingham, one by William Pitt. None of these chiefs, alone, had the power to establish himself as the unquestioned ruler. None controlled parliament; none dominated the king; none exercised the royal patronage. The result was a continual factional strife for supremacy.

The king, though no longer a creature of the ministry, was yet in part dependent on the Whig chieftains. They were the outstanding leaders of the country. All together they controlled parliament. If the king had attempted to defy them all, they would probably have united to drive him from the throne. Therefore, he called upon one or another of them to head a ministry. At the same time he resisted their efforts to place themselves above the throne. To the factional strife among the Whigs was added a continual warfare between them and the court. Such struggles, tearing at the vitals of the government, threatened to reduce it to a state of impotence.

Such was the situation when the ministry was confronted with acts of resistance, both in the colonies and at home. What should be done? The king's friends, the Bedfords, and the Grenvilles opposed concessions to "rioters"; all favored strong measures for the suppression of unrest. But the Whig factions differed as to methods. The Bedfords urged the use of harsh repressive measures against the people, without too tender a regard for civil liberties. Grenville wished to safeguard constitutional rights and to enforce the law by lawful means.

The followers of Pitt and of Rockingham had other views. Both wished to make concessions to the colonies in order to avoid a resort to force. Both insisted that, in dealing with popular unrest, the government should respect the traditional civil liberties of English subjects.

In 1766 it appeared that the future would be decided by Pitt. He had defended the colonies in the Stamp Act controversy. Would he also come forward as the leader of the oppressed at home? If he did that, he would become a powerful antagonist of the court. He towered above all men as the hero who had led the nation to its greatest triumphs during the war. He had exhibited driving energy, oratorical power, and the ability to inspire the people.

It soon appeared that he was not destined to arouse the nation against the oligarchy as he had aroused it against a foreign foe. His long effort to live strenuously at the peak of high endeavor had undermined his health. A man who strained continually after greatness, he found himself out of tune with the times, once the stimulations of the war had subsided. Moreover, the postwar strife within the kingdom did not suit his temperament. His reverence for the aristocracy deterred him from assuming the leadership of the discontented masses in a struggle that verged on civil war; his sympathy for the rank and file alienated him from the oligarchy; and his desire to preserve the constitutional liberties of the subject did not appeal to angry men when such liberties were being used in an assault on the *status quo*.

Ironically, Pitt became the chief means by which the court party gained full control of the government. In 1766 George III asked him to head a ministry and raised him to the peerage as the Earl of Chatham. Thus he ceased to be the Great Commoner; thus he retired from the House of Commons, long the sounding board for his stirring oratory.

> Here dead to fame lies patriot Will
> His monument his seat,
> His titles are his epitaph
> His robes his winding sheet.

To serve as the chief lieutenant of the newly created earl, the king chose the Duke of Grafton, an amiable, tolerant sportsman, who lacked the moral force that emanates from strong convictions and a blameless personal life. Soon after the new ministry was launched, the health of Chatham gave way, in December 1766. For nearly two years he remained an invalid, stricken by a mysterious malady that forced him into seclusion and unfitted him for public work. Grafton described a visit to him in 1767: "Though I expected to find Lord Chatham very ill indeed, his situation was different from what I had imagined; his nerves and spirit were affected to a dreadful degree: and the sight of his great mind bowed down, and thus weakened by disorder . . . filled me with grief and concern." [7]

This tragic illness placed Grafton at the head of the ministry. It had been formed on an all-party basis. And now it happened that the king's friends among the ministers proved to be bolder and more aggressive than the followers of Chatham. In the absence of the great leader the ministry was reconstructed in such a way as to give the court the deciding voice. At this critical point the Bedford faction united with the king's friends. The political revolution of 1767 appears to have been engineered by Lord Mansfield. It occurred at a time when popular unrest, in both England and America, seemed to threaten the fundamentals of society. "A series of weak administrations and perpetual strong opposition," wrote Mansfield, "will lead to destruction." [8] Grafton, the chief minister, added: "The scarcity of corn, and the high price of provisions of every kind, had been continued for two years, and more; and its pernicious consequences were now felt through the spirit of discontent and riot which broke out in many parts of the kingdom, but was most serious in and about the metropolis."[9] In the face of this tension the pliant Grafton yielded and admitted several re-pressionists into his ministry. Lord North became chancellor of the exchequer in the autumn of 1767. In December three Bedford men received high offices: Gower, Sandwich, and Weymouth. All these men shared the attitude of the court regarding American resistance and unrest in England. The changes took place during the absence of Chatham. When he resigned in October 1768 the conquest of the ministry by the court had been achieved.

iii

Before the court could meet effectively the challenge of the American resistance it was imperative that the opposition within England should be suppressed. Once the court had gained full control of the government (as it had by the end of 1767) it could take strong measures against its civilian foes at home.

First, it struck at the disaffected populace, using soldiers to disperse crowds that were demonstrating against the government. In March 1768 John Wilkes returned to London and again became a storm center of social strife. He submitted to trial on libel charges that had grown out of his writings in 1763. Sentenced to serve a term of two years in prison, he again received tumultuous ovations in the streets from shouting partisans who hailed him as if he were the king. On April 17, the secretary of state, Lord Weymouth — the man whose personal life was "a long drawn-out debauch" — sent a special letter to the chairman of the quarter sessions at Lambeth. Referring to the "very riotous" disposition among the common people, Weymouth gave directions for the use of troops in the event of "indecent tumult and disorder," and added: "I hope you will not delay a moment calling for their aid, and making use of them effectually, where there is occasion; that occasion always presents itself, when the civil power is trifled with and insulted; nor can a military force ever be employed to a more constitutional purpose, than in support of the authority and dignity of the magistracy."[10]

On May 10 a large crowd assembled at St. George's Fields (outside the prison in which Wilkes was held) and clamored for his release in order that he might attend the opening of parliament, to which he had been recently elected. In the course of the demonstration the crowd clashed with the king's troops. Five or six civilians were killed and fifteen wounded. A soldier and a magistrate, who were tried on the charge of murdering an innocent bystander, were acquitted. The "Massacre of St. George's Fields" announced a change in the policy of the government. Thereafter, the employment of armed force revealed, in a grim fashion, the will of the court to assert its authority.

Nor did the government shrink from further action against Wilkes. He obtained a copy of Weymouth's letter and charged, in print, that the ministry had plotted the Massacre of St. George's Fields. Again he was accused of libel, whereupon the House of Commons, controlled by the court, expelled him from his seat (February 4, 1769). His constituents re-elected him three times, twice without opposition, and after each victory the House cast him out. Following his fourth election the House gave the seat to a court candidate who had obtained fewer than a third of the votes received by Wilkes. The whole proceeding was mockery of elections. It expressed both the contempt of the court party for the people and its determination to rule by arbitrary power. As a result of bribery and corruption, parliament had been made a party to its own degradation. And, most important, the exclusion of Wilkes was a direct violation of existing law. The House had not only expelled him; it had also disqualified him — an action outside and beyond its legal authority. When men entrusted with the power to govern used that power to violate the law, it appeared that the constitution had been overthrown and that government by law had given way to government by men. The king's men, in this instance.

The court next turned its attention to the press, which in 1769 reached the peak of its severity in criticism of the king and his ministers. In the first attack on Wilkes, in 1763, the government's hostility so intimidated the printers that none with an established business would work for him. The chief victim chosen for the next assault was Henry S. Woodfall, publisher of the savage "Letters of Junius." In the ensuing trials, Lord Mansfield, chief justice of the court of the King's Bench, applied his doctrine that deprived alleged libelers of jury trial and placed them at the mercy of the king's judges. The new campaign against the press seems to have disarmed the opposition. Junius soon desisted. In January 1773 he wrote: "In the present state of things, if I were to write again, I must be as silly as any of the horned cattle that run mad through the city. . . . I . . . [refer] to the cause and the public. Both are given up. I feel for the honor of this country, when I see that there are not ten men in it who will unite and stand alike upon any one question. But it is all alike, vile and contemptible." [11]

When Chatham returned to London in 1769 the ministry was pursuing a course which he regarded as a betrayal. Of his experience as a minister he said: "I was duped, I was deceived." [12] He assailed the court party and denounced Grafton. "There was in his conduct from the time of my being taken ill a deviation from everything that had been settled and solemnly agreed to by his grace both as to measures and men, till at last there were not left two planks together of the ship which had been originally launched." [13] Chatham believed that the constitution had been overthrown and that on its wreckage had risen a new despotism. The House of Commons had become the slave of the king's servants. The "ministers held a corrupt influence in parliament." An invisible government was at work; "there is something behind the throne greater than the king himself." It operated first "by secret treachery, then by official influence, afterward in public councils." [14]

In September 1769 an observer of the English scene reported: "Never did the people engage in the struggle for liberty under so many disadvantages. Never did ministers attempt to establish despotism, possessed of such power, or supported by such regular, well-disciplined force. Never was public virtue at so low an ebb nor ministerial influence (by means of places, pensions, etc.) so unlimited. Never were the people so unarmed, so unskilled, so unprepared to exert force, nor the Administration so well furnished with every means of subverting the constitution." [15]

The opposition to the oligarchy had reached its summit in 1768–1769, when the excitement over Wilkes was at its crest, and when Junius was pounding the court with his most savage invective. By the end of 1771 the opposition had collapsed. Violent disturbances in the streets, attacks on leading noblemen, an assault on the palace itself — all these manifestations of popular unrest caused a wave of revulsion. Men who feared mob rule put aside their differences and drew together under the court. Burke observed in August 1770 that "the dread of pushing things to a dangerous extreme, while we are seeking for a remedy to distempers that all confess, brings many to the support, and most to a sort of ill humored acquiescence in the present scheme of court government." [16]

The vigorous campaign of the court against press criticism seems to have intimidated the warriors of the pen, whose initial weakness had been disclosed by their unwillingness to sign their names to their abusive publications. The partisans of Wilkes had subsided under the determined animosity of the court. The royal troops had given the populace some stern instruction in the duty of obedience and submission. Repressive measures had succeeded. Moreover, a sharp conflict broke out within the popular party in London. And, fortunately for the government, the economic condition of the country improved. Trade revived abroad; the unemployed were able to find work; and for a time the pressure of poverty was relieved.

In addition, the court profited by a series of changes affecting national leadership. Within the span of about two months occurred the deaths of two of the outstanding Whig leaders. George Grenville died in November 1770; the Duke of Bedford in January 1771. Since both men had agreed in general with the court party on colonial issues, and since the American question was still vital, it was natural for the leaderless followers of Grenville and Bedford to turn to the court. Many had already done so. Lord Chatham, still suffering from ill health and subject to fits of melancholy, pronounced his maledictions on the times — and retired. Lord Rockingham, shy, moderate, and ineffectual, carried on the struggle, almost alone.

Meanwhile, the public sank into a state of lethargy. "After a violent ferment in the nation," wrote Burke in 1771, "as remarkable a deadness and vapidity has succeeded. . . . I do not suppose that there is anything like this stupor in any period of our history."[17]

By the end of 1771 the king had installed in office the dignitaries who, with one exception, were to guide the country through most of the American war. In January 1770 Lord North, responding to the king's urgent plea, became the First Lord of the Treasury and chief minister. A year later Sandwich (Admiralty), Thurlow (attorney general), Suffolk (secretary of state), and Wedderburn (solicitor general) received the posts which they held thereafter until late in the war. Gower (Lord President of the Council), Mansfield (chief justice), Jenkinson, and Barrington (secretary at war) had been appointed earlier. Other important members of the North administration who were to serve during the war included Richard Rigby (paymaster general), Lord George Germain, and Lord Weymouth. Before 1771 these men had not formed a unified group. North, Barrington, Mansfield, Germain, and Jenkinson had belonged to the party attached to the king. Suffolk and Wedderburn had been followers of Grenville. Sandwich, Rigby, Weymouth, and Gower had been members of the dissolute Bedford faction (the "Bloomsbury gang"). However, there was one common denominator in their past careers. They had all favored the Stamp Act; they had all opposed its repeal. Since enforcement would have required the use of troops, they were prepared for the test of force. For this reason they constituted, in 1771 and thereafter, what may with accuracy be termed a party of war.

iv

During the critical years 1768–1771, when the king's friends were tightening their grip on the kingdom, they abstained from drastic actions against the colonies. Once they had overcome their foes at home, they were ready to give the Americans the same treatment that had mitigated unrest in England. The success of the repressive actions of 1768–1772 promised that a kindred result might be attained in America, with comparable promptness and ease. The colonies, now deprived of strong support, would be isolated, and the court might act without fear of domestic enemies.

However, the internal dangers that had unified the oligarchy had not entirely disappeared. The opposition in England had been repressed but not destroyed. It was urgent, therefore, that the oligarchy remain united and firm in its adherence to the court. A contest with foreign adversaries would not only cement that unity but would also weaken and embarrass domestic opponents, who would have to choose between supporting the government, remaining passive, and giving aid and comfort to the enemies of the state.

On August 1, 1772, George III wrote to Lord North urging a conciliatory attitude toward France in connection with a minor dispute then under negotiation. He concluded with these words: "We must get the colonies into order before we engage with our neighbors."[18] Eight days later he wrote again to North, stating bluntly: "I have therefore also looked forward to a time of war."[19] He proposed at this time a series of changes to strengthen the administration of the American colonies, particularly as regards their "internal police."

It is evident that in the midsummer of 1772 George III anticipated a war. He did not designate the antagonist. Would it be France? Or the thirteen colonies? He did not intend to become involved in war with his brother monarch, if he could help it. In his letter of August 1 to North he wrote: ". . . when I consider how very unsettled everything is in France, and more so the character of the monarch, I am convinced that they do not foresee the danger they are running of drawing themselves into discussions with us which if not conducted with the greatest temper may draw both nations into that which they ought assiduously to avoid. I am glad Lord Stormont [the English representative at Paris] views it in this light. . . . I am averse to make a point of honor of such a trifle . . . I would . . . consider whether he [Stormont] might not grant a part . . . to put an end to this tiresome correspondence." [20]

The king's thoughts of war were uttered when the government was considering the affairs of the British East India Company. That subject was the chief item of business before parliament during the winter of 1772–1773. The court took the initiative in steering through the debates its bill for a new scheme of British operations in India. The subject was complicated, and the speakers concerned themselves with the many involved and technical aspects of the company and its practices. Attached to the bill was one feature which attracted little attention during the debates. It pertained to the sale of tea in the American colonies.

When most of the Townshend duties of 1767 had been repealed in 1770, the king's friends had insisted upon retaining one duty, in order to assert the right of taxation. The duty selected for this purpose was the 3*d.* duty on tea — an import tax to be collected in the American ports of entry.

The India Act of 1773 offered various aids to the East India Company, which had approached the brink of bankruptcy. Its assets included a large stock of unsold tea, stored in warehouses in England. One important market for its tea had dwindled — that of the American colonies, which annually absorbed about six million pounds. At this time the colonists were getting nearly all their tea from Holland, where they could buy it more cheaply than in England.

Prior to 1773, the British East India Company had been prohibited by law from exporting tea from England to the colonies. Since the company had received a virtual monopoly of the business of importing tea into England, the government had sought to favor other traders by reserving to them the privilege of buying the company's tea in England and of exporting it to America. The Act of 1773 made a most important change in this arrangement. It authorized the company to export its teas directly to America. The company was required to pay only one British duty—the Townshend 3*d.* tax, to be collected in America.

Had the king's friends deliberately sought a means of reviving the excitement in America they could scarcely have devised a more effective arrangement than that provided by the India Act of 1773.

The new plan meant that the East India Company would gain a monopoly of the market for tea in America. Having a large stock of unsold tea on hand, and receiving special financial aid from the British government, the company was in a position to dump its tea in the colonies at low prices and thereby to drive its colonial competitors from this branch of the American trade. The American importers of Dutch tea were due to be undersold. If the company could be thus favored in one commodity, it might be favored in others—chinaware, spices, and East India fabrics. By this sort of manipulation of privileges and prices other English concerns might be favored at the expense of American merchants until the latter would have to go out of business altogether.

This threat was particularly repulsive to the colonists because it was directed at them through the agency of a company which symbolized, in its plundering of India, the sort of exploitation which they feared might be visited upon them.

To the colonists the new plan appeared to be a clever, sinister device to trap them into an acceptance of a parliamentary tax. They were to get tea cheaply—more cheaply than consumers in England. This temporary benefit appeared to be a bribe to induce them to pay the Townshend duty and thereby to acknowledge its legality. Moreover, the device for collecting the tax was extremely effective. The East India Company would now import most of, or all the tea brought into the colonies. The king's revenue agents in America could collect the tax from only one taxpayer. The company would gladly co-operate, in return for the monopoly and other concessions it was about to receive.

Yet, on the other hand, if the Americans should submit and buy the company's tea, they would acknowledge the taxing authority of parliament. Britain could then impose other taxes, and the cherished principle — no taxation without representation — would be abandoned.

In brief, the colonists were now called upon to submit to a monopoly for the benefit of a hated corporation and in so doing to admit the claim that Britain might tax away as much of their wealth as it might please her to demand.

Another feature of the new plan recommended itself to the ministry. It was devised in such a way that English friends of America could not logically support the colonists, if it should provoke another wave of resistance. The duty in question had been enacted when the presumed champion of the colonies, the Earl of Chatham, was nominally at the head of the ministry. In the years 1770–1773 neither he nor other vocal friends of America had objected to its retention. When Lord North presented the India Company plan in April 1773 it was adopted without any objection. Thus the opposition in Britain was not in a position to protest, if the government should undertake to enforce the collection of the duty.

In 1792 an English publicist, John Almon, charged that the arrangement of 1773 was a trick of the ministry to force the issue of American taxation. It is most difficult to believe that the authors of the India Act did not consider its probable effects. Perhaps they anticipated that the colonists would submit and that Britain's authority would be decisively asserted. Perhaps they anticipated a resistance that might lead to war. One point suggests the latter conclusion. Almon asserted that the ministry selected Boston as the test port, citing as evidence the fact that only at that town did the king's officials refuse to issue clearance papers permitting the tea ships to return to England without landing their cargoes. Thus it appears that only at Boston was the company compelled to unload (or to attempt to unload) its tea. In the opinion of the ministry, Boston was the hotbed of resistance. If the court wished to risk an act of violence it was most likely to get it there.

v

The news of the Boston Tea Party arrived in England late in January 1774. The cargoes of three vessels — tea worth £15,000 — had been destroyed. The British government had been openly assailed, for the victimized East India Company had simply tried to do what parliament had directed it to do. Had a government ever been more daringly attacked? The response in England was drastic. The enemies of America were infuriated. They had suffered much from the earlier resistance. They had repeatedly stifled their indignation when past offenders had escaped without punishment. This was the last straw! Who could defend such wanton lawlessness — such an act of vandalism? Smoldering resentments broke out into a flame of wrath. Law and order — justice and decency — all things good — were at stake. This was the opportunity to settle matters once and for all, while the colonies were so completely in the wrong. The men who demanded retribution were now assertive, determined, truculent. Men who had wavered were at last convinced that Britain must act. A few onetime apologists for the colonies abandoned their cause and sided with the government. The steadfast friends of America were caught off guard. Called upon to defend the indefensible, and taunted by bold and confident antagonists, they were, for the moment, silenced, dispirited, overborne by a torrent of condemnation. "The violence committed upon the tea cargo," wrote Chatham in March 1774, "is certainly criminal; nor would it be real kindness to the Americans to adopt their passions and wild pretensions, where they manifestly violate the most indispensable ties of civilized society."[21]

If the leaders of the court party had not anticipated American resistance to the attempted collection of the tea tax, they were indeed the most unknowing men who have ever ruled a state. The speed and decisiveness with which they acted after the Tea Party signify that they were not surprised or unprepared. Before the heat of resentment had time to cool in England they rushed through parliament five far-reaching punitive measures. Any one of these acts was likely to provoke resistance; all together they made an armed conflict inevitable. George III directed the legislative campaign. He voiced his contempt of the opposition, kept a close watch and a constant check on the votes and debates, and urged Lord North to drive ahead. Nearly two hundred placemen held seats in the House of Commons. Within about four months the momentous legislation was prepared, considered, and enacted. The road was cleared and the members cheered as the king's five-coach express, "Coercion," rolled swiftly to its destination.

The punitive acts offered the colonists no alternative other than resistance or complete submission. The legislation, if enforced, would have deprived them of every right and privilege for which they had been contending. Had they submitted, they would have accepted the view that the British government possessed a complete, final, and absolute authority over them. They would have placed themselves entirely at its mercy. So drastic were the acts that one must conclude that the court now intended to break the colonial opposition, to deprive the colonies of their right of self-government, and to expose them to any exaction that Britain might choose to demand.

All together the punitive acts implied that the province of Massachusetts was in a state of rebellion. They did not undertake merely to punish the authors of the Tea Party. They undertook to stop the entire maritime trade of Boston and to remodel the government of the province. To justify such sweeping measures the ministry was obliged to assume that the people collectively were responsible for the Tea Party and other acts of resistance. If the ministry had not intended to force a general settlement, it would have singled out the authors of the Tea Party and have taken action only against them. Instead, the punitive acts implied that the responsible persons were so entwined in a mass of popular disaffection that they could not be separated from it, and that in consequence a corrective must be applied to the whole. By refusing to permit the province to offer any defense, the ministers convicted it of guilt without considering counterevidence. Claiming for parliament the supreme authority over Massachusetts, they made use of the supreme law of the land to declare the province in a virtual state of rebellion.

There is no doubt that the court had decided to impose a settlement on the colonies. But there was a serious difficulty. The ministry might be fatally weakened by opposition at home. British expressions of sympathy and acts of assistance might so encourage the colonists as to defeat the ministry's plans. First of all, the friends of America in England must be discredited and repressed.

Two or three days after the arrival of the news of the Tea Party, Solicitor General Wedderburn delivered his savage attack on Franklin. The foremost dignitaries of the court party attended and shouted their approval as Wedderburn rained his blows upon the helpless American. Franklin was in touch with the leading English friends of America. His humiliation served notice on all. Moreover, he was immediately dismissed from his position in the colonial post office. This was another ominous warning.

George III operated on the rule that his appointees should hold their offices during his pleasure. By 1774 he had established a number of grim precedents in the practice of forcing opponents out of office. Four of the greatest Whig leaders had fallen victim in the recent past: Grenville, Rockingham, Shelburne, and Chatham. One of the heroes of the Seven Years' War, General Jeffrey Amherst, had been dismissed from high office for noncompliance with the king's wishes. So harsh and abrupt was the king's action that Amherst was virtually disgraced. Another leading opponent, Colonel Isaac Barré, follower of Chatham, was denied an army promotion due to him and was passed over by a junior acceptable to the court. In February 1774 the king abruptly relieved Charles James Fox of his duties as a junior Lord of the Treasury. With such shining examples before them the placemen were no doubt sensitive when the apparatus of patronage operated at full force. The king scrutinized the votes cast by his appointees in parliament and pointed out the delinquents to Lord North. Officeholders were told their duty, and candidates for positions and honors were reminded anew of the conditions of success.

At this time the king also displayed a lively interest in the press. A new star had arisen recently in the political sky — the Reverend John Horne, friend of America and critic of the court. His printer, Henry S. Woodfall, had previously suffered the displeasure of the court for publishing the "Letters of Junius." Horne was accused of libeling the speaker of the House of Commons. Neither the speaker nor the House seemed disposed to press the case until the king wrote on February 13, 1774, to Lord North, as follows: "Now that this affair has come forward, the House must with spirit proceed. The half-measures taken on the former occasion have certainly taken off the dread that used very necessarily to be had of offending that House, and therefore makes a due degree of severity absolutely incumbent on the House to inflict on the author and also on the printer." [22]

In the debates on the punitive bills, the spokesmen of the court party subjected the opposition to a barrage of abuse. Particularly bellicose was a member from Wales, Charles Van, who spoke for the ministry to the delight of the House. "The town of Boston," he exclaimed, "ought to be knocked about their ears, and destroyed." If the Americans should oppose the punitive acts, he would do "as was done of old, in the time of the ancient Britons." He "would burn and set fire to all their woods and leave their country open." "If we are to lose that country, I think it better lost by our own soldiers, than wrested from us by our rebellious subjects." [23]

In a later debate, a member from Bristol, Henry Cruger, an American, answered a court speaker who had ridiculed the colonists and had branded them as cowardly. According to one report, Cruger, in refuting the charge, confided that he "was an American himself and lived in Parliament Street — which set the House into a laugh; and attempting to go on, [he] could not be heard." [24] In the House of Lords, the Lord President of the Privy Council, Lord Gower, exclaimed: "My lords, let the Americans talk about their natural and divine rights! their rights of God and nature! I am for enforcing these measures."[25]

All the punitive bills passed both houses by large majorities. The first on the list, the Boston Port Bill, went through without recorded opposition in the final voting. Before the indignation in England over the Tea Party had spent itself, the court had committed the kingdom to a course almost certain to end in war. The policy of coercion now had behind it the king, the court, the ministry, both houses of parliament, the army, and the treasury. It was embedded in the supreme law of the land. The opposition within England had been reduced in numbers; the court party had gained adherents. Those who continued to oppose in England must now stand against the organized power of the state. They must challenge the supreme law of the land. They must speak for outsiders who had been stigmatized as disloyal, rebellious, and criminal.

Soon after the punitive acts had become law, the court decided to dissolve parliament and to hold a general election. The existing parliament had yet another year to run. It was now deemed wise to appeal to the country, without waiting for the appointed election date. The American response to the punitive acts had dispelled all hopes of peace. Preparations for war must proceed without delay. It would embarrass and weaken the ministry if it should have to halt during a war and wage an electoral campaign. Better to hold the election at once. With a new parliament at its side the ministry could act with certainty of support, free from political interruptions. Besides, the wave of hostility to the colonies had not subsided in England.

The election proceeded with a speed verging on haste. The old parliament was dissolved September 30; the election returns were available in mid-November; the new parliament assembled on November 29. The court party, prepared in advance and braced for the contest, utilized the machinery of bribery and patronage with the skill that had gained such decisive victories in the elections of 1761 and 1768. The returns as reported by North on November 14 indicated an impressive majority for the court. It had captured at least

321 of the 558 seats in the House of Commons. Four days later the king pronounced the New England colonies to be in "a state of rebellion" and said that "blows must decide" whether they were to be subject to Britain or independent. "We must either master them or totally leave them to themselves and treat them as aliens."[26] Having received its electoral mandate in favor of an American war, the court now enjoyed full freedom of action, secure in the backing of a compliant parliament entrenched in power for seven years.

vi

On the eve of the war the literature of England reflected the general state of society. It was an age without great poets, dramatists, essayists, or novelists. Pope, Fielding, and Swift had been dead twenty years or more. The prevailing temper was more conducive to study of the past than to creative works of the imagination. The two chief men of letters were Edward Gibbon, the historian, and Samuel Johnson, the lexicographer. Over the lesser literary figures Dr. Johnson presided as a czar. Having experienced bitter poverty in his early life, he accepted a handsome pension from George III in 1762. He regarded the colonists with contempt, called them "rascals, robbers, pirates," and said that he could love anyone but an American. "Sir," he declared, "they are a race of convicts, and ought to be thankful for anything we may allow them short of hanging."[27] Although he professed to despise political pamphlets, he printed early in 1775 his anti-American tract, *Taxation no Tyranny*. He was not paid for this labor, but evidently he considered it a Grub Street production — a return to the court for his pension, comparing himself to a hired craftsman who must satisfy an employer. He submitted to deletions from the tract which were requested by his superiors. Among the passages thus stricken out was an allusion to the previous exemption of the colonists from British taxes. "We do not put a calf into the plow," he had written. "We wait till he is an ox."[28] The dumb creatures in America, he assumed, were destined to be beasts of burden for his pension-givers. His patrons permitted him to say merely that the longer the colonies had been spared from British taxes, the better they could pay.

Written as an answer to the resolves and acts of the First Continental Congress, and bearing the marks of the officialdom of the court party, the *Taxation* tract assailed all the major claims and arguments of the colonists. Government, it held, is absolute in its power. The colonists, subject as they were to the boundless authority of Britain, did not possess any inherent rights. Nor had they a valid title to representation in parliament. They had sacrificed that when they went to America. "What they have voluntarily quitted, they have no right to claim." If they wished to have direct representation they might, when they grew rich, move to England, buy estates there, and thus get the right to vote.[29]

Johnson described the leaders of the insurgents as "zealots of anarchy," "dictators of sedition," "croakers of calamity," "incendiaries that hope to rob in the tumults of a conflagration and toss brands among a rabble passively combustible." The Continental Congress was a "seditious meeting, punishable by law."[30] The Americans, who multiplied "with the fecundity of their own rattlesnakes," had "obeyed no law they could violate," had "imparted no good they could withhold," had "entered into associations of fraud to rob their creditors." They were now in a state of rebellion. "The madness of independence has spread from colony to colony, till order is lost and government despised, and all is filled with misrule, uproar, violence, and confusion."[31] All this was evidence of black ingratitude. The late war had been "incited by their outcries, and continued for their protection, a war by which none but themselves were gainers." At great cost Britain had delivered them from the French and had brought them security. "With what kindness they repay benefits, they are now showing us." They were revolting—and it was necessary to subdue them. "Chains need not be put upon those who will be restrained without them." "When it is urged that they will shoot up like the hydra," one "naturally considers how the hydra was destroyed."[32] "Let us give the Indians arms, and teach them discipline, and encourage them now and then to plunder a plantation." "Why do we hear the loudest yelps for liberty from the drivers of Negroes?" "It has been proposed that the slaves should be set free. . . . If they are furnished with firearms for defense . . . they may be more grateful and honest than their masters." The privileges of the colonists which had been abused "will be taken away, and those who now bellow as patriots, bluster as soldiers, and domineer as legislators, will sink into sober merchants and silent planters."[33]

III. April and May, 1775

> Unhappy it is though to reflect that a brother's sword has been sheathed in a brother's breast, and that the once happy and peaceful plains of America are either to be drenched with blood or inhabited by slaves.[1]
>
> — WASHINGTON TO GEORGE WILLIAM FAIRFAX, MAY 31, 1775

BY the end of 1774 the court had created an appearance of unity in England. But its policy did not call upon its adherents to embrace hardships or to make personal sacrifices in war. The purpose of the policy was to enable the devotees of pleasure to continue to enjoy their luxuries. On the other hand, the ordinary people of England could not be expected to risk their lives. Why should they fight for a government that oppressed them? In view of such aims and attitudes, why did the ministers undertake the war? Because they hoped that America could be subdued at a small cost in English lives. They acted on a comforting view of the colonial resistance which they derived from several of their agents who had served in the colonies. Chief among them were Thomas Hutchinson, former governor of Massachusetts; Cadwallader Colden, lieutenant governor of New York; Lord Dunmore, governor of Virginia; and General Thomas Gage, commander of Britain's troops at Boston. Their reports gave a fairly consistent account of the American scene.

As servants of the ministry, these informants could not admit that the colonists had any valid grievances. The king, it was said, ruled his subjects in America with wisdom and justice. The revolt had been fomented by a few "demogogues," "factious spirits," and hotheaded, "ill-designing" men who had deceived and excited the populace. The people could be brought to their senses quickly by firm measures. They would not fight—or they would not fight long.

They would be frightened by the British troops. When the test came, their courage would fail.

The king reported the views of General Gage as stated in an audience on February 4, 1774: "He says that they will be lions, whilst we are lambs; but if we take a resolute part, they will undoubtedly prove very meek."[2] After an interview with Hutchinson on July 1, George III said that he, the king, was "now well convinced" that the colonists would submit.[3]

According to the king's informants, a major weakness of the Americans was their lack of unity. One colony would not aid another in distress. The Continental Congress was certain to be a fiasco. Its plan for an all-American boycott of British trade was doomed to failure. Boston, Philadelphia, and New York would not abide by it. In Virginia, Lord Dunmore surmised that it might provoke a civil war. Once goods had become scarce, the people would plunder the homes of the rich.

Previous concessions by Britain, it was asserted, had simply encouraged the colonists to resist. At all costs there should be no more appeasement. New concessions would merely foment new disorders. A determined show of force was now imperative. Let the ringleaders be arrested and tried for treason. Once the American friends of the king had been assured the support of his army, an upsurge of loyalty would invigorate the legal governments. The rebellion would die; law and order would prevail.

During the last weeks of 1774 the ministry matured its plans for military action. By the end of January, it had placed an embargo on private shipments of arms to the colonies. Generals Howe, Burgoyne, and Clinton had been ordered to Boston, along with four additional regiments. "The war," wrote Horace Walpole, "is determined on . . . and every hostile measure is to be prepared."[4]

In a secret letter dated January 27 Lord Dartmouth embodied the fateful instructions to Gage. The letter was not dispatched until about February 22. By that time the new parliament had given its approval. On February 2 the House of Commons, by a vote of 296 to 106, adopted a motion of Lord North's that declared the existence of a rebellion in Massachusetts. At that historic session 430 members attended — "as great a number as has been known to be present at the same time." [5]

Copies of the secret letter to Gage were dispatched by the *Nautilus* and the *Falcon*. The *Nautilus* sailed from Plymouth March 13 and reached Gage at Boston April 14. The letter instructed him to act at once. Britain's authority, it said, must be upheld. The people of New England were seeking independence; therefore it must be decided promptly how the king's troops could be used most successfully "to defend the constitution and restore the vigor of government." A small force, if used against the colonists at once, might be more effective than a larger army employed after they had acquired "confidence from discipline." The letter then advised Gage that the "king's servants" believed that "the first and most essential step . . . toward re-establishing government would be to arrest the principal actors and abettors in the provincial congress (whose proceedings appear in every light to be acts of treason and rebellion)." Even though such a step should be "a signal for hostilities, yet . . . it will surely be better that they should be brought on, upon such ground, than in a riper state of rebellion." [6]

On April 14 the provincial congress was meeting in Concord. Foremost among its "principal actors and abettors" were John Hancock, its president, and Samuel Adams, the guiding spirit of the New England resistance, already known in London as a leading "politician of the world" and as a master of the art of "forwarding a rebellion." Reports circulating from Boston warned that Gage intended to seize the two leaders. Both were on the alert, prepared to elude their would-be captors.

On the day Gage received his authorization to begin the war, the British frigate *Somerset* took up a new position between Boston and Charlestown. On the next day, the grenadier and light infantry companies were relieved of routine duties, and army transports were assembled near the warships. Observers at once notified Adams and Hancock of these preparations, which foretold a ferrying of troops from Boston to the mainland. At Concord the reports set men to work on the task of removing the stores of war which the insurgents had assembled there.

With preparations nearly completed, Gage, on the eighteenth, sent men to patrol the roads leading to Concord, with the object of intercepting insurgent couriers and of locating the hiding place of Hancock and Adams. The night of the eighteenth was chilly. In the evening a force of eight hundred grenadiers and light infantrymen marched through Boston Common to the inner bay. By eleven o'clock they were in the process of crossing the back bay to Lechmere Point. By half past two in the morning they had landed. Although they marched quietly and quickly they encountered on all sides so many evidences of a countryside astir that their commander, Lieutenant Colonel Smith, sent back to Boston for reinforcements. At daybreak they arrived at Lexington Green, where they met a band of militiamen. The house of the Reverend Jonas Clark, the hiding place of Hancock and Adams, was only a half mile away. As the regulars and the insurgents met, an unidentified shot was fired. Then came a volley from the cheering regulars, directed at the retreating minutemen. Eight of the latter were killed; ten were wounded; the rest fled to safety. Only one British soldier was wounded. If the regulars did not take the active part in this affray, the minutemen must have been exceedingly poor shots. Behind the deed lay the secret instruction from the king to Gage: ". . . a smaller force now, if put to the test, would be able to encounter them with greater probability of success than might be expected [later] from a greater army. . . ."[7]

The regulars reached Concord without further incident. Then began the engagement which lasted until they had retreated to the shelter of the British guns at Charlestown. On the morning of the nineteenth, between nine and ten o'clock, Lord Percy set out from Boston with a relief force of about eighteen hundred troops of the first brigade. Taking a roundabout route through Roxbury, Percy and his men arrived at Lexington at about two o'clock in the afternoon and there met Smith's force, which had retreated under a hail of bullets fired from houses, thickets and stone walls, all the way

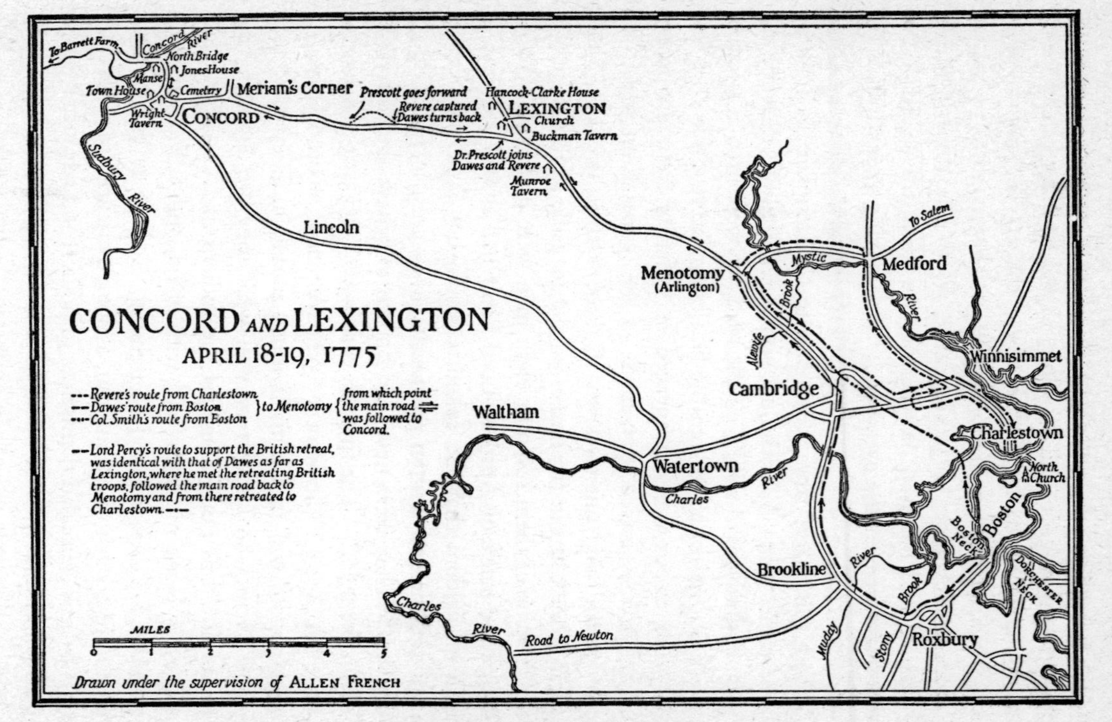

Concord and Lexington

From the *Atlas of American History*, edited by James Truslow Adams. Courtesy of Charles Scribner's Sons

from Concord to Lexington. Percy tells the end of the story: "I ordered the grenadiers and light infantry to move off, covering them with my brigade, and detaching strong flanking parties which was absolutely necessary, as the whole country we had to retire through was covered with stone walls. In this manner, we retired for fifteen miles under an incessant fire, which like a moving circle surrounded and followed us wherever we went, till we arrived at Charlestown at 8 in the evening . . . and having expended almost every cartridge." [8]

During the retreat from Lexington to Charlestown the fighting became rather grim. A British eyewitness reported: ". . . before the column had advanced a mile on the road, we were fired at from all quarters, but particularly from the houses on the roadside . . . Several of the troops were so enraged at suffering from an unseen enemy, that they forced open many of the houses from which the fire proceeded, and put to death all those found there. . . . Many of them were killed in the houses on the roadside from which they fired; in some of them seven or eight men were destroyed." [9]

Before the battle of April 19 Lord Percy had shared the view of British officialdom that the colonists would not fight. "Whenever we appear," he had written previously, "they are frightened out of their wits." "They were never yet known to behave themselves decently in the field." [10] The first test convinced Percy that he had been wrong. On April 20 he wrote: "Whoever looks upon them as an irregular mob, will find himself much mistaken. They have men amongst them who know very well what they are about, having been employed as rangers against the Indians and Canadians, and this country being much covered with wood, and hilly, is very advantageous for their method of fighting. Nor are several of their men void of a spirit of enthusiasm, as we experienced yesterday, for many of them concealed themselves in houses, and advanced within ten yards to fire at me and other officers, though they were mortally certain of being put to death in an instant." [11]

Reports of the battle spread throughout the colonies like wildfire. Riders fanned out to the south, west, north, and northeast, spinning a web of fact and rumor that soon covered all the settlements. One courier rode from Boston to Philadelphia in five days and a few hours, although normally it took six days to reach New York from Boston by stagecoach. Passing through Pomfret, Connecticut, he brought the news that prompted Israel Putnam to leave his work in the field and to hasten to Cambridge. Everywhere the people were electrified with excitement. It was the most stirring news story in the annals of the colonies. Far away in Kentucky a band of pioneers named their settlement Lexington. At New York the patriots responded with a parade, an attack on the royal arsenal, and enlistments of troops. The first accounts to arrive, sent by patriot enthusiasts, told of the aggression, brutality, and defeat of the British, and pictured the innocence, heroism, and victory of the Americans. The war could hardly have started in more favorable circumstances. An army of more than two thousand men had invaded the countryside. It had failed to achieve its objectives, and had been driven back in ignominious retreat, suffering casualties three times those sustained by the defenders. And now the British army cowered in Boston, cooped up in the peninsula, surrounded by the victors. Plain farmers had done all this. They had proved themselves more than a match for the king's best troops. The victors were the same sort of people who inhabited all the settlements; if they could vanquish the redcoats, then so could others. The victory therefore gave a mighty impetus to the American cause.

ii

When the excitement provoked by the battle was at its height, Samuel Adams and John Hancock set out on a journey to Philadelphia, where they were to serve as delegates of Massachusetts in the Second Continental Congress, scheduled to convene May 10. They followed on the heels of the couriers who spread the stirring news of April 19. Arriving at Hartford, April 29, they held a secret conference with Governor Jonathan Trumbull and learned of Connecticut's plan for a surprise attack on Ticonderoga. A leading promoter of this design was a wealthy merchant of Wethersfield, Silas Deane, one of Connecticut's delegates to the Continental Congress, who now became a traveling companion of Adams and Hancock. Before the three arrived at New York they were joined by their fellow delegates of Massachusetts, Thomas Cushing, John Adams, and Robert Treat Paine; and by the two others of Connecticut, Eliphalet Dyer of Windham and Roger Sherman, a merchant from New Haven.

The eight travelers were en route to a congress which the British government regarded as treasonable. Dyer had refused to make the trip to Philadelphia by water, fearing capture by a British warship. "Tho I love honor," he wrote, "yet I had rather tarry a little longer before I have the honor of being hanged for my dear country."[12] Adams and Hancock were now celebrated fugitives from the British army. As the delegates journeyed through the settlements they were given a hero's reception. The countryside was in arms, and the towns hastened to provide guards for the protection of the travelers. They became so accustomed to welcoming parties that at Stamford they unwittingly appropriated the places of honor at a wedding feast. After this embarrassing incident, a dozen men arrived "with bayonets fixed" and "formed our guard, swearing they would see us safe on our way until relieved by another guard. We arrived at Haviland's in Rye, that night, with our guard, and the next morning they were relieved by twelve more from Greenwich . . . extremely well mounted and armed, and their two officers in scarlet and gold."[13]

At New York they found the people aglow with patriotic feeling. "Before Mr. Watts's door a battalion of about eight hundred men, in uniforms and bayonets fixed, with a band of music, received us with the military salute from the right as we passed them in front. . . ." The procession moved through the town, by Wall Street and Broadway, till it halted at Faunce's Tavern, where the party dined. "Instantly a guard of grenadiers was set at each door where we lodged, and relieved regularly in the usual way." The parade had been viewed by an "amazing concourse of people"—"thousands on foot trudging and sweating through the dirt," while the "doors, the windows, the stoops, the roofs of the piazzas were loaded with all ranks, ages, and sexes." [14]

"On Monday morning, the company of grenadiers, under Captain Lasher, formed before our headquarters, and the principal gentlemen of the city, with their delegates, being assembled, a procession was made to the ferry, where the Rhode Island packet lay to receive us. The crowd had become almost as great as on the Saturday before, and we passed the ferry (after three huzzas from the shore) . . . music playing on board, and armed boats on each side. When arrived, the grenadiers landed first and formed; then we landed, and parted." [15]

By this time the eight New Englanders had been joined by four New York delegates: John Alsop, Philip Livingston, William Floyd, and James Duane. At Newark the party dined with a "genteel company of gentlemen"; at Elizabethtown they received a salute from four companies of militia; at Woodbridge "all were in arms"; at Brunswick they lodged "with a strong guard." [16] At Princeton they were greeted by a company under arms and by the president of the college and the students. Thence they went by way of Trenton to Bristol, where again they stopped for the night.

On the tenth of May the party entered Philadelphia. "Early in the morning a great number of persons rode out several miles, hearing that the eastern delegates were approaching, when, about eleven o'clock, the cavalcade appeared . . . first, two or three hundred gentlemen on horseback, preceded, however, by the newly chosen city military officers, two and two, with drawn swords, followed by John Hancock and Samuel Adams in a phaeton and pair. . . . Next came John Adams and Thomas Cushing in a single-horse chaise: behind followed Robert Treat Paine, and after him the New York delegation and some from the province of Connecticut. . . . The rear was brought up by a hundred carriages, the streets crowded with people, of all ages, sexes, and ranks. The procession marched with a slow, solemn pace. On its entrance into the city, all the bells were set to ringing and chiming, and every mark of respect that could be, was expressed."[17]

iii

The sixty-three members of the Second Continental Congress who met in May and June of 1775 composed the most distinguished assembly of the revolutionary era. The five titans of the age were there: George Washington, Benjamin Franklin, Samuel Adams, John Adams, and Thomas Jefferson. The only comparable gatherings were the First Continental Congress and the Constitutional Convention of 1787. Franklin and Jefferson did not attend the former; the two Adamses and Jefferson were not present at the latter. About one half of the members achieved an enduring fame. Several were young men at the beginning of their public careers: Jefferson and James Wilson were thirty-two; John Jay only twenty-nine. Of the twenty-five most important members, twenty-one were under forty-five years of age; fifteen were in their twenties or thirties.

Seven of the members had already acquired continental or international reputations. For the moment the glare of publicity fell upon John Hancock and Samuel Adams, heroes of the opening engagement of the war and symbols of the first patriot success. As reported fugitives from the British government, they attracted that romantic interest which the curious bestow upon hunted men. These colorful figures overshadowed a familiar Pennsylvanian of considerable renown. When only thirty-five years of age, John Dickinson had written the *Letters from a Farmer in Pennsylvania* and had thereby become widely known in England and throughout the colonies. But for the moment this prophet was less honored in his community than the celebrities from afar. Such was one of his colleagues in the Pennsylvania delegation — Benjamin Franklin, the patriarch of the revolutionary movement. Now in his seventieth year, he had arrived in Philadelphia at a critical time — only five days before the convening of the Congress. The day after he landed, the Pennsylvania assembly chose him as one of its delegates, in place of Joseph Galloway, who had cast his lot with the king. Franklin had been absent from Philadelphia during the past ten years, so that it was inspiring to see again the venerable scientist and humanitarian, whose international renown exceeded that of any other American. Strange it was to observe the cool, self-possessed philosopher seated imperturbably in the frail craft of insurrection, as it tossed about in the stormy seas of revolution. The prestige of this veteran of innumerable political battles was greater than ever, by reason of the persecution he had suffered at the hands of the Privy Council and the stoical fortitude with which he had endured it. His loyalty to the American cause had been tested in the fiery furnace and had been found to be without a flaw. No member was more in demand, for of all present he had the latest and most complete knowledge of affairs in England. Since the Congress would have to ground its actions on the plans of the ministry, the information he brought was sought with avidity.

To the casual onlooker at Philadelphia, in the second week of May, the most conspicuous figure was a tall, stately member who, alone among the delegates, wore a military uniform. Washington had arrived on May 9, directly from Mount Vernon. His uniform was that adopted for a newly formed independent company of Fairfax County — a band of insurgents he had trained during the winter of 1774–1775, with an eye to fighting the king's troops. That company might have suffered the fate of the minutemen of Lexington, had the British army been in the vicinity of Mount Vernon in April 1775.

Washington was now forty-three. "In stature he a little exceeded six feet; his limbs were sinewy and well-proportioned; his chest broad; his figure stately. . . . His complexion was florid; his hair dark brown; his head in its shape perfectly round. His broad nostrils seemed formed to give expression and escape to scornful anger. His eyebrows were rayed and finely arched. His dark blue eyes, which were deeply set, had an expression of resignation, and an earnestness that was almost pensiveness."[18]

For twenty-two years he had periodically been in close touch with British officials and British measures, and his experience of them had not suffused his memory with kind thoughts of the mother country. On the whole, British officials had exhibited an ignorance of American conditions and an arrogance toward "primitive" America which tended to make them satisfied with an indolent and inefficient conduct of colonial affairs, as if the settlers did not deserve more. A sense of superiority dictated that Britain should rule the colonies, but — due to the inferiority of the Americans — she need not rule them well.

In contrast to such an attitude, Washington felt a strong pride in his native land. Except for a short trip to the island of Barbados, he had not visited any other. His love of country life and his delight in the out-of-doors indicate that he appreciated the beauty of the scenes among which he spent his early life. His desire for pre-eminence and his urge to exercise his gift for leadership denote that he esteemed the people with whom he associated. Without a trace of the recluse in his nature, he sought to realize his purposes through the medium of people; even at Mount Vernon he was seldom without companions. He strove by excelling to achieve greatness, and hence he had a passion for efficient management. He knew that efficient action required firsthand knowledge of the country and its needs. British contempt affronted his American pride; British ignorance imposed an obstacle to the solution of American problems; British superiority denied to him the opportunity to lead his fellow men. With confidence in himself and in his countrymen, he was not long in reaching the conclusion that he and they could manage their common concerns better than British officials could.

As a youth, he had lived on the fringes of the aristocratic society of Virginia. He aspired to gain a place — the highest — at its center. He desired to become wealthy, to be a great landowner, and to enjoy the respect of good men of all ranks. This he must accomplish largely by himself. His father died when he was eleven, and for five years he lived with his half brother, Lawrence. He received little formal schooling, and his book learning was slight. His reading was directed toward practical ends; he knew little of imaginative writing, and his literary judgments were not well informed. Business, farming, men, and haunts of field and forest were his principal teachers. He studied enough of arithmetic and geometry to become proficient as a surveyor. As a writer, he could make his meaning sufficiently clear, for he often struck off homely, strong, and effective phrases, along with many awkward expressions, replete with errors in spelling and infractions of the rules of grammar. His written exercises in mathematics and map-making were works of art, denoting a gift for practical affairs comparable to youthful genius in other lines of endeavor.

His early life had given him an exceptional sense of responsibility. Circumstances and ambition led him as a youth to cultivate the virtues of manhood. The record of his early years shows no traces of frivolity. It is the story of a serious young man who had resolved to become great and who knew he must achieve that end by his own exertions. As a boy he seems to have been a young man; as a young man he occupied the positions of middle age; at the crest of his career he stood above his contemporaries like a colossus. At sixteen he surveyed land for Lord Fairfax in the Shenandoah Valley; at nineteen he held the rank of major; at twenty-one he went as agent of Governor Dinwiddie on an arduous, important mission to the French and Indians in the upper Ohio valley. At twenty-two, a lieutenant colonel, he led Virginia's first military expedition beyond the Alleghenies, and at twenty-three he became commander in chief of the colony's forces in defense of the western frontier. From 1763 on, he consistently resisted British encroachments upon American rights. Now, at Philadelphia in May 1775, he appeared as a commanding figure — a man tested by adversity, well known to other leaders of the colonies, and untouched by rumor of failure or weakness — a self-possessed American, trusted by men to whom he imparted in good measure some of his own confidence, courage, and resolution.

IV. Washington

Certain it is, our whole substance does already in a manner flow to Great Britain and whatsoever contributes to lessen our importations must be hurtful to their manufactures.[1]

—WASHINGTON TO FRANCIS DANDRIDGE, SEPTEMBER 20, 1765

BEFORE the summer of 1774 Washington had not been one of the more conspicuous opponents of the British measures which inspired the colonial resistance. For ten years after 1763, the contest had been fought mainly with the weapons of argument and debate. This polemical warfare had brought into the foreground a group of men who were versed in the constitutional history of England. It had popularized writers and orators—men like James Otis, John Dickinson, and Patrick Henry. By reason of writings published in 1774, John Adams, Thomas Jefferson, and James Wilson gained sudden distinction. Franklin owed his eminence in the cause of resistance largely to his pen. In the port towns, leaders like Samuel Adams had achieved renown as organizers and directors of the common people.

Washington was not a writer, an orator, a constitutional lawyer, or an organizer of urban masses. He was a planter and a businessman—and not a particularly articulate one. Consequently, he had not gained notoriety during the years of agitation and discussion. However, by May 1775 the great debate was nearing its end, and the time for action had come. Suddenly he moved to the center of the stage. A hurried glance at his early career might give the impression that he stumbled into the leadership of the American cause without knowing why. The fact is that in May 1775 he was one of the most forward and determined of the leaders—fully the equal of Samuel Adams in fixity of purpose and maturity of conviction. His military uniform was an arresting expression of his forwardness. He alone among the members of the Congress outwardly proclaimed his willingness to take up arms and to levy war against the king's agents. His attitude in 1775 was not hastily assumed or superficial. It was the result of personal experiences reaching as far back as 1755. Many things had happened which explain why he became one of the most determined opponents of Britain's rule.

Early in May 1755, on the eve of the French and Indian War, he joined the army of General Edward Braddock, in the capacity of aide-de-camp to the British commander. Washington was then twenty-three; the general was about sixty. A month had not passed before the two were engaged in heated arguments. Braddock had some disagreeable experiences with local contractors which moved him to denounce the colonists as a whole. Washington defended his compatriots, fearing, as he said, that the general would represent them "in a light we little deserve." Instead "of blaming the individuals as he ought, he charges all his disappointments to a public supineness, and looks upon the country, I believe, as void of both honor and honesty." "We have frequent disputes on this head," continued the youthful patriot, "which are maintained with warmth on both sides, especially on his, who is incapable of arguing without [it], or giving up any point he asserts, let it be ever so incompatible with reason."[2]

Then followed disappointments arising from the British management of the campaign. Washington urged a rapid advance to the French post, Fort Duquesne, at the forks of the Ohio. Braddock agreed, but his slowness dismayed his energetic aide, who complained in June: "All my sanguine hopes [were] brought low when I found that instead of pushing on with vigor, without regarding a little rough road, they were halting to level every mold hill, and to erect bridges over every brook, by which we were four days getting twelve miles."[3]

Soon came the defeat of Braddock on the Monongahela, within seven miles of Fort Duquesne. Praising the conduct of the British officers and the Virginia troops, Washington blamed the British regulars for the disaster. "The dastardly behavior of the English soldiers," he wrote, "exposed all those who were inclined to do their duty to almost certain death; and at length, in despite of every effort to the contrary, [they] broke and ran as sheep before hounds, leaving the artillery, ammunition, provisions, and every individual thing we had with us a prey to the enemy; and when we endeavored to rally them in hopes of regaining our invaluable loss, it was with as much success as if we had attempted to have stopped the wild bears of the mountains."[4]

After Braddock's defeat, Governor Dinwiddie placed Washington in command of Virginia's frontier defenses, with the rank of colonel. The British government had adopted a rule for military operations in America to the effect that an officer (usually an Englishman) who had received his commission directly from the king should outrank an officer (usually a colonist) who had received his commission from a colonial governor. This rule meant that Englishmen controlled military affairs in the colonies. In 1755, Governor Sharpe of Maryland placed Fort Cumberland under the command of a certain Captain Dagworthy, who claimed that he held his commission directly from the king. Dagworthy ignored orders from Washington and insisted that the Virginian serve under him. Washington emphatically refused and appealed to Governor Dinwiddie, who consented that Washington should go to Boston for a conference with Governor William Shirley of Massachusetts, then commander in chief of the British forces in America. Early in 1756 Washington made the journey and secured from Shirley an order which authorized him to take command at Fort Cumberland. Later in the year, when he was being censured in Virginia for the loose conduct of soldiers at the fort, he wrote: "The unhappy differences which subsisted so long about the command did, I own, prevent me from going to Fort Cumberland, to enforce those orders, which I never failed to send there; and caused, I dare say, many gross irregularities to creep into that garrison. . . . But whose fault was that? Ought it not to have been attributed to the officer commanding there [Captain Dagworthy], whose business it was to suppress vice in every shape?"[5]

Once the command at Fort Cumberland had been settled, it soon involved Washington in other troubles with the royal government. His superiors insisted on garrisoning the fort with considerable force. He objected to this, pointing out that only a very few people lived in its vicinity. It was so isolated, "lying quite out in a corner, quite remote from the inhabitants"—so far from "where the Indians always repair to do their murders"—that it did not afford protection to the settlements.[6] When raids occurred, the frontiersmen fled toward Winchester, about fifty miles to the southeast, and the Indians pursued them thither, without interference. Since the garrison usually did not learn of such forays until a month afterward, it offered no succor. It was worse than useless because it immobilized troops who were needed where the frontiersmen were being attacked.

Washington urged that most of the soldiers be withdrawn from the fort and that Winchester be made the chief center of operations. During a visit to Williamsburg he endeavored to win Governor Dinwiddie to his views. The latter's response was noncommittal. Washington wrote in August 1756: "Now whether I am to understand this [as] ay or no to the plain simple question asked, vizt. 'Is the fort to be continued or removed?' I know not. But in all important matters I am directed in this ambiguous and uncertain way."[7]

Dinwiddie went so far as to authorize Washington to get the views of his officers as to the retention or abandonment of the fort. The Virginian evidently construed this as an official approval of his plans. Thereupon he withdrew most of the garrison in order to place the men where they could defend the settlers. But just at this time there arrived in the colonies a new British commander in chief, Lord Loudoun. Though ignorant of conditions on the Virginia frontier, he rejected Washington's plan and ordered the garrison to return. A withdrawal from Fort Cumberland, he thought, would "not have a good appearance at home."[8] Imperial strategy, it seems, transcended for the moment the safety of the families on the Virginia frontier. Washington sided with the latter. For the sake of maintaining Fort Cumberland, he wrote in December, "the best lands in Virginia are laid open to the mercy of a cruel and inhuman enemy." The people, he continued, "have long struggled with the dangers of savage incursions, daily soliciting defense, and willing to keep their ground. . . . The disposition I had made of our small regiment gave general satisfaction to the settlements, and content began to appear everywhere. The necessary measures for provision and stores were agreeably concerted, and every regulation established for the season. But the late command reverses, confuses, and incommodes everything. . . . Whence it arises, or why, I am truly ignorant; but my strongest representations of matters relative to the peace of the frontiers are disregarded as idle and frivolous; my propositions and measures, as partial and selfish; and all my sincerest endeavors for the service of my country perverted to the worst purposes." The orders he received were "dark, doubtful and uncertain; today approved, tomorrow condemned." He lamented that he was left "to act and proceed at hazard, accountable for the consequence, and blamed without benefit of defense." [9]

In November 1758 a force of Americans and British, of whom Washington was one, advanced to the site of Fort Duquesne, which they found deserted and in ruins. The Indian allies of France had fallen away and her cause in the Ohio valley had collapsed. A new British stronghold, Fort Pitt, soon rose upon the ruins of Fort Duquesne. These events made the frontiers of Virginia secure. In December 1758 Washington gave up his duties as commander in chief of the colony's forces and retired to private life at Mount Vernon, which estate he had acquired by virtue of the death of his half brother, Lawrence.

ii

For the next fifteen years Washington devoted his energy to the management of his farms and other business affairs. In these pursuits he soon ran into difficulties with British merchants which remind one of his earlier disagreements with the British army.

At first he concentrated on the production of tobacco. As a planter, he found himself involved in the network of laws and commercial relations which bound the colonies to Britain. In large measure the colonial policies of Britain had been shaped with an eye to regulating the trade which was carried on by planters like Washington. He therefore came into contact with British colonial policy at its most essential points.

That policy decreed, first of all, that the tobacco which Washington produced could not be sent from Virginia directly to a foreign country. It must be carried first into a British port, even though the final market for two thirds of Virginia's crop was on the European continent. Nor could he sell his tobacco to a foreign buyer, inasmuch as a British act prohibited foreign merchants from trading with Britain's colonies. He must transport his tobacco across the Atlantic only in British vessels: foreign ships could not legally visit British colonial ports. He must buy his supplies of European goods in Britain, for parliament had decreed that all European goods en route to America must be carried into Britain and unloaded there before they could be transshipped to the colonies.

The planters who, like Washington, lived in the tidewater area of Virginia commonly depended upon British merchants for the sale of their tobacco. Ships from England went up the rivers of the colony, visiting the various plantations, where they took on board that part of the year's crop which the planters chose to export. Such tobacco, while on shipboard, remained the property of the planter, and he assumed all the risks which attended the voyage across the Atlantic. Ordinarily, the ship belonged in whole or in part to a merchant who resided in London or in another English town. To such a merchant the planter consigned his tobacco shipment, with instructions regarding its sale. After the merchant had sold the tobacco, the proceeds technically belonged to the planter. However, he was obliged to pay a number of charges that had been incurred either in transit or at the English port. The merchant deducted such charges from the gross proceeds before any cash was credited to the planter's account.

Import duties payable in England composed the first charge which the planter had to pay. He must also pay to the merchant the costs of the shipment: freight charges, insurance premiums, and a commission for handling the tobacco. Other expenses involved warehouse and inspection fees and the cost of unloading and carting the consignment, while the planter bore all losses which arose from shrinkage or deterioration of the tobacco, if such loss occurred before the merchant made a sale.

In the vessel which carried the tobacco to England the planter usually sent a written order which told the merchant how to use that part of the proceeds which would belong to the planter after all charges had been deducted. From shops and warehouses in England the merchant selected goods which the planter had ordered. All sorts of manufactured articles, thus purchased, went out to Virginia in the vessels which sailed to fetch the next year's tobacco crop.

It often happened that bad market conditions in Europe depressed the price of tobacco, and that the gross proceeds from a shipment failed to pay both the English charges and the cost of the manufactured goods which the planter had ordered. In such a case, the merchant might fill the order, thereby supplying the goods on credit and protecting himself by taking a lien on the planter's next crop. The gravest difficulty, however, befell the planter in time of severe depression, when the sale of tobacco in England did not yield enough money to meet all the English charges. On such occasions, the merchant had to pay, first of all, the import duties, in full. This meant that the remaining part of the gross proceeds would not pay the sums due to the merchant on account of freight, insurance, and commission. For such unpaid charges the planter then became indebted to the merchant. In prosperous times the planter often borrowed money outright in order to purchase land, slaves, or plantation stock. By reason of these underlying conditions, the debts of the planters became larger, year after year, as short-term loans secured by crops were converted into mortgages on their estates.

The debtor planter experienced many troubles. He must pay the merchant a yearly interest charge—a sum which, when deducted from the proceeds of his tobacco sales, cut down his buying power for manufactured goods. In addition, he had to send his tobacco to one merchant—his creditor—in order to pay existing debts and to obtain new credit. Compelled thus to trade with a single firm, he lost the benefit of competitive bidding for his crop. Debtor planters appreciated the truth of Franklin's maxim that necessity never drives a good bargain. In hard times many a planter would regard himself as "in the clutches" of his merchant creditor.

iii

Washington bought and sold in England through the firm of Robert Cary and Company. His letters to that house abound with allusions to his disappointments and distress. Once his tobacco could not be exported because vessels failed to arrive from England. On another occasion he objected that he had to pay higher freight rates than other shippers. Protesting against the cost of insurance he observed that "a person had better risk the loss . . . than part with so large a proportion of the year's produce to secure the rest."[10] When some of his tobacco was damaged on shipboard he wrote that he could "prove that the craft which received it had twelve or fifteen inches of rain water in her bottom entirely discolored by the juice of the tobacco; nothing but a miracle therefore could save it from destruction."[11]

The price which Cary secured for his tobacco in England frequently did not satisfy him. He heard that his neighbors' tobacco brought higher prices than his own. The crop of one year he thought had been sold for a third of its value, and another went at a price so low "that the freight and other incident charges swallowed up the sales and rendered me very unprofitable returns, much less so than I could have had in this country without risking the hazard of a boisterous element."[12] In 1768 he wrote: "I have lost (at least) four years out of five by my consignments, having better prices offered in this country than my tobacco has sold for in England."[13]

Nor did the services of Cary and Company as a buyer satisfy him. The goods he ordered were numerous and varied: all kinds of plain and fashionable clothing, drugs, wines, fruits, notions, tools, household utensils, paper, handkerchiefs, playing cards, and snuff. A carriage and harness for four horses cost him £352. He wanted to secure busts of Alexander the Great, Julius Caesar, and other military leaders; for his library he sought busts of Sallust, Terence, Horace, and Erasmus; for his chimney piece he purchased statuary and ornamental pottery.

At different times he objected to the high prices, to the poor quality, and to the inferior style of the goods which he received. In 1760 he noted that "woolens, linens, nails, etc. are mean in quality but not in price, for in this they excel indeed, far above any I ever had."[14] A set of hoes he found to be worthless, "for they are scarcely wider or bigger than a man's hand."[15] A dozen scythes did not suit him — "some of one length, some of another; some crooked and some straight."[16] A shipment of 1766 included some wheat riddles so worthless that one would either have to send them back or keep them as "useless lumber. . . . I expressly desired sand sieves for the purpose of sifting out the dust and retaining the wheat, instead of which the wicker is so open that not only the dust but all the wheat passes through likewise . . . which renders them of no service."[17]

Goods arrived at Mount Vernon poorly packed, broken, and without invoices. Seeds were ruined on shipboard. Cloth was moth-eaten; goods were not of the right size, though he had sent exact measurements. He received two dozen whipsaws when he had ordered only two. For a case which would have cost four guineas in Virginia he was charged seventeen. Other goods failed to arrive, or put in their appearance many months after he expected to receive them. "We often have articles sent us," he said, "that could only have been used by our forefathers in the days of yore. 'Tis a custom . . . with many shopkeepers, and tradesmen in London when they know goods are bespoke for exportation to palm off sometimes old, and sometimes very slight and indifferent goods upon us, taking care at the same time to advance 10, 15, or perhaps 20 per cent upon them."[18] When ordering a spinet he "begged as a favor that Mr. Cary would bespeak this instrument as for himself or a friend, and not let it be known that it is intended for exportation."[19]

Such were Washington's business troubles when the news of the Stamp Act shook the colonies. His cup of bitterness became exceedingly bitter. He thought that the colonies had been contributing enough to Britain through the channels of trade. "For certain it is," he wrote, "that our whole substance does already in a manner flow to Great Britain." The immediate purpose of the new taxes was to maintain in America a British army, ten thousand strong. For the first time in peace the colonies were to be filled with the sort of military men he had encountered during the late war. He denounced the act as "an unconstitutional method of taxation," and pointed out that the colonies simply did not have the money that was required by the act. Since it taxed most legal documents, the courts would have to close, whereupon they would be unable to protect the rights of creditors. If that should be the result of the act, "the merchants of Great Britain trading to the colonies will not be among the last to wish for the repeal of it."[20]

In the opposition to the Stamp Act Washington was not surpassed by any other American leader. But since he was neither an orator nor a writer, his influence was exerted behind the scenes, and he did not gain thereby a continental reputation. However, it was not then necessary for him to address the world because one of his colleagues at Williamsburg in the Virginia assembly did that for him. He was content to have his views and indignation expressed by a young orator of "bold, grand, and overwhelming eloquence"—Patrick Henry.

iv

As a painstaking, systematic businessman, Washington kept exact accounts of the cost and profit of raising tobacco. They told him that it did not pay. Consequently, in the mid-1760's, he decided to abandon tobacco as a large-scale, commercial crop. Thereby he sought to escape his thralldom to British merchant monopolists and creditors — a bondage that was enforced by British law. This was perhaps the most important decision of his life, for it led him into conflict with the British government at several critical points. He now sought to achieve economic independence and to develop new sources of income that would free him from the entanglements of British trade.

It is highly probable that Washington was strongly influenced in this decision by the Stamp Act. He perceived in 1765 that the centering of American trade in Britain permitted the British government to tax it at will. Only by means of diversified industries, he thought, could the colonies free themselves from the danger. In September he wrote: "The eyes of our people, already beginning to open, will perceive that many luxuries which we lavish our substance to Great Britain for, can well be dispensed with whilst the necessaries of life are (mostly) to be had within ourselves. This consequently will introduce frugality, and be a necessary stimulation to industry. If Great Britain therefore loads her manufactures with heavy taxes, will it not facilitate these measures? They will not compel us, I think, to give our money for their exports, whether we will or no; and certain I am none of their traders will part from them without a valuable consideration."[21]

The margin of profit in the tobacco industry was so slight that parliamentary taxation of the planters threatened to consume their surplus. Washington was farsighted when in 1765 he anticipated that Britain might impose taxes on manufactured goods sent to the colonies. That was exactly what parliament did by levying the Townshend duties of 1767. Washington then entered into a non-importation association and in 1769 directed his London merchant not to send him any articles subject to such taxes ("paper only excepted").[22]

If Washington was to discontinue the exportation of tobacco, he must also find another means of supplying himself with manufactured goods. He therefore undertook to produce them at Mount Vernon. His spinners and weavers were soon making considerable quantities of linens, woolens, cottons, and linsey-woolsey. His records proved that such goods could be produced at lower cost than the price he had to pay for comparable articles obtained from England.

Such domestic industries in America did not serve the welfare of the empire, as viewed by British officials. Their first rule of policy decreed that the colonies should provide a profitable market for British wares, of which cloth ranked first in importance. To this end the imperial authorities had, by various legal devices, endeavored to check the growth of American industries that threatened to produce the sort of things that Britain desired most urgently to sell to the colonies. Numerous acts and orders, extending backward to the seventeenth century, aimed to deter the Americans from manufacturing iron and steel products, hats, leather goods, and cloth of all varieties.

The imperial trade resembled a tennis game in which Britain sent over manufactured goods and the colonists returned raw materials. Britain made the rules and acted as referee. Finding that so many of his returns were called out of bounds and that they did not yield him credit on the financial score, Washington decided to quit the game. When he abandoned tobacco as an export crop he took himself out of the imperial trade. He practically withdrew from the empire, since it was first and last a commercial organization. If the other planters had followed his example, one major branch of the imperial trade would have been lopped off. British manufactures would have lost a market; British shipowners would have lost business; British merchants would have lost an important source of profit. And the crown would have suffered seriously, for in the 1760's it derived about £400,000 a year from taxes levied on the tobacco shipments of the colonies.

To manufacturing, Washington added another enterprise—the fishery. Again he utilized the resources of the plantation, for his hands made their catches in the Potomac, taking large quantities of whitefish, herring, and shad. On the farm he replaced tobacco with wheat. His yield of that crop increased nearly twentyfold in a period of four years. At his mill he ground his wheat into flour which, along with the fish, he exported to the West Indies. Thereby he obtained sugar, molasses, rum, coffee, fruits, and nuts, as well as money which he used to buy the finer goods that could not be manufactured at Mount Vernon.

As a producer of wheat and fish, Washington did not act as British officials thought a good Virginian ought to act. Britain did not favor an increased production of those commodities. Pennsylvania, New York, New Jersey, and New England already supplied all the wheat and fish that the empire needed. Perhaps those colonies were producing too much. The surplus had to be sold largely in the West Indies. Britain's islands there, having passed the peak of their development, could not provide a market sufficient to take off all the current output. If more was to be produced, it would have to be sold to the West Indian possessions of France, Holland, and Spain. That would merely serve Britain's competitors. It would supply them with cheap provisions and enable them to cut their production costs and thereby to undersell their British rivals. Thus at a second point Washington's new activity did not serve the welfare of the empire, as it was viewed in London.

v

A third enterprise with which Washington busied himself proved to be exceptionally absorbing—his speculations in western lands. The society of his day lived by a process of expansion. Pioneers opened a clearing in the forest; farmers moved in with their families; young men took younger wives; the settlement quickly swarmed with children who were soon seeking farms of their own. After two or three generations, these vigorous replenishers of the earth had occupied all the good land in their vicinity and a farther frontier beckoned to landless sons and daughters. In 1767 Washington urged a friend in distress to go west, "where there is a moral certainty of laying the foundations of good estates to your children." To men of wealth the great west afforded the means of acquiring more. "The greatest estates we have in the colony," continued Washington, were made "by taking up . . . at very low rates the rich back lands which were thought nothing of in those days but are now the most valuable lands we possess."[23] For fortunate promoters who amassed large holdings there were various ways to wealth. One might sell on a rising market, or rent to industrious tenants, or work one's land with imported servants.

The colonists, said Lord Dunmore, "do and will remove as their avidity and restlessness incite them. They acquire no attachment to place, but wandering seems engrafted in the nature; and it is a weakness incident to it that they should ever imagine that the lands farther off, are still better than those upon which they are already settled."[24]

By 1763 the tide of settlement had overflowed the great valley of Virginia and was ready to surge across the mountains into the lands adjoining the southern tributaries of the Ohio. Virginians had participated in the late war in order to clear the way for the occupation of this fertile area. Soil, climate, and the needs of the settlers all decreed that it should be a wheat and cattle land—not an extension of the tobacco country of the seaboard. The Potomac, flowing with majestic sweep past Mount Vernon, offered a natural highway to link an old Virginia with a new. The prospectus of a plan for improving the navigation of the river urged that thereby "we might . . . greatly increase our exports of wheat, gently lead our people off from tobacco . . . and render a vast extent of back country useful to trade."[25] In the upper Ohio valley Washington saw a land ideally suited to the type of settlement in which he was now most interested—one devoted to diversified farming and to domestic manufacturing.

Unhappily for all concerned, this vision of a great interior commonwealth was not attractive to the king's principal advisers in London. They had quite a different conception of the destiny of inland America. It is true that shortly before and during the French and Indian War they had acted on ideas akin to Washington's views of a future appropriate to the west. They had then sought to extend settlements beyond the mountains. The advance of the pioneers strengthened the hold of Britain on the territory claimed by the French. Since the frontier farmers were also soldiers, the crown encouraged them to go into border zones where they met the vanguards of the Spaniards and the French. To encourage such pioneers the king's officials offered them land in the upper Ohio valley. In March 1749 the Privy Council authorized a grant of 200,000 acres to a group of Virginians who organized the Ohio Company. The scene of this grant was the land about the forks of the Ohio. Many leading Virginians took part in the adventure, among them three Washingtons (including George), Robert Carter, George Mason, Thomas Nelson, and four members of the Lee family. In the negotiations that produced this grant there appeared a source of future conflict between the Virginians and the crown. British officials conceived of the new company as a club with which to beat the French. The Virginians regarded it mainly as an agency through which the Ohio country might be occupied by settlers.

A few years later, the governor, Robert Dinwiddie, when seeking soldiers for the war, offered land to volunteers and promised that 200,000 acres in the west would be set aside for that purpose. As the leading soldier of Virginia, Washington became entitled to a share of this proffered bounty.

During the period of the French war, the short-run aim of the British government had harmonized with the objectives of the Virginians. Both desired to encourage settlement. The crown wished to use the pioneers mainly to drive out the French. The colonists desired to open the west to farmers who would overspread the land and build new communities. This difference of aims quickly became apparent after the expulsion of the French had removed the menace which, for a time, had held the crown and the Virginians together in an artificial partnership.

Once the French had been expelled from the Ohio valley the British government dropped its earlier policy of encouraging settlement there, and adopted a new one which tended to discourage it. The crown no longer needed to extend a frontier zone of farmer-soldier settlers into an area claimed by an enemy. Now it appeared that the occupation of the Ohio valley would not promote the welfare of the empire. The settlers would produce grain and livestock — commodities with which the empire was already overstocked. Moreover, new communities in the west would not be accessible to British traders. To transport goods across the mountains would be so expensive as to prevent the settlers from buying British products. They would be obliged to make most of the things they needed. Isolated in the interior, they would not contribute to the growth of British trade.

On the other hand, the interior produced commodities that influential men in England deemed to be far more valuable than additional supplies of wheat and meat products. Such were the furs and deerskins of the Indian trade. They did not compete with British goods; in fact, they afforded a market, inasmuch as they were obtained from the Indians in return for manufactured articles. The fur trade was the great prize that Britain had gained through the conquest of Canada, eastern Louisiana, and Florida. The incompatibility of fur trade and settlement was an old story. The settlers drove back the Indians and destroyed the fur-bearing animals.

Britain's plans for the utilization of the resources of North America did not assume their full form until the middle of 1774. The final decision was not reached until after a good deal of experimentation. The matured policy exhibited two main features. First, it decreed that the larger part of the interior should be closed to settlement and reserved to the Indians and the fur trade. The crown established a western limit of settlement by making a line to divide the lands reserved to the Indians from those open to settlers. This "dividing line" or "boundary line" was drawn in agreement with the Indian tribes. The red men ceded to the king their claims to the land east of the line and retained full title and possession to the land lying west of it. By this means the two parties designated an Indian country into which settlers were not allowed to enter.

While the king's advisers were working out this policy, they recognized that the rapidly increasing population of the thirteen colonies could not safely be excluded from unoccupied land, without room for expansion. To relieve the pressure of expanding settlement, the government offered a special outlet. Land-hungry farmers might move to certain seacoast areas — to Florida, Nova Scotia, Cape Breton Island, or Prince Edward Island. The development of those areas promised to benefit the empire. They might produce such things as wine, silk, and fruits (in Florida) or timber and naval stores (in the north). Britain needed such commodities, and none of them would compete with the products of established industries. Settlements on or near the seacoast would be easily accessible to British traders. For such reasons the king's advisers chose to settle the seacoast areas in preference to the Ohio valley. The former were opened freely to settlement, and liberal grants of land were made to British promoters who would people them with workers.

If Britain's plans of 1774 had been realized, the growth of North America would have produced a belt of settled territory, semicircular in shape, extending along the Atlantic seacoast and the Gulf of Mexico, from the mouth of the St. Lawrence to the mouth of the Mississippi. The interior beyond the mountains would have remained an Indian country, closed to settlement and reserved to the fur trade.

vi

When Washington found that tobacco-growing was unprofitable, he decided to supplant it with operations in western lands, using the bounty claims as a wedge to open to settlement the valley of the Great Kanawha. To this end he originated a project and enlisted the interest of other veterans. He purchased many bounty claims, "as a lottery," at low prices, since the royal government was slow in making good its promises and the claims for a time had little value. He embarked upon this course in 1767.

His efforts soon bore fruit. In December 1769 the Council of Virginia authorized him to locate 200,000 acres for the benefit of the veterans. He met with other claimants at Fredericksburg, where they chose him as their agent and decided to locate their grants on the Great Kanawha. Late in 1770 he made a trip to that river, explored the country, and selected a site for the grants. At another meeting at Winchester his associates decided to survey the site he had chosen. In November 1771 he reported that "we have surveyed ten of the largest tracts we can find in the district allowed us, and have been able to get 61,796 acres."[26]

The chosen site on the Great Kanawha was then well to the westward of the fringe of settlement. At the start, Washington hoped to find tenants to work his land. This interest raised the question of a government for the area; and that in turn magnified the importance of the crown, as the recognized creator of such authority. British policy did not at the time countenance the establishment of a government in the Kanawha country. The better sort of independent settlers would not occupy an area devoid of a civil authority; only those would be attracted who had little or no respect for an organized government. But persons of that sort made the worst possible tenants, for they were such as would desert a landlord at their pleasure "without paying any rents."[27] This handicap obliged Washington to postpone his tenancy plans and to engage bonded servants to make the initial improvements on his tract. Even so, the problem of government remained, for the settlement could not prosper without an effective civil authority. The British government, claiming as it did the supreme power over the west, would hold the whip in its hand, as long as its pretensions were recognized by the colonists.

In April 1774, Washington's agent, John Floyd, surveyed for him two thousand acres, located on the west bank of the Great Kanawha, forty miles above its junction with the Ohio. About a year later Washington completed plans for the development of his land. Having obtained servants, he engaged an overseer, whom he directed to go to the site and begin improvements. "Use every diligence in your power," he advised, "to get as much land as possible ready for corn, and continue planting even with ripe rare corn, as long as you think it shall have time to come to perfection. You may, in the meanwhile, be putting up houses for the convenience of yourselves to live in, but do not spend any time fencing in the field till it is too late to plant, as the corn can take no injury till some time after it is up which will be time enough to begin fencing." [28]

At the critical point he received a rude shock, for on March 21, 1775, Lord Dunmore, the governor of Virginia, suddenly canceled his claims. Washington registered a strong protest. On the very day that the British army at Boston prepared to march to Concord the governor at Williamsburg replied, confirming the invalidation of the Kanawha grant, on the pretext that Washington's surveyor was not qualified to make surveys.

By this time Washington was deep in the activities of the American resistance. He had come forward in the summer of 1774 to take a leading part in the opposition to the punitive acts. He spoke with considerable asperity of the Quebec Act, which aimed a mortal blow at his western plans. That act detached from the thirteen colonies the land west of Pennsylvania, north of the Ohio, and east of the Mississippi, and added it to the royal province of Quebec. The authors of this drastic measure intended that the land thus severed from the thirteen colonies should be reserved to the Indians and the fur trade. It did not interfere, directly, with Washington's Kanawha tract. But indirectly it did. Presumably, the Indians were to continue to live on the north bank of the Ohio, with the sanction and protection of the crown. If so, could the settlement of the lands along the south bank proceed with safety?

If there was one law that governed the peopling of the colonies, it was the rule that settlement should advance inland along a river and that the pioneers should simultaneously occupy both banks. It was not comfortable to dwell with hostile Indians on an opposite shore, adept as they were in the art of slipping noiselessly across a stream. On the north bank of the Ohio, opposite the mouth of the Great Kanawha, the situation was especially serious. There dwelt the Shawnee nation, traditional foes of the colonists. Most disconcerting was the fact that these warriors claimed the ownership of the land across the river from their villages, and insisted that it be pre-

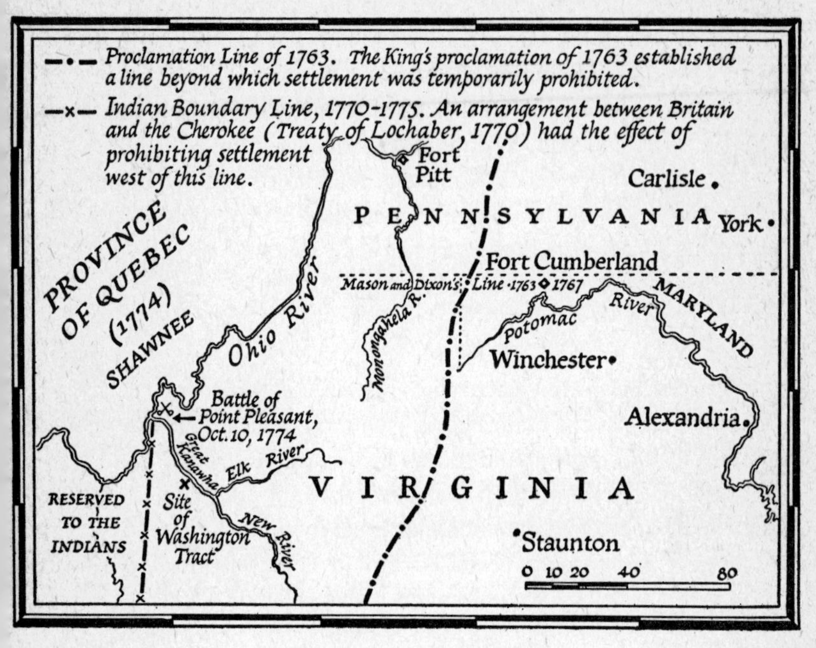

Washington and the West

Based on Plates 60 and 61 of the *Atlas of American History*, edited by James Truslow Adams. Courtesy of Charles Scribner's Sons

served as their hunting domain. They wished to be free to roam at will over the very land that Washington had chosen for his settlement. Back in 1769 a Shawnee chief had warned a band of intruders led by Daniel Boone: "Now, brothers, go home and stay there. Don't come here any more, for this is the Indians' hunting ground, and all the animals, skins, and furs are ours; and if you are so foolish as to venture here again you may be sure the wasps and yellow-jackets will sting you severely." [29]

The strife between the Shawnee and the pioneers exploded in Dunmore's War of 1774. It arose from friction between the whites and the Indians who passed to and fro across the Ohio River. The chief engagement, the battle of Point Pleasant, occurred in October at the mouth of the Great Kanawha. The war had begun in earnest after it became known on the frontier that the Quebec Act had extended the province of Quebec so as to include within it the Shawnee villages, and had, by inference, sanctioned the Shawnee claims to the valley of the Great Kanawha. Dunmore's zeal in pressing for war gave color to the charge that he had provoked it in order to weaken the colonists at the onset of their renewed struggle with the British government.

* * *

Washington's experience with Britain's policies was such as to exasperate a patient man. Before 1760 those policies had encouraged him to suffer hardship and to risk his life in the struggle against the French, on the supposition that victory would open the west to settlement. No one had done more to expel the French. For this service the royal government promised him a land bounty in the west. After the war he devoted much arduous labor to his Kanawha project. He kept within the legal bounds set by Britain, for his proposed settlement was located east of the dividing line, as it was drawn in 1770. Then, in 1774, parliament unceremoniously detached from Virginia the land north of the Ohio, and in so doing created a condition unfavorable to the development of his Kanawha tract. At this time, also, the British colonial secretary, Lord Dartmouth, instructed Dunmore to stop the granting of western lands. Washington protested vigorously against the Quebec Act and the other punitive measures. For such opposition, presumably, he was penalized by the invalidation of a title he had acquired at no little hazard, expense, and labor.

V. Congress Votes for War

> I have no notion of being hanged for half treason. When a subject draws his sword against his prince, he must cut his way through, if he means afterward to sit down in safety.[1]
>
> — JOSEPH REED, SEPTEMBER 29, 1775

IN mid-May the Second Continental Congress was called upon to consider an absorbing question. Should it establish an American army and incorporate into it the thousands of militiamen who surrounded the British troops in Boston? Affirmative action would endorse the resistance of April 19 and approve the view of Massachusetts that the British troops had begun the war by shooting down innocent citizens, almost within sight of their homes. Every member of Congress who should vote for such military assistance would give aid and comfort to armed men, branded as rebels, who were levying war against the British state.

The presence of the delegates in Philadelphia fanned there the excitement that had been kindled by the news of Lexington and Concord. In early morning and late afternoon militia companies paraded on the Common, performing their exercises with a proper martial spirit, to the admiring gaze of numerous spectators. The king's friends were dispirited; many hastened away from the unfriendly city. The Philadelphians supported the delegates so vigorously that no man was "hardy enough to express a doubt of the feasibility of their measures."[2]

The popular excitement invaded Congress and animated the members. "The drum and fife are hourly sounding in every street."[3] For a time the members were drawn together in a community of patriotic purpose. The farmers who drove the British from Concord to Boston set in motion a wave of enthusiasm on which Congress was carried into the war. They also simplified its task. It was far easier to take over an army in being than to devise one *de novo*. How would Congress have been affected by an American debacle, had one occurred on April 19? The delegates would have met in the gloom of defeat, not in the glow of victory. The king's friends would have been emboldened; the insurgents would have been cast down. There would not have been an established army at hand for Congress to adopt. The members might not have made the decision for war and the American cause might have collapsed.

The first important item of business which the Second Congress considered was a plea for aid from the leaders of Massachusetts. On May 11 John Hancock presented their appeal. "We have the greatest confidence," they said, "in the wisdom and ability of the continent to support us."[4]

Despite the initial success of the New Englanders, they stood on uncertain ground. They had incurred the wrath of a powerful government, and, for the present, they were the main target of its military might. The British army remained in Boston, a formidable force. Well-founded reports foretold the coming of substantial reinforcements. Generals Clinton, Burgoyne, and Howe were on the way. Letters written by British soldiers in Boston expressed defiance, determination, and confidence in Britain's ultimate success. At the end of March, parliament adopted a drastic act which forbade the New Englanders to trade with foreign countries and prohibited them from engaging in one of their principal industries—the North American fishery. Thus they had to choose between losing a main source of livelihood or involving themselves in a destructive contest with the British navy.

Massachusetts had now undertaken to maintain an army of 13,800 men. The shortage of powder and cannon was acute. Seacoast towns, exposed to British warships, had already been depopulated, thereby diminishing the colony's restricted means of support. To sustain their war effort the people must depend upon a recently improvised government, not yet a year old. How long could one colony, even with the aid of three small neighbors, carry on an unequal contest with one of the great powers of the world?

ii

The plight of Massachusetts arose from a set of false assumptions on which the North ministry acted after 1772. The first attributed to that colony practically all the blame for the troubles in America. More specifically, the town of Boston was branded as the primary instigator of disaffection. Lord Dartmouth, the British colonial secretary, stated the attitude of the ministry in a letter of April 15, 1775, to General Gage: "I have hitherto avoided taking any notice of what has been passing in the provinces to the south of Hudson's River, because the objects of your command are more immediately confined to the New England colonies; and there is little room to expect that you will be able to extend any military operations beyond these colonies, in the principal of which a rebellion has been declared by parliament to exist, and therefore the suppression of that rebellion must be the first object of your attention."[5]

A second assumption of British officials was the view that the people of Massachusetts would quail when put to the test of opposing disciplined soldiers who were instructed to shoot. Repeatedly, the king's advisers spoke of colonial "riots" and "mobs," and likened them to their counterparts in English cities. Experience in England had proved that "rioters" quickly dispersed when the government made use of troops. Gage wrote to Dartmouth in January 1775: ". . . it's the opinion of most people, if a respectable force is seen in the field, [and if] the most obnoxious leaders are seized . . . government will come off victorious, and with less opposition than was expected a few months ago."[6]

The third assumption of British policy was the notion that other colonies would not give more than token aid to Massachusetts. In addition, British officials insisted that the leaders of the colony were striving for independence. Finally, the theory culminated in the charge that Massachusetts had placed itself in a state of open rebellion.

These assumptions produced specific results. The theory that Massachusetts was the principal culprit encouraged the ministry in the plan of concentrating its force against that colony. The idea that its people would not fight encouraged the resort to arms. The notion that the other colonies would not act in a common cause fostered the illusion that Massachusetts might be isolated and dealt with singly. The accusations concerning independence and rebellion provided a justification for using the strongest measures of repression.

In applying these assumptions, the ministry framed the punitive acts of 1774 in such a way that they bore almost wholly on Massachusetts. All the British military activities were directed against that colony. Only its leaders were marked for arrest and punishment. At the outset only Massachusetts was designated by parliament as in a state of rebellion. The first trade act of March 1775 not only excluded the four New England colonies from the fishery; it expressly authorized the other colonies to engage in it, and virtually invited them to do so.

All the assumptions which prompted the ministry to begin the war were either false or of doubtful validity. The New Englanders of 1774 were quite a different sort of people from the Londoners who periodically assembled in "mobs." The latter did not possess firearms, nor were they organized in military units. The colonists owned effective weapons, which they knew how to use. Their militia companies assembled every year for training and drill. The impulse to defend themselves with firearms had been instilled by decades of Indian warfare.

Was Massachusetts the chief instigator of American discontent? Virginia had led in opposing the Stamp Act. Philadelphia, New York, and Charleston had refused to accept the East India Company's tea in 1773, thereby nullifying a British law. Twelve colonies had sent delegates to the First Continental Congress. Of its members, a Philadelphian, Joseph Reed, wrote: "There are some fine fellows come from Virginia, but they are very high. The Bostonians are milksops to them."[7] Under the leadership of the resolute Virginians, the First Congress set itself up as an independent legislature. It enacted laws for the purpose of injuring British trade. It undertook to create an organization, in the form of local committees, to enforce its measures. It authorized such bodies to use force to prevent the king's agents from enforcing British statutes. It adopted resolves which, in effect, denied that the colonies were subject to the authority of parliament. All these things it did with the avowed purpose of nullifying British laws and of forcing the British government to agree to measures acceptable to its members.

In the winter of 1774–1775 independent military companies were formed in several colonies. The governor of Maryland reported on December 30, 1774: "The spirit of resistance against the tea act, or any mode of external taxation, is as strong and universal here as ever. I firmly believe that they will undergo any hardships sooner than acknowledge a right in the British parliament in that particular."[8] The night before the Second Congress convened, a Philadelphia loyalist, Samuel Curwen, took part in the conversation of a group that included Washington, Benjamin Harrison, and Richard Henry Lee. They discussed chiefly the ways and means of blocking the channel of the Delaware River. Curwen "could not perceive any disposition to accommodate matters."[9]

In view of the falsity of the view that imputed guilt solely to Massachusetts, why did the ministry make use of it? In 1774 and early in 1775 it offered a method of crushing opposition in America at a minimum cost. It justified the government in an effort to isolate one colony and to direct against it the full force of its power. Once the resistance in Massachusetts had been broken, the other colonies would be intimidated: what had been done to one might be done to another. To make a horrifying example of Massachusetts required the use of troops. To justify that, it was necessary to assert that the colony was guilty of dreadful misdeeds. Hence the accusation that leaders seeking independence had plunged the province into a state of open rebellion.

At the very time the ministers began the war on the theory that Massachusetts was the sole culprit they had privately rejected it. Late in October 1774 General Gage acknowledged that the resistance was continental in scope. "Nobody," he wrote, ". . . could have conceived that the acts made for Massachusetts Bay could have created such a ferment throughout the continent, and united the whole in one common cause."[10] In February 1775 Dartmouth informed Gage that the ministry was on the point of adding Virginia, Maryland, and Pennsylvania to the list of culprits. Only two weeks before he received the instructions to begin the war, Gage reported, on March 28, 1775, that the "winter has passed without any great bickerings between the inhabitants of the town and his majesty's troops."[11]

The attempted chastisement of the Bay Colony was the ministry's answer to the measures of the First Continental Congress. In face of the most positive evidence that twelve colonies were deeply involved in the resistance, the ministry chose to designate one province as alone responsible. The king's troops were ordered into action only in Massachusetts. Only that colony was branded by parliament as in a state of rebellion. Only its leaders were threatened with the gallows.

iii

The Massachusetts delegates at Philadelphia had a delicate task to perform. They must obtain the full support of the Congress for their colony. "Every post," wrote John Adams, "brought me letters from my friends . . . urging in pathetic terms the impossibility of keeping their men together without the assistance of Congress."[12] As supplicants for aid, the Massachusetts delegates were obliged to act with circumspection. They could not dictate to Congress the terms on which assistance was to be granted. They must use the arts of persuasion and stand ready to make concessions. They must strive to dispel mistrust of their motives and fear of their influence. They must convince doubting delegates of the justice of their cause and of the urgency of their need.

While Congress was considering the all-important question of aid to Massachusetts it received news of a change in the policy of the North ministry. In mid-April parliament enacted a retaliatory law directed against South Carolina, Virginia, Maryland, New Jersey, and Pennsylvania, thereby dispensing with the fiction of one-colony guilt. Copies of the act arrived in America at the end of May. It prohibited the five designated colonies from engaging in any trade with foreign countries. It applied to them a curb similar to the one that had been imposed on New England. Only four of the thirteen colonies — Georgia, North Carolina, Delaware, and New York — were now in a privileged category, free from the British stigma of disloyalty.

If the authors of this act intended to induce the four favored colonies to desert their partners and to withdraw from the union, they were soon disappointed. The act did not break the unity of Congress or deter its members from adopting extreme measures of resistance. It served merely to expose the falsity of Britain's earlier policy which attributed all blame to Massachusetts.

The *Journals of the Continental Congress* do not record a formal resolve for the creation of a Continental army. The question was: should the members vote to levy war against the British state and thereby expose themselves to the penalty for the crime of treason? As early as May 21 John Adams ventured to "guess" that an army would be posted in Massachusetts, "at the continental expense."[13] Three days later Congress selected as its president the "arch-traitor," John Hancock, and on the twenty-sixth it condemned Britain as the aggressor in the engagement of April 19. About this time it received word that the trade of South Carolina, Virginia, Maryland, Pennsylvania, and New Jersey had been subjected to the vengeance of parliament. On June 3 the delegates approved the borrowing of £6000 for purchasing powder "for the continental army."[14] Such is the first official notice that the critical step had been taken. But even yet it was not decisive, for there was no reference to the inclusion in the Continental force of the New England troops at Boston. The final arrangements were evidently completed by June 7. On the eighth a great celebration was staged in Philadelphia. Early in the afternoon the members gathered on the Common to watch a "parade of the three battalions [of] militia of the city and liberties, with the artillery company . . . a troop of light horse, several companies of light infantry, rangers, and riflemen, in the whole above two thousand men, who joined in one brigade, and went through their manual exercises, firings, &c. &c."[15]

The final decision is recorded in the *Journal* for June 10 in a resolve which, for the first time, used the expression, "the American army before Boston."[16] On that day Congress made provision for obtaining an adequate supply of powder. It was then, also, that John Hancock, in official capacity, notified the authorities of Massachusetts and New York of the fateful decision. Writing to James Warren that day Samuel Adams pointedly alluded to "the American Army before Boston."[17] Other arrangements were soon announced. On the fourteenth a Virginia delegate reported: "We have determined to keep ten thousand men in Massachusetts Bay, and five thousand in different parts of the New York government, at the expense of the continent."[18] Congress then authorized the printing of $2,000,000 in paper currency (bills of credit) to be used for paying the troops and for purchasing army supplies. The climax was reached on June 15 when Washington was unanimously elected commander in chief.

While Congress was moving step by step toward the creation of the American army it paused occasionally to adopt other measures of an anti-British cast. For one thing it rejected Lord North's plan for "conciliation," which arrived in the form of a resolution of the House of Commons, approved on February 27, 1775. The plan professed to offer to the colonies a concession on the subject of taxation. It proposed that each assembly should agree to provide Britain with an annual revenue, the amount to be prescribed by the ministry. The money should be paid to British officials and spent as directed by parliament. The assembly would have only the privilege of determining the mode of raising the money. It was as if a person should demand from others an annual payment, the sum to be fixed by him, and the money to be spent by him, for purposes which he alone should determine. The payers would have only the privilege of deciding whether they would take the money, say, from their savings accounts, their cashboxes, or their checking accounts. If they did not comply, the levy would be exacted by force. Although veiled in obscure language, the North plan proposed such a complete surrender by the colonies of the essentials of the taxing power that American leaders quickly detected the subterfuge. Immediately after the House of Commons approved the plan the ministry authorized Gage to begin the war.

iv

On June 20 the newly elected commander in chief wrote to his brother: "I am embarked on a wide ocean, boundless in its prospect and from whence perhaps no safe harbor is to be found."[19]

Washington's activities during the twelve months before June 1775 led naturally to his acceptance of the army command. Early in May 1774 he had attended the regular session of the Virginia House of Burgesses at Williamsburg. The electrifying news of the Boston Port Bill spurred the members to devise resolves in protest. Suddenly, the governor dissolved the house, it having adopted a resolve which urged resistance and intimated the possibility of civil war. The members met immediately at Raleigh Tavern, there to propose the assembling of a Continental Congress, on the theory that the British measures against Massachusetts imperiled all the colonies. Soon afterward, dispatches from the north told of insurgent activities in Maryland, Philadelphia, and Boston. Twenty-five of the burgesses then issued a call for a provincial convention to assemble on August 1. Washington was one of the signers of this appeal. The impetus for it arose from a Boston proposal for a "general association against exports and imports, of every kind, to and from Great Britain."[20]

Early in July Washington, back at Mount Vernon, busied himself with plans for the August convention. The citizens of Fairfax

County appointed him to a committee to prepare a set of resolutions on the unfolding crisis. One of the other members, George Mason, visited Mount Vernon on Sunday, July 17. There the two men whipped into shape a paper containing twenty-four resolves. Washington took it to a second meeting at the Fairfax County courthouse, where the citizens approved it on July 18. Hence the name, "the Fairfax Resolves."

Washington was later accused of something akin to "railroading" the Resolves through the meeting. As the presiding officer, he refused to read a letter submitted by his friend, Bryan Fairfax, to whom he explained: ". . . as no person seemed in the least disposed to adopt your sentiments . . . except a Mr. Williamson . . . I forbore to offer it."[21] Fairfax replied: "Mr. Williamson told me the other day that he found afterward that there were a great many of his opinion in the court house who did not care to speak because they thought it would be to no purpose. . . ."[22] Washington evidently was not to be deterred by timid souls who shrank from attending a public meeting, or — if present — feared to speak.

The Fairfax meeting having selected him as one of its delegates to the August convention, he returned to Williamsburg, armed with the Fairfax Resolves. They provided the substance of a program adopted by the convention. The members also chose him as one of seven delegates to present the plan to the forthcoming Continental Congress. Washington's continental fame was enhanced by his militant stand in Williamsburg. A South Carolinian informed a Bostonian "that Colonel Washington made the most eloquent speech at the Virginia convention that ever was made. Says he, 'I will raise one thousand men, subsist them at my own expense, and march myself at their head for the relief of Boston.'"[23] When John Adams learned of the action of the Virginia convention he wrote: "The spirit of the people is prodigious; their resolutions are really grand."[24] The convention voted to pay the expense of its delegates to the Philadelphia Congress. Washington's assessment amounted to more than £90.

The most important influence of the Fairfax Resolves appears in one of the principal measures of the First Congress — the Continental Association. This was a plan for establishing an independent government in the colonies — one that was to function in opposition to the British government, for the purpose of nullifying British laws.

Both the Fairfax Resolves and the Continental Association provided for nonimportation of goods from Britain, to be effective about six weeks after approval. Both proposed a ban on the importation of slaves. Both suggested an embargo on American exports to Britain, to take effect about one year after adoption. Washington insisted on this delay to avoid any charge of a plot to default on colonial debts due to British merchants.

The unique feature of the Fairfax Resolves, which gave unusual importance to the work of the First Continental Congress, was a plan for enforcing the nonimportation agreements. In every community, an extralegal committee was to be authorized to stand watch over local merchants and other importers. If a committee should detect a violator of the nonimportation agreements, it was to compel him either to send back his goods or to place them in its custody. It was also to publish the names of all violators, in order that they might be boycotted and exposed to public contempt.

If the First Congress had merely recommended nonimportation agreements, on a voluntary basis, its activities would not have appeared unduly serious to British authorities. But when the Congress introduced the idea of compulsion, its work assumed, in British eyes, a most offensive aspect. Merchants were required to conform, whether they approved or not. They were to be subjected to a supervising authority, armed with coercive powers. The earlier nonimportation agreements had been private and voluntary. Individuals merely pledged to act for themselves; there was no organized official means of enforcement. When the Congress undertook to create the machinery to enforce its measures, and to authorize penalties and punishments, it ceased to be a recommending body and became a legislature. Its acts now acquired the force of law. It had set up a new government. And for what purpose? That

British laws might be nullified; that the British government might be rendered futile; that British authorities might be forced to bow to the will of Congress.

It is not known whether Washington or Mason originated the Fairfax Resolves. The only manuscript copy, in Mason's handwriting, is in Washington's papers. The Resolves were given their final form at Mount Vernon. Washington presided at the meeting which adopted them. As a delegate of Fairfax County, he presented them to the Virginia convention at Williamsburg. There they were incorporated into the plan which the Virginia delegation submitted to the First Continental Congress. At Philadelphia the Virginians held a commanding position. Washington was their most important leader. Two of his fellow delegates, Patrick Henry and Richard Henry Lee, were of his mind at this time. He also had the confidence of three of the other members, as indicated by the fact that on October 24 Benjamin Harrison, Peyton Randolph, and Richard Bland authorized him to sign their names "to any of the proceedings of Congress."[25] The work of Washington and Mason at Mount Vernon in July blossomed in the most decisive action taken by the First Continental Congress in October.

Equally important, the Fairfax Resolves contained the seed from which the Continental army developed. It was evident at once that local committees charged with the duty of enforcing nonimportation agreements would need the assistance of an organized military force. Hence, when the Virginia convention of August 1774 adopted the essential feature of the Fairfax Resolves, it also authorized the establishment, in each county, of an independent military company. Independent, that is, of the royal governor, who commanded the regular militia organization.

Before he left to attend the First Continental Congress, Washington took a hand in the preparations for establishing the Fairfax company. During the following winter he devoted his attention mainly to the task of placing Virginia on an independent military footing. He continued to collaborate with George Mason, who assisted in devising plans for the new organization. For various companies Washington acted as purchasing agent, ordering military equipment through a Philadelphia merchant, William Milnor. The articles purchased included sashes, epaulettes, colors, fifes, drums, muskets, bayonets, powder boxes, and treatises on military discipline. The planners envisaged a formal, disciplined army to be used in conventional warfare — not a band of Indian fighters. Each company was to consist of sixty men, with seven elected officers and four corporals appointed by the captain. When enough companies had been established they were to be formed into a regiment. The uniform included a hunting shirt, cap, and gaiters. Each soldier furnished his own musket and powder.

Late in December the governor, Lord Dunmore, described the progress of the resistance. "The associations," he wrote, "first . . . recommended by the people of this colony, and adopted by what is called the Continental Congress, are now enforcing throughout this country with the greatest vigor. A committee has been chosen in every county, whose business it is to carry the association of the Congress into execution, which committee assumes to inspect the books, invoices, and all other secrets of trade and correspondence of merchants, to watch the conduct of every inhabitant without distinction, and to send for all such as come under their suspicion . . . to interrogate them respecting all matters which, at their pleasure, they think fit objects of their inquiry; and to stigmatize, as they term it, such as they find transgressing what they are hardy enough to call the laws of Congress, which stigmatizing is no more than inviting the vengeance of an outrageous and lawless mob to be exercised upon the unhappy victim. Every county, besides, is now arming a company of men, whom they call an Independent Company, for the avowed purpose of protecting their committees, and to be employed against government if occasion require."[26]

The evolution of the companies pointed to a final colony-wide organization to be headed by Washington. By May 1775 he had been chosen to command the companies of seven counties. His new activities added to his fame abroad. From England a friend wrote to him early in March 1775: "It is reported in London, that you are training the people of Virginia in the use of arms."[27] He informed his brother about this time that ". . . it is my full intention to devote my life and fortune to the cause we are engaged in. . . ." The uniform of buff and blue which made him so conspicuous at the Second Congress was that of the Fairfax company. He wore it throughout the Revolutionary War.

V

When Washington took command of the American army he believed that the struggle would end in the independence of the colonies and the establishment of a new nation. Everything he did thereafter tended to attain that result. Since he was to play the leading role in achieving independence, it is essential to consider the ideas on which he acted, as he had expressed them, prior to June 1775.

He thought that the main troubles of the colonies flowed from the assertion by parliament of an assumed right to tax the colonies. Without delving into constitutional theories, he emphatically denied that parliament possessed such a right. "An innate spirit of freedom," he wrote, "first told me that the measures which administration hath for some time been . . . pursuing are repugnant to every principle of natural justice."[28] He said to a friend that "the parliament of Great Britain hath no more right to put their hands into my pocket, without my consent, than I have to put my hands into yours for money."[29] He judged that all the offensive acts of Britain were intended to subject the colonies to parliamentary taxes. The ministry's measures, he thought, revealed a "premeditated design and system" to impose "an arbitrary government" upon America.[30] "I observe . . . that government is pursuing a regular plan at the expense of law and justice to overthrow our constitutional rights and liberties."[31] He feared that an unlimited power claimed by rulers who were "removed from the impressions of . . . compassion arising from personal . . . connections, which soften the rigors of the most despotic governments, must, if continued, establish the most . . . intolerable species of tyranny . . . that was ever inflicted upon mankind."[32] By 1775 he had lost faith in petitions. "Shall we," he asked, "whine and cry for relief, when we have already tried it in vain? . . . What reason is there to expect anything from their justice? . . . there is no relief but in their distress."[33] Besides, the colonists were contending for a right—not seeking a favor. In taking this position he recognized that from a sovereign "there can be but one appeal."

What did he expect from the appeal to arms? He placed the blame for the distress of the colonies not only on the ministry but on parliament as well. Foreseeing that Britain would not yield unless to force, he anticipated a costly war, predicting that "more blood will be spilt on this occasion, if the ministry are determined to push matters to extremity, than history has ever yet furnished instances of in the annals of North America."[34] And after the ministry did push matters to extremity, he wrote in May 1775: "Unhappy it is . . . to reflect that the once happy plains of America are either to be drenched with blood or inhabited by slaves."[35] The fruit of such an ordeal was not likely to be a happy family reunion. If the colonies were not to be crushed, they must win. A war, he thought, would inflict such a "vital wound" on the country as "time cannot cure or eradicate the remembrance of."[36]

Congress adopted its first statement of war aims on May 26, 1775. It imputed to the ministry and parliament—not to the king—the responsibility for the British measures to which it objected. The two major offenses complained of were Britain's attempt to levy taxes on America and the effort to change "the constitution and internal police of some of these colonies."[37] The Congress then denounced the British army as the aggressor in Massachusetts, and directed that the colonies be placed in a state of defense in order to prevent the execution of offensive British measures by the British troops. Finally, the statement directed that a "humble and dutiful petition" be presented to the king, to express the ardent wish of the members for the restoration of harmony, in a manner consistent with the "undoubted rights and true interests of these colonies."[38]

The petition thus authorized was adopted by Congress early in July. John Dickinson composed it. Humble in tone, it begged the king "to procure us relief from our afflicting fears" occasioned by the measures of the ministry.[39] Dickinson betrayed an ignorance of the king's personal opinion, for the petition, by the plainest inference, acclaimed the Earl of Chatham, now branded by the king as a "trumpet of sedition." So also it betrayed ignorance of the personal influence of George III and of his strong approval of all the obnoxious American measures. After mentioning "the irksome variety of artifices, practised by many of your majesty's ministers, the delusive pretenses, fruitless terrors, and unavailing severities that have, from time to time, been dealt out by them," it professed an attachment "to your majesty's person, family, and government, with all devotion that principle and affection can inspire."[40]

Dickinson justified the humble tone of the petition on the ground that it was adopted in company with strong measures of resistance. "War is actually begun," he explained in a private letter, "and we are carrying it on vigorously. This conduct and our other publications will show that our spirits are not lowered. . . . If they reject this application with contempt, the more humble it is, the more such treatment will confirm the minds of our countrymen to endure all the misfortunes that may attend this contest."[41] Franklin, the member best informed concerning the attitudes of the British authorities and therefore the one best qualified to predict the fate of the petition, made an exact statement of its meaning and significance. "It has been with difficulty," he wrote, "that we have carried another humble petition to the crown, to give Britain one more chance, one opportunity more, of recovering the friendship of the colonies, which, however, I think she has not sense enough to embrace, and so I conclude she has lost them forever. . . ."[42]

One publication to which Dickinson alluded was a letter to the inhabitants of Canada, prepared by a committee consisting of Samuel Adams, John Jay, and Silas Deane, and adopted by Congress on May 29. "We are informed," it told the Canadians, "you have already been called upon to waste your lives in a contest with us." A "despotic administration," designing "to extirpate the rights and liberties of all America," had issued "cruel edicts" which threatened "fetters of slavery" and a "common ruin," employing "insidious stratagems and maneuvers of peace more terrible than the sanguinary operations of war." By denying to the Canadians an elected assembly, an "arbitrary ministry" had exposed them to a "torrent of oppression" and subjected them to "unmerited degradation." The letter then invited them to throw off the yoke of British rule and "to join with us in resolving to be free." It hinted strongly at the involvement of France in the American war. Disavowing any aggressive designs of Congress on Canada, it next sounded a note of warning: "We presume you will not, by doing us injury, reduce us to the disagreeable necessity of treating you as enemies." The letter closed with a word of hope that through the agency of an appeal to the king, "he will at length be undeceived, and forbid a licentious ministry any longer to run riot in the ruins of the rights of mankind."[43]

vi

It is difficult to appreciate the dangers which beset the colonial leaders in 1775. By the resort to arms they exposed themselves to the charge of treason. Their resources were meager and their military forces were in an embryonic state. Success was doubtful in the extreme. Each leader had to act as an individual and to assume a personal liability for every statement to which he signed his name. None had behind him a strong organization capable of giving financial or other means of support. Each must rely upon hastily improvised bodies that were creatures of a public opinion suddenly inflamed. Would the interest of the people in the insurgent cause endure? Perhaps it might evaporate, thereby exposing the leaders to the vengeance of a formidable and possibly vindictive foe.

As the contest unfolded, the British authorities changed their view as to the nature of treason in relation to the American resistance. In the first stage they indicated that the unpardonable crime was that of striving for independence. Such was the accusation leveled at the leaders of Massachusetts. This charge created the impression that such activity was the one crime that could not be forgiven. Any colonial leader, therefore, who did not wish to incur the imputation of treason must take pains to disavow the aim of separation.

In January 1775 the ministry adopted another view. Attorney General Thurlow ruled, when declaring Massachusetts in rebellion, that the state of being in arms against the British government constituted treason. British law had long recognized the act of levying war against the state as treason, and this definition was now applied to the colonial resistance. However, when Congress made its military decisions in June 1775, the view still prevailed in America that independence-seeking was the only unforgivable crime. Some of the members probably comforted themselves with the hope that they could take up arms against the government and remain within the framework of law, as long as they were contending for their "constitutional rights." No one, of course, could give a legal coloring to armed resistance if the aim was to free the colonies altogether from Britain's rule. It was not until the end of February 1776 that the colonists learned that parliament had legalized the Thurlow definition of treason in America and that all the leaders who had taken up arms were liable to punishment for a heinous crime.

One cannot measure the sentiment for separation during the months when independence-seeking was conceived of as the main form of treason. Even if a leader was disposed to speak for himself, he had to think of his close associates. In only a very few cases can a positive desire for independence be established by evidence antedating 1776. But that does not mean that there was not, as early as May 1775, a widespread disposition to acquiesce in independence. If only a few had originally regarded it as a positive good, many now accepted it as an inevitable outcome of the refusal of

Britain to respect American rights. Prudence still dictated that such a view should not be expressed in writing. A person who was convinced that independence must come might continue to sign statements that he did not desire it — that he hoped that Britain would surrender for the sake of conciliation.

A number of American leaders indicated an awareness of their exposure to the charge of treason. The penalty for the crime in English law was rather gruesome. According to Blackstone, the convicted traitor was to be hanged and taken down while alive. Next, his entrails were to be removed and burned, while he yet lived. Then his head was to be cut off and his body divided into four parts.

VI. Parties in Congress

> The Congress are very diligent in making every needful provision in their power for the support of the American cause and at the same time do not neglect any possible means of reconciliation with Great Britain.[1]
>
> —ROGER SHERMAN, JULY 6, 1775

IN the excitement aroused by Lexington and Concord Congress made its decision to take up arms. Cautious members had been swept along in the surge of patriotic feeling. As it abated, they regained composure and grew assertive. We have gone far, they now said; let us await the results of this initial action before we do more. We have shown Britain that we are neither weak nor disloyal; we must postpone more drastic measures in the hope that the ministry will yield to our demands. The unity of Congress soon vanished as differing opinions and clashing interests divided the members into factions. The pervading issue was independence. Directly or indirectly, every motion, every resolve, touched upon this absorbing subject.

In a general way Congress divided into three parties. They did not have formal organizations or designated leaders; they were merely groups of members with common points of view. One is called the militants, the second the conciliationists, the third the moderates.

The conciliationists were the smallest and least important of the three parties. The views of fifty-five of the sixty-three members of the Second Congress have been ascertained. Of these fifty-five, only nine, or 16 per cent, were conciliationists. The leading members of the group were John Dickinson of Pennsylvania, and John Jay, James Duane, and Robert R. Livingston of New York. The main strength of the party was concentrated in the three colonies of Pennsylvania, New York, and Maryland.

With few exceptions, the conciliationists gave their primary allegiance to the defense of American rights. Only two of the group, Dr. John J. Zubly of Georgia, and John Alsop of New York, eventually abandoned the American cause. The party as a whole expressed a strong sense of attachment to Britain and labored to achieve a settlement that would restore the imperial relationship as it had existed before 1763. Self-government and autonomy within the framework of empire — such was the goal of conciliation. To attain this end the party favored dignified and peaceable means of resistance. As far as possible, the contest should be waged on the high plane of reasoned debate. Another dutiful petition to the king was always in order; another noble statement of American grievances was always worth while. The pen was mightier than the sword. Shun any act that would needlessly inflame feelings on either side; avoid intemperate language and violent deeds.

The conciliationists endorsed certain forms of resistance, including the nonimportation agreements. They either approved of the establishment of the Continental army, or supported it after it had been created. But they wished to fight a defensive war. If the colonists must arm themselves, then let them assume a defensive position and stand ready to protect themselves if the adversary should attack. Abstain from offensive operations; do not molest the foe or sting him into action. Wait in readiness to receive his blows.

The conciliationists put their faith in the friends of America in England, hoping that the opposition to the ministry would compel it to change its course. A manly, respectful resistance would dignify the American cause and impart honor to its adherents across the sea, thereby enabling them to support it without fear of criticism. Conversely, rude utterances and violent deeds would so disfigure it as to render it ugly and indefensible.

The chief leader of the conciliationists, John Dickinson, was now forty-two — a few months younger than Washington. When John Adams visited Dickinson in 1774 he was much impressed by the latter's splendid estate, with its "beautiful prospect of the city, the river, and the country," its "fine gardens," his "very grand library," and "his coach with four beautiful horses." Adams found his host to be "very modest, delicate, and timid" — "ingenious as well as agreeable." "He has an excellent heart, and the cause of his country is near it." "He is a shadow; tall, but slender as a reed; pale as ashes, one would not think at first sight that he would live a month; yet upon a more attentive inspection, he looks as if the springs of his life were strong enough to last many years." [2]

On the surface, Dickinson's writings appear to abound with contradictions. No pamphleteer surpassed him in the art of flaying the actions of the ministry. In the *Letters from a Farmer* he described in forceful prose many instances of the injustice of the British measures. But at the same time he condemned rough forms of resistance and urged that decorous appeals be made to the sense of justice of the British rulers. Was he illogical in assuming that authors of past injustices would suddenly become just and unselfish, if appealed to in a mild and dutiful manner?

The flaw in his position resulted from his false appraisal of conditions in England between 1763 and 1776. As a young man, in his twenty-first year, he went to London to study law. There he remained, between the years 1753 and 1756, imbibing the prevailing legal doctrines that had been popularized by the Glorious Revolution of 1688. Those doctrines extolled the civil liberties of the subject. The England that Dickinson came to know at first hand was the England of the old Whig champions of freedom and toleration. It was a rather free and easy time. The Glorious Revolution, having been accomplished without bloodshed, offered a perfect model of resistance to a man of Dickinson's temperament and Quaker background.

The happy years he spent in England suffused his mind with pleasant thoughts of the "homeland." With ample means to gratify his tastes, unburdened with responsibilities, free from the drudgery of routine work, exempt from the wear and tear of the conflicts of business or profession, enjoying the spirits of youth, and sensitive to a new world of art, letters, and historic shrines, the young student saw the most attractive side of English life and returned home, his memory stocked with pleasant recollections. Moreover, he had been in London at a time when Britain, needing the assistance of the colonies in its conflict with France, treated them with a tender indulgence.

To this good old England Dickinson afterward looked with nostalgia. He did not realize that it had passed away. There was as yet no Wordsworth to tell him that England had become "a fen of stagnant waters"—that "altar, sword, and pen, fireside, the heroic wealth of hall and bower" had "forfeited their ancient English dower of inward happiness." He did not appreciate that "the late war, the most glorious and advantageous that ever had been carried on by British arms" (as he phrased it), had left the nation deeply in debt and had forced the government to seek more revenue from taxes. He did not perceive that England's lenient treatment of the colonies could not outlast its need of their assistance against the French. He did not realize that a postwar oligarchy, firmly entrenched in power, was prepared to jettison the Whig heritage of civil liberty in order to protect itself from the hosts of angry men who demonstrated in the streets.

He preferred to comfort himself with the illusion that the good old days would come again. The American measures were but the work of a few misguided rulers. The true spirit of England would soon assert itself. This exercise in tyranny was an aberration; it could not last. "I cannot but pity a brave and generous nation, thus plunged in misfortune by a few worthless persons. . . . The present cause is that of Bute, Mansfield, North, Bernard, Hutchinson, &c., not of Great Britain. Let her renounce their detestable projects, which point at her as their ultimate object, and reconcile herself to her children, while their minds are capable of reconciliation."[3]

ii

A feeling of affection for Britain was not the only impulse which animated the conciliationists. All had another thing in common. Each was either a man of ample means or a spokesman of men of fortune. The spirit of conciliation flowed most readily from large sources of wealth that were located within easy reach of British troops. The two principal centers, New York and Philadelphia, lay exposed to occupation by the enemy. Whenever the British authorities so decided they could take possession of either city with an army landed under the shelter of the British fleet. What, then, would be the fate of their uncompromising foes whose property would fall into their hands? A poor man had little to save but his life. That could be managed by a judicious retreat. It would not be so easy for a man who owned a house stocked with costly effects or a fine suburban estate — whose warehouses were filled with goods and whose rented buildings were as immovable as the valuable city lots on which they stood. An insurgent who retreated to safety must leave behind his wealth to the confiscating proclivities of the enemy. Yet it might not be prudent to be too outspoken in support of the king. The insurgents also knew how to confiscate. Whatever one's sympathies, one might best serve one's cause by keeping a foot in each camp. One might take part in the resistance and still profess loyalty to the king and strive for conciliation.

The party of conciliationists drew its importance from its influence in the two strategically located provinces of Pennsylvania and New York. In each they represented an established aristocracy that did not stand to profit from the political consequences of independence. In both instances the ruling families resided in the older parts of the province. They governed through the assembly and the executive council. Although each colony had a governor appointed in England, the provincial aristocracy was so strong that it could defy and defeat him if he attempted to deprive it of its liberties, power, or property. Its grip on the assembly was the result of a restricted franchise or an unequal scheme of apportioning seats. In Pennsylvania, a high property qualification for voting excluded from the polls the employed workers of Philadelphia, then called the mechanics. Three eastern counties (Philadelphia, Bucks, Chester) plus the capital city sent twice as many delegates to the assembly as did the eight interior and western counties. The New York oligarchy consisted of the wealthy merchants of the port town and the landlords holding great estates in the Hudson valley. The voteless inhabitants included the mechanics of the city and tenants on the princely domains of the magnates.

In both provinces the unprivileged inhabitants, seething with discontent, protested against the rule of the oligarchies and the policies they stood for. Cheap lands, low taxes, adequate protection of the frontiers, more currency, greater opportunities for the small man in business and the skilled trades — such were some of the aims which inspired the disfranchised or poorly represented farmers and workers to demand more votes for themselves and more seats in the assembly. Fearing that such votes and seats would be used to knock the props from under aristocracy and to do away with its benefits and protecting laws, its leaders stoutly resisted the popular cry for democratic reform.

The connection of the colonies with Britain figured decisively in the provincial struggles between the many and the few. The colonial aristocracy modeled itself on the English aristocracy, with respect to fashions, manners, and the arts of living. It was the settled policy of Britain to encourage the colonial gentry; to this end the highest offices granted to Americans by the king were given to the men "of largest estates, least encumbered with debt." When a colonial upper class had been menaced by a populace in arms, the British government had usually sent troops to the rescue. The political structures of both New York and Pennsylvania rested on charters granted by the king; both provinces had governors and councils appointed in England. British authorities, after 1763, shuddered at the idea of democracy and could be counted on to oppose levelers and reformers in every conceivable way. If the colonies should declare independence, they would be obliged to establish governments on a new basis of authority. Since the resistance was a popular movement, it was inevitable that new governments would rest directly on the people as a whole. To base government on popular sovereignty was to invite its complete democratization. Then farewell to the political power of the aristocracy, which owed its origin to acts of an English monarch and which had long been upheld by antidemocratic arts and practices.

iii

The five titans of the Revolutionary age — Washington, Samuel Adams, Franklin, John Adams, and Jefferson — belonged to the militant party. In the spring of 1775 it was not a large group. It consisted of about one third of the members of Congress whose views have been identified — eighteen in all. Its other outstanding leaders were Patrick Henry and Richard Henry Lee of Virginia, Roger Sherman of Connecticut, John Sullivan and John Langdon of New Hampshire, George Clinton of New York, and Christopher Gadsden of South Carolina.

The militants either favored independence as a positive good or regarded it as a means essential to victory and as an inevitable outcome of the war. They had long since lost faith in petitions, having become completely disillusioned as to the attitude of the British authorities. They also foresaw that Britain would not yield submissively to armed resistance of a purely defensive sort. They realized that their preparations for war would cause the ministry to increase its forces and spur it to use them aggressively when they were ready. In warfare, according to the militant view, victory would go to the adversary who acted vigorously on the offensive. The colonies must strike quickly before Britain could muster its full strength. At the same time, the militants did not expect to vanquish so formidable a foe with a sudden knockout blow. Consequently, they anticipated a protracted, costly war.

John Dickinson

Richard Henry Lee

From portraits by Charles Willson Peale

Some militants undoubtedly desired independence for its own sake. Others, like Washington, visualizing a long, hard war, realized that the struggle would so inflame feelings as to burn away the tie with Britain, in the event of an American victory. To all the militants, independence seemed a condition indispensable to success. It would provide the aggressive spirit and the freedom of action that could never be attained so long as Americans regarded themselves as colonists and therefore as dependents and inferiors. The psychological effect of recognizing one's foes as superior beings was destructive of morale. Moreover, victory might require aid from France. If so, what reasons would move that inveterate enemy of Britain to intervene? Why should France, a monarchy with a colonial empire, assist a band of insurgents who were fighting against both monarchy and empire? France could have but two objectives: to weaken its ancient rival and to strengthen itself. To attain those ends the French must help the colonies to gain their independence. The Bourbon monarchy could not have the slightest interest in helping the subjects of Britain to patch up a quarrel with their king in order to pacify his empire and thereby to render it more menacing than ever to France.

Having committed their lives and fortunes to the hazards of war, the militants must achieve victory — or else. Common folk would have to do the fighting. Why should they? Independence provided the most impelling motive. It offered an inspiring prospect — nothing less than the creation of a new nation, a great republic, dedicated to the rights of man. The Americans had arrived at a crossroads of history. Backward the road led to monarchy, serfdom, oppression. Ahead was visible the trace of a new path leading to emancipation, freedom, and self-government — to dignity, opportunity, and advancement for the common man. Congress stood at the crossroads and debated. Should it take the road backward to the oppressions of the old world or build a new road to the summit discernible in the distance? It had called the people to arms. Could it expect them to fight to preserve the symbols of their former servility, sufferings, and degradation? All the American leaders whose vision encompassed the great west quickly realized the necessity for independence. For the moment, the king claimed title to the fertile valleys of the interior. His advisers did not intend that the land should be available to settlers. Independence would break the hold of the dead hand of the crown on this magnificent country and vest the title of it in a new authority, to be created by and responsive to men who wished to make it an abode of freemen.

Independence acted as a magnet drawing together the leaders of the colonial democracy. They were the first to stand out as militants, and they formed the largest part of that group. But several prominent militants did not belong to the democratic wing of the party. Washington, John Adams, and Roger Sherman were not full partners of Samuel Adams, Richard Henry Lee, and Franklin. But the militants who failed to subscribe wholly to the creed of democracy did not fear the common people. They were men of strong or masterful character who had confidence in their ability to lead their countrymen, or at least to hold their own in the rough-and-tumble of a democratic society.

A large majority of the New England members belonged in the militant camp. By making Massachusetts the scapegoat, the British government had put the New Englanders in the front line. First to receive a hard blow, they were the first to become fully aware of the issues of the struggle. Incensed by the punitive acts, they drove the king's friends among them to the shelter of the British army in Boston. As the insurgent ranks were purged of opponents, the bolder spirits took command.

To substantial citizens of New England, independence did not mean what it meant to men of fortune in many other colonies. The puritan insurgents were not seeking to rid themselves of the British connection in order to introduce democracy; they already had it. They did not intend to remodel their basic institutions of town meeting and representative assembly; rather they strove to preserve them. The innovations that threatened to turn everything upside down in New England were originated by the British authorities — not by the colonists. The former were the revolutionaries; the latter were the defenders of the old order. When it appeared that separation was imperative in order to safeguard established rights, the prospect of independence did not appear to be alarming, or even novel. Connecticut and Rhode Island had always been virtually independent. In none of the New England colonies had the political tie with England amounted to very much. From earliest times the people had supported, governed, and defended themselves. They were not dismayed by the thought of moving the edifice of government from the base of the British monarchy to the foundation of popular sovereignty. Four colonies and innumerable towns had been founded in New England by the people themselves, without any authorization from Britain. Popular sovereignty did not frighten the Puritans. It was an old story to them.

Samuel Adams personified the democracy of New England. Born in Boston, educated there and at Harvard, residing in Massachusetts continuously, he strove to protect and invigorate the Puritan way of life as embodied in the village school, the town meeting, the Congregational Church, and the representative assembly. That aim made him a man apart — consistent, integrated, fearless. "He eats little, drinks little, sleeps little, thinks much, and is most decisive and indefatigable in the pursuit of his projects."[4] Strong, hearty, and sociable, he enjoyed the company of people and was more at home among common folk than in high society, though by no means a boor. "He affects to despise riches, and not to dread poverty, but no man is more ambitious of entertaining his friends handsomely, or of making a decent, an elegant appearance than he. He has lately new-covered and glazed his house, and painted it very neatly, and has new-papered, painted, and furnished his rooms, so that you visit at a very genteel house, and are politely received and entertained."[5]

His astuteness, his knowledge of the springs of human action, and his large store of information — all animated by constant reflection — produced a hardheaded realism that made him almost immune to deceit. He appraised the situation in Britain with remarkable accuracy. Not a particularly impressive speaker, he exerted his influence in writing, in devising effective plans of action, and in organizing the provincial democracy. He had the ability to foresee the effect of events on public opinion, coupled with the knack of preparing news reports capable of producing in the public mind the response he desired. In such work he moved with the utmost speed in order to create the first impression and to obtain action while the people were aroused.

His place in Congress differed materially from his earlier position in Boston; and in adjusting himself to his new duties he exhibited qualities that made him appear like another man. Previously, he had worked with people who knew him and agreed with his views. He had engaged in a sharply defined contest with a clearly recognized antagonist. As the conflict increased in bitterness, he acted with directness, daring, and energy. So apparent was his leadership that his fame had spread to the other colonies and to England. At Philadelphia it was not his part to lead like-minded friends in forays against a common foe. The majority of his associates now suspected him. As a man condemned by Britain of a high crime, he was on the defensive. For the moment it was not his office to guide, to inspire, to direct. Men who were nominally his partners strove to thwart his plans. He must observe the strictest caution in dealings with his friends, lest unguarded statements implicate them in the charge of treason that had been leveled at him.

In this difficult situation he acted with exceptional patience and restraint. He displayed a conciliatory manner, agreeing to the proposals of others when necessary to preserve unity. He spoke little, kept in the background, and concealed resentments and disappointments. He made allowances for the prejudices of his opponents and put their measures in the best possible light when he wrote to his friends at home. All this he did while acting with men who mistrusted him and whose hesitation threatened to defeat his cause and to cost him his life. With all his patience he kept steadily at work, winning a concession here, gaining a point there, securing every action that would push Congress forward and commit it to independence. After mid-March 1776 his position improved and his influence increased. The evacuation of Boston relieved the pressure on his colony and lessened its dependence on Congress. His task as a supplicant had been performed. Meanwhile, Britain had condemned the other members of Congress as traitors, so that he was no longer a scapegoat to be shunned by timid men.

iv

The largest group in Congress — the moderates — consisted of about half the total membership, or twenty-eight of the fifty-five delegates whose views are known. This party had strength in all the colonies, and particularly in the middle area and the south. Philip Schuyler and Philip Livingston of New York, William Livingston of New Jersey, James Wilson and Robert Morris of Pennsylvania, Thomas Johnson of Maryland, Benjamin Harrison of Virginia, and two delegates of North Carolina, William Hooper and Joseph Hewes, acted with the group. South Carolina contributed four members: John Rutledge, Edward Rutledge, Thomas Lynch, Sr., and Henry Middleton. New England was represented by Silas Deane, John Hancock, and Thomas Cushing.

Like the other two groups, the moderates stoutly defended American rights. They resembled the conciliationists in their disavowal of a desire for independence. Like the militants, they had lost faith in petitions and believed that Britain would not yield unless compelled to do so by force. Their distinctive view was the idea that vigorous, offensive military action would cause Britain to back down and give in to the demands of Congress. A strong show of force would demonstrate that America could not be conquered. Perhaps the British surrender would come through a change of ministers; perhaps the ministry would have a change of heart. At this point, the moderates differed from the militants. The latter foresaw that Britain would not retreat before its colonies in arms but would redouble its efforts to subdue them.

It is difficult to account for the motivation of the individual moderate. The position offered, temporarily, an escape from both the evils of unconditional submission and the dangers implicit in independence. Since the group was the largest one in Congress, it may have appealed to some men who courted the popularity that is conferred by affiliation with the majority. Such a motive has been attributed to Hancock and Deane. By disavowing the aim of independence, the moderates warded off the most serious charge that might have been brought against them. Many disliked the democracy of New England and feared that its influence would revolutionize the other colonies, once the tie with Britain had been severed. Men might honestly hope that a strong show of force would bring victory without the hardships and losses incident to a struggle for independence. There are also intimations that some moderates favored separation but preferred to wait for an opportune time before avowing such hazardous views. Nineteen of the group signed the Declaration of Independence.

As the largest party, the moderates determined the policies of Congress. In 1775 they acted with the conciliationists to defeat any proposal savoring strongly of independence. They united with the militants to enact measures providing for adequate support of the army and for a vigorous prosecution of the war. Thus for many months the policy of Congress was that of war short of independence. Superficially, the policy seemed to align the moderates chiefly with the conciliationists. In reality, the moderate position was much closer to the militant. The two decisive actions of 1775 were the creation of the army and the prosecution of the war. Together they made independence inevitable.

On June 12, 1775, General Gage issued a proclamation which branded the leaders of Massachusetts as traitors and offered pardons to all insurgents who would lay down their arms, "excepting only from the benefit of such pardon Samuel Adams and John Hancock, whose offenses are of too flagitious a nature to admit of any other consideration than condign punishment."[6] Such was the status of the man the moderates supported as president of Congress. Benjamin Harrison, a moderate leader, is reported as saying, when he escorted Hancock to the president's chair: "We will show Britain how much we value her proscriptions."[7] Jefferson relates that in the debate on the petition to the king John Dickinson remarked that the only word in it he objected to was "Congress," whereupon Harrison replied: ". . . there is but one word in the paper, Mr. President, of which I approve, and that is the word 'Congress.'"[8]

When the moderates learned that military resistance had failed to force the ministry to yield, they were driven from their first position to that of the militants. The two parties then had enough strength to carry the motion for independence. In the end nearly all the moderates voted for or signed the Declaration.

The fullest statement of a moderate's view was written by Thomas Johnson of Maryland, the delegate who nominated Washington for the command of the army. Johnson wrote to General Horatio Gates a revealing letter which fell into the hands of the British. Dated August 18, 1775, it gives a striking version of the motivation of the Dickinson petition to the king.

Johnson described the petition as an answer to Lord North's "conciliation" plan, which he denounced as "designed to wear the face of peace and embarrass us in the choice of evils—either to accept and be slaves or reject and increase the number and power of our enemies." Johnson then asserted that the Dickinson petition was intended to embarrass the ministry in a comparable manner. It would give Lord North "only a choice of means injurious to his villainous schemes." In Johnson's opinion the colonies were already independent, for he said that "our second wish" was a "reunion" with Britain on the principle of liberty. To strengthen themselves, he continued, the colonists must unite America and divide Britain. A "peaceable" line was the most likely to accomplish that. If the king should grant the petition, the ministry must make a total and abject submission to the colonies. If the petition should lead to a negotiation, "Britain . . . must be ruined by the delay. If she subdues us at all it must be by a most violent and sudden exertion of her force." However, it was most likely that the king would reject the petition. Such a rejection would convince moderate Americans that there was no peaceful alternative, thereby driving them "to own the necessity of opposing force by force." The rejection of the petition would also intensify the opposition in Britain to the court. One purpose, therefore, was to influence British politics. "If we can keep up a strong party in England headed by such characters as Lord Chatham . . . [then] Bute, Mansfield, North, and a corrupt majority cannot draw the British force fully into action against us." The British friends of America "will certainly continue so long as they see we do not desire to break from a reasonable and beneficial connection with the mother country." But if "they should once be convinced by our conduct that we design to break from that connection I am apprehensive that they will henceforth become our most dangerous enemies."[9]

Johnson's appraisal of the petition did not commend itself to General Gage. The British commander at Boston, in transmitting the Johnson letter to Dartmouth, observed: "The Congress in that petition appears to have treated the king with . . . treachery and deceit. . . . They all desire peace and a cessation of hostilities, at the very time that they are raising forces, attacking the king's forts and territories, oppressing his faithful subjects, robbing and plundering them of their properties. Nor has the Continental Congress scrupled to publish to the world the most notorious falsehoods. . . ." Gage then expressed the hope that no man in England "will be longer deceived by false professions and declarations but [will] see, through all the disguise, that this is no sudden insurrection in America, but a preconcerted scheme of rebellion."[10]

v

The point of agreement on which the moderates and the conciliationists united was stated by Thomas Johnson when he expressed the hope that the ministry would be rendered impotent, if "we can keep up a strong party in England headed by such characters as Lord Chatham." The hope proved to be an illusion, based as it was on a misconception of the political situation in England. It assumed that there existed "a strong party" in opposition to the court. No such party existed. The friends of America were in a hopeless minority. Chatham, a sick, aging man, without influence at home, had virtually withdrawn into a retirement of despair, from which he aroused himself spasmodically to utter a solo cry of anguish to an unheeding House of Lords. The moderate program collapsed when the weaknesses of the English Whigs quickly demonstrated that it rested on an unsound basis.

The fundamental difference between the militants and the other two parties arose from contrasting appraisals of the political situation in England and of the likely effects on English politics of the methods of the American resistance. The conciliationists believed that petitions, nonimportation, and a defensive military posture would attain adequate guarantees of American rights. The moderates believed that vigorous, offensive military action would effect political changes in England which would lead to a pro-American settlement. Only the militants foresaw that the resort to arms would intensify the government's determination and embroil the colonists in a sanguinary war which they could not win without enlisting the driving force of independence.

What accounts for the superior insight of the militants? They had the best information about conditions in England and were the most realistic in their judgments. What, then, were the sources of information on which Washington, Samuel Adams, and other militant leaders depended?

One of the major figures of the militant group, Richard Henry Lee, served as a link uniting two elements in Congress — a southern and middle area bloc headed by Washington, and the New England militants, led by John and Samuel Adams. The importance of Lee at this time arose largely from his close affiliation with Washington. The two men viewed the contest in the same light and cooperated effectively. Forty-three years old when the Congress convened in 1775 (one month older than Washington), Lee was "a tall, spare man" described by John Adams as "masterly" and "agreeable" — "a scholar, a gentleman, a man of uncommon eloquence." [11] His brother William wrote to him from England in 1774: "You are personally obnoxious to the king and his junto, as having shown more spirit in support of your rights than the people of this country." [12]

As a young man, Lee identified himself with the yeomen of interior Virginia who were asserting democratic ideas in opposition to a corrupt oligarchy. In opposing the British government he continued a crusade which he had begun in local politics at the end of the French and Indian War. Virginia had provided large sums of money to finance the war, at a time when a small group of old families ruled the colony without opposition. With the connivance of a popular official, many of the aristocrats "borrowed" money from the public treasury. Unhappily, no accounts were kept of these "loans," nor were arrangements made for repayment. Although he belonged to the inner circle of select families, Lee had no sooner entered the House of Burgesses than he forced an investigation of the irregularities. A picked committee soon whitewashed the suspects. But about a year later their chief died and the ensuing disclosures verified Lee's charges. The victims of the exposure, who happened to be the Royalist leaders in the colony, never forgave the young reformer.

Among the five brothers of Richard Henry Lee were two whom the father (who died in 1750) had not endowed with landed estates. Arthur, the youngest, and William, a year older, were obliged to shift for themselves. Both were energetic, forceful, assertive, and restless. Arthur had been educated at Eton and at the University of Edinburgh, where he received the degree of Doctor of Medicine. He began medical practice at Williamsburg only to discover that politics interested him more. Foreseeing the coming struggle, he decided to return to England and to devote himself to a novel project for gathering information to be transmitted to leaders in America. He departed in 1768, accompanied by William, who had decided to seek his fortune in London as a merchant.

The two brothers arrived in England at a critical time. Popular unrest shook the country and the oligarchy resorted to stiff measures of repression. The young Virginians plunged into the battle as partisans of John Wilkes. Arthur wrote letters in the style of Junius, became intimate with the radical leaders, and persuaded them to champion American rights as a part of the Wilkes movement. Without regular occupation, he made British politics his principal study. His superior education, his achievements in science, and the prestige of family gained him entrance to varied circles. In the meantime he carried out his original plan and became a one-man committee of correspondence. Soon after his arrival he started an exchange of letters with Samuel Adams that continued until the beginning of the war. Through the influence of Adams he was appointed successor to Benjamin Franklin, then the agent of the Massachusetts assembly in London. Both Samuel Adams and John Adams testified that they received their best intelligence of English affairs from Arthur Lee. When Congress appointed its first secret agent in England, it selected him for the assignment. His brother William, successful as a merchant, gave him an important source of information in the City, and assisted him in the American correspondence. William did so well in London politics that he was elected one of the two sheriffs of the City in 1773 and an alderman in 1775. In the latter capacity he went with a delegation of London officials to present to the king a petition praying that Britain's military operations in America be ended.

The view of British affairs expressed by Washington and the Adamses coincided at most essential points with the views set forth in the letters of Arthur Lee. There were many reasons for trusting his reports. By 1775 he had been at the center of events for seven years and had mastered the art of ferreting out information and appraising it. He wrote to relatives or friends whose fortunes, even lives, would be affected by his reports; hence he had the strongest motives for stating the truth. Above all, his dispatches giving advance information had for years been verified by subsequent events.

His letters had the merit of describing the England with which the colonists had to deal — not a mythical England of the past. Year by year his reports recorded the process by which the court party tightened its grip on the country and repressed internal dissent. They laid bare the weakness of the Whig opposition and traced its waning influence. They exposed the attitude of the court toward the colonies and revealed its undeviating purpose of subjecting them to its will. They described the apathy of the people and their acquiescence in the loss of old liberties. There was no reason to expect effective aid for America from any source in England. The ministry was settled in its hostility; parliament was servile and corrupt. The colonies could not depend upon any group in England and must rely mainly upon themselves. "Believe me, sir, the harmony and concurrence of the colonies is of a thousand times more importance in this dispute than the friendship or patronage of any great men in England."[13] ". . . I would wish my countrymen to remember that salvation cometh not from the East nor from the West, but from themselves. The Scripture tells us that to put our trust in princes and in great men is futile."[14]

Such warnings of the impotence of the British friends of America had the maximum force when they came from Arthur Lee. Of all the colonists, not excluding Franklin, he and his brother William were closest to, and most familiar with, the British opposition to the court. Both saw it from the inside and knew its leaders personally. During a period of a half dozen years they had watched it disintegrate to an almost hopeless state of weakness and despair.

On the eve of the war the militants of New England received confirmation of the views of Arthur Lee from another observer—Josiah Quincy, Jr. Son of a Boston merchant, Harvard graduate, successful lawyer, and protégé of Samuel Adams, young Quincy went to England in the autumn of 1774 in order to ascertain the fate in store for the colonies. He remained there until mid-March, when he embarked for home at the suggestion of a small group of "the most stanch friends of America," who commissioned him to reveal orally in Boston views that they feared to put into writing. Before his departure he reported in letters home the results of his observations.

The court, the ministry, and parliament, he had discovered, were implacable in their hostility to America. No concessions would be made. Petitions were futile and nonimportation agreements would not move the government. The people appeared to be hostile to the court but they were helpless — "the servants of their masters." "How easy it is for the ministry to frown and flatter them into silence. How easy to take the spoils of the nation, and for a season, fill the mouths of the clamorous."[15] The Whig leaders dared not defend the colonies boldly, lest the insurgents submit meekly and bring ridicule upon their friends in England.

In letters intended to be shown in Boston, Quincy addressed his compatriots. If you fail, he warned them, "how ineffably contemptible will you appear; how wantonly and superlatively will you be abused and insulted by your triumphing oppressors."[16] "Whoever supposes that shouts and hosannas will terminate the trials of the day entertains a very childish fancy."[17] "Your courage — your courage, I repeat it — will be brought to the test."[18] "Prepare, prepare, I say, for the worst."[19] "Your countrymen must seal their cause with their blood."[20] "If my countrymen deserve to be free — they will be free."[21]

While Quincy was journeying to Boston in the early spring of 1775, Benjamin Franklin was en route to Philadelphia. "He will be received, and carried in triumph to his house, when he arrives amongst us."[22] "Dr. Franklin is an American in heart and soul. You may trust him; — his ideas are not contracted within the narrow limits of exemption from taxes, but are extended upon the broad scale of total emancipation. He is explicit and bold upon the subject, and his hopes are as sanguine as my own, of the triumph of liberty in America."[23] Quincy, who wrote this tribute to the great American, died at sea late in April. Franklin landed at Philadelphia early in May, in time to attend the first session of the Second Congress. There he added his massive strength to the militant party and contributed his great store of knowledge of English politics. His reports agreed with those of Josiah Quincy and Arthur Lee, thereby giving the militants a single appraisal derived from reports of three astute observers of the English scene. Before leaving for America, Franklin had summarized the fruit of the experience of ten years spent in Britain. He wrote: "When I consider the extreme corruption prevalent among all orders of men in this rotten old state . . . I cannot but apprehend more mischief than benefit from a closer union. I fear they will drag us after them into all the plundering wars which their desperate circumstances, injustice, and rapacity may prompt them to undertake; and their wide-wasting prodigality and profusion is a gulf that will swallow up every aid we may distress ourselves to afford them. Here numberless and needless places, enormous salaries, pensions, perquisites, bribes, groundless quarrels, foolish expeditions, false accounts or no accounts, contracts and jobs all devour revenue, and produce continual necessity in the midst of natural plenty. I apprehend, therefore, that to unite us intimately will only be to corrupt and poison us also."[24]

VII. Washington and Congress

> Resolved unanimously upon the question, whereas, the delegates of all the colonies, from Nova Scotia to Georgia, in Congress assembled, have unanimously chosen George Washington, Esq., to be general and commander in chief of such forces as are, or shall be, raised for the maintenance and preservation of American liberty; this Congress doth now declare, that they will maintain and assist him, and adhere to him, the said George Washington, Esq., with their lives and fortunes in the same cause.[1]
>
> —RESOLVE OF JUNE 17, 1775

IN spite of the disagreements that divided Congress into factions, the delegations unanimously elected Washington to the command of the army. That men differing among themselves on many issues could agree in such an important decision is one of the outstanding facts of the Revolution. Its effects on the events that followed can hardly be exaggerated. Each faction had its special reasons for joining in the selection of Washington and for supporting him thereafter.

He appealed to the militants because he shared their views of the character and purposes of the British government and its policies. Both believed that the colonies could defend their rights only by vigorous armed resistance. As neither expected that Britain would yield without a severe struggle, both foresaw a war that would tax the resources of the colonies to the limit. Both believed in an active course—in the rule that a strong offense is the best defense. Both were disposed to act quickly and to do everything required to break the military power of Britain in America. Neither had the slightest faith in the hope of the conciliationists that a defensive posture would overawe Britain into submission. "Better it is," wrote Washington, "to fight an enemy at a distance than at one's door."[2] He therefore preferred to carry the war to the enemy, rather than to wait for him to attack. "It is not sufficient for a man to be a passive friend and well-wisher to the cause. This, and every other cause of such a nature, must inevitably perish under such an opposition. Every person should be active in some department or other. . . . It is a great stake we are playing for, and sure we are of winning if the cards are well managed. Inactivity in some, disaffection in others, and timidity in many may hurt the cause. Nothing else can." [3]

Washington made his initial affiliation with the New England militants while attending the First Continental Congress at Philadelphia in September 1774. He received then a letter from Robert Mackenzie, a British captain at Boston, with whom he had served during the French and Indian War. Mackenzie denounced the people of Massachusetts and warned him "of their fixed aim of total independence." [4] Washington arranged a meeting with the delegates of the province (Samuel Adams, John Adams, Thomas Cushing, and Robert Treat Paine) at which he was attended by two friends, both militants—Richard Henry Lee and Dr. William Shippen of Philadelphia. The interview satisfied him completely, and he replied to Mackenzie in a letter that might have been written by Samuel Adams. He admitted that the people of Massachusetts were "irritated . . . every day receiving fresh proofs of a systematic assertion of an arbitrary power" employed "to overthrow the laws and constitution of their country, and to violate the most essential and valuable rights of mankind." Regretting that Mackenzie had been misled by "venal men . . . whose business it is to misrepresent facts," he then denied that the people of Massachusetts were "rebellious, setting up for independence, and what not." And, he continued, "I think I can announce it as a fact, that it is not the wish or interest of that government, or any other upon this continent, separately or collectively, to set up for independency." But, he added, "none of them will ever submit to the loss of those valuable rights and privileges which are essential to the happiness of every free state, and without which life, liberty, and property are rendered totally insecure." The letter closed with the warning that if the ministry should "push matters to extremity" such "a vital wound" would be "given to the peace of this great country as time cannot cure, or eradicate the remembrance of."[5]

A New England militant, Elbridge Gerry, first expressed a preference for Washington as commander in chief. Writing on June 4 in behalf of himself and Joseph Warren to the Massachusetts delegates in Congress, Gerry said: "I should heartily rejoice to see this way the beloved Colonel Washington."[6] The New England generals, he thought, would acquiesce in the appointment as a mark of respect to "our sister colony, Virginia." All the New Englanders in Congress gave their approval, and many wrote favorable letters home in order to assure the general a friendly reception. "This appointment," said John Adams, "will have a great effect in cementing and securing the union of these colonies. . . . I hope the people of our province will treat the general with all that confidence and affection, that politeness and respect, which is due to one of the most important characters in the world. The liberties of America depend upon him, in a great degree."[7]

During the decisive first year of the war no member of Congress gave Washington more wholehearted support than did Samuel Adams, who wrote in mid-July 1776: "I am exceedingly pleased with the calm and determined spirit which our commander in chief has discovered in all his letters to Congress."[8] Adams was always on guard against British maneuvers for a peace negotiation. "It is my opinion that no such offers will be made but with a design to take advantage of the delay they may occasion. We know how easily our people, too many of them, are still amused with vain hopes of reconciliation."[9] When such a proposal was in the air in June 1776 Adams suggested that it should be disposed of by Washington. "I conceive," he wrote, "that the general in whose wisdom and valor I confide, will without hesitation apply all his force to annoy and conquer immediately upon the enemies' approach. . . . I am very sure he will give no advantage to the enemy, and that he will conduct our affairs in so critical a moment in a manner worthy of himself."[10]

Washington also received continuing support from Richard Henry Lee. Their partnership in the American cause began in the spring of 1774, when Lee twice called at Mount Vernon. At Philadelphia both Virginians visited often at the home of Dr. Shippen, whose wife, a strong partisan of the American cause, was a sister of Lee. After Washington left for the army camp he corresponded regularly with Lee, who supplied him with late news and used his influence to get things done in Congress. "I shall take it kind of you," wrote the general, "to give me from time to time such authentic intelligence of the maneuvers of the ministry as you think may be relied on." [11] Lee was probably the most important unofficial link between the army and Congress. "It has been a capital object with us," he informed Washington, "to make your arduous business as easy as the nature of things will admit." [12] When the general was criticized by ultrademocrats for insisting on discipline in the army, Lee backed him up and assured him that all men of common sense approved his course, stating that armies without discipline "are fit only for the contempt and slaughter of their enemies." [13]

ii

Few traces of the relations between Washington and the conciliationists survive. One of the group, a Virginian, Edmund Pendleton, did not favor his appointment as commander in chief. His known militancy and boldness could not have endeared him to men as cautious as Dickinson. Congress never selected a conciliationist to confer with him, nor did he correspond with any member of the group. In the first half of 1776 his impatience with its point of view increased in asperity. He regarded its obstructionism as a chief peril to the success of the cause that had become his absorbing interest.

Even so, the conciliationists continued their support of the army and did not find fault with its commanding general. The reasons for their co-operation are apparent. They feared that the war and independence might produce a social and political upheaval in America that would sweep away the aristocratic governments and replace them with democratic models that would offer little or no protection to men of large property. This danger would be increased many times if the army were under the command of a zealous reformer intent upon destroying social distinctions and reducing all men to a single level.

Washington's affiliations, his wealth, his manner of living, his social relationships—all gave the maximum assurance that, as long as he directed the army, it would not be used to put over a sanguinary revolution within the colonies. No American had a greater respect for order, regularity, and established rights. Where could the conciliationists find a more acceptable general to exercise the tremendous power implicit in the army command? Where indeed!

His acceptability to gentlemen of the old school is strikingly illustrated by two letters exchanged with an elderly friend in Virginia—Landon Carter. After the evacuation of Boston, when the continent was resounding with his praise for his first great victory of the war, Washington took time to write to his venerable neighbor a personal letter giving an account of his success. What joy must have animated the friend of "declining age" when he received this message from the hand of the continental hero of the hour. "I assure you I indorsed it 'the history of the evacuation of Boston' . . . and I read it with great pleasure to all our friends around."

For the first time a correspondent of Washington's addressed him, in the text of a letter, as "Dear George." "Permit me to say that you have made good the prediction of my first acquaintance with you. . . . Go on my dear sir, and impress every memory as 'the man who resolved never to forget the citizen in the general.' . . . Time will discover that your social virtue has (like the one of Pompey of old in the style of Cicero) been the favored means of so much good to your country. For I cannot help foretelling that, where you cannot be present, with your humanity, discipline, forecast, and prudence, we shall still be at a loss."

Although promising not to trouble Washington with "strictures on the jargon of the times," the elderly Virginian could not resist the temptation to speak his mind. "I could wish," he continued, "that ambition had not so visibly seized so much ignorance all over the colony, as it seems to have done." The Virginia convention then in session "abounds with too many of the inexperienced creatures to navigate our bark on this dangerous coast, so that I fear the few skilful pilots who have hitherto done tolerably well to keep her clear from destruction will not be able to conduct her with common safety any longer."

Warming to his subject the venerable observer commented on the connection between independence and the trend of the times. "I need only tell you of one definition that I heard of independency. It was expected to be a form of government that, by being independent of the rich man, a countryman would then be able to do as he pleased. And it was with this expectation they sent the men they did, in hopes they would plan such a form. One of the delegates I heard exclaim against the patrolling law, because a poor man was made to pay for keeping a rich man's slaves in order. I shamed the fool so much that he slunk away; but he got elected by it. Another resisted drafting the militia by lot, to be ready for any immediate local emergency; and he got first returned that way. When we used to have legislators, that rascal would have been turned out; but now it is not to be supposed that a dog will eat a dog. I know who I am writing to, and therefore I am not quite so confined in my expression, for a more decent language would not explain my meaning so well.

"And hence it is that our independency is to arise. Papers it seems are everywhere circulating about for poor ignorant creatures to sign, as directions to their delegates, to endeavor at an independency. In vain to ask to let it be explained what, what is designed by it! If the form of government is to preserve justice, order, peace, and freedom, I believe there are few who would refuse; but when these only modes of social happiness are left so much cancelled, or not touched upon in the least, what sensible creature ought to trust an ignorant representative to do what he pleases, under a notion of leaving his constituents independent?"[14]

iii

Washington agreed with the moderates in favoring prompt and vigorous actions of all sorts against the British army in America. Until early October 1775 he joined with them in disavowing a desire for independence. Both, however, refused to state categorically that they would, in all circumstances, continue to maintain the connection with Britain. For the present, independence was a door through which they declined to go, yet they insisted on leaving it open as the last way out of their difficulties. As men of substantial wealth they shrank from the uncertainties that were likely to attend the annihilation of the old authority on which the governments of the colonies had long rested.

If there was a party in Congress devoted to Washington, it was the moderate group. In him they saw a symbol of their hopes for attaining American freedom without exposure to the turmoils of a social upheaval. The support he received on various issues from the militants or the conciliationists greatly strengthened his position and in so doing enhanced the influence of the moderates—his main reliance. As the largest group in the Congress, and the one closest to the man of the hour, they drew to themselves delegates who relished popularity and who liked to swim with the current. Such a man, obviously, was Silas Deane. Quickly perceiving the commanding position of Washington, he decided to attach himself to the general. On June 16, 1775, he wrote to Mrs. Deane: "General Washington will be with you soon, elected to that high office by the unanimous voice of all America. I have been with him for a great part of the last forty-eight hours in Congress and committee, and the more I am acquainted with, the more I esteem him. . . . I wish to cultivate this gentleman's acquaintance and regard, not from any sinister views, but from the great esteem I have of his virtues. . . .

I know you will receive him as a friend, and what is more—infinitely more—his country's friend who, sacrificing fortune, independent ease, and every domestic pleasure, sets off at his country's call. . . . Let our youth look up to this man as a pattern to form themselves by, who unites the bravery of the soldier with the most consummate modesty and virtue. I will say no more."[15]

The first president of Congress, Peyton Randolph, was a Virginia moderate and confidant of Washington. When Randolph returned to Virginia late in May 1775 the presidential chair was offered to John Hancock, who accepted with alacrity. By identifying himself with the southern and middle area moderates, Hancock offended his colleague from Massachusetts, John Adams. In personal relations with Washington, Hancock sounded a note that approached flattery and adulation. He offered to serve in the army under the general in any capacity, even if it were "to take the firelock and join the ranks as a volunteer."[16] Washington regretted that "so little is in my power to offer equal to Colonel Hancock's merits and worthy his acceptance."[17]

From Pennsylvania Washington chose for the office of quartermaster general a popular Philadelphia moderate, Thomas Mifflin. Explaining his choice to Richard Henry Lee, Washington said that he selected Mifflin "from a thorough persuasion of his integrity, my own experience of his activity, and finally because he stands unconnected with . . . this, that or t'other man. . . . There is more in this than you can easily imagine."[18] For his private secretary Washington chose another Philadelphia moderate, Joseph Reed.

In referring to Pennsylvania politics, Washington alluded to the sharp division between defenders of the aristocracy and a popular party dedicated to democracy. To the former group belonged two wealthy Philadelphia business partners, Robert Morris and Thomas Willing. Both were strong partisans of Washington and as such expressed the prudential considerations that impelled men of wealth to accept his leadership. Neither Willing nor Morris voted for independence. However, by abstaining, they enabled other delegates of their province to cast an affirmative ballot. Morris had long worked vigorously for the cause, mainly behind the scenes. Once the fateful decision had been made, he wrote, July 20, 1776, to Joseph Reed: "My confidence in the abilities of General Washington is entire. His life is the most valuable in America, and whenever an engagement happens, I sincerely hope he will think how much depends on it, and guard it accordingly."[19] Despite his failure to speak out for independence, Morris impressed John Adams as "an excellent member of our body."

Three moderates of conservative views who held key positions in influential delegations were Thomas Johnson of Maryland, Thomas Lynch, Sr., of South Carolina, and Benjamin Harrison of Virginia. Johnson was an early business associate of Washington in a project for improving the navigation of the Potomac. In the summer of 1774 the two men co-operated in devising the resistance to the punitive acts — at the time when Washington sponsored the drastic and decisive program embodied in the Fairfax Resolves. As the senior delegate of South Carolina, Lynch was one of Washington's mainstays in Congress. He impressed John Adams as "solid, firm, judicious."[20] To Samuel Adams he appeared to be a "man of sense and virtue."[21]

Lynch's early affiliation with the Virginia friends of Washington was indicated by his nomination of Peyton Randolph for the presidency of the First Congress. The views of the South Carolinian illustrate clearly the attitude of a moderate. He pressed for a vigorous conduct of the war on the theory that "resolution and firmness ought to rule our councils."[22] Counting on the destruction of the British army in America and the conquest of Quebec to bring the ministry to its knees, he expected that Washington would achieve both objectives by the spring of 1776. He endorsed the general's "design to hover like an eagle over your prey, always ready to pounce it when the proper time comes."[23]

Unsympathetic to equalitarians and levelers, Lynch heartily approved of Washington's efforts to tidy up the army. Speaking of new rules adopted in October 1775, he told the general: "You will not now suffer your officers to sweep the parade with the skirts of their coats or bottoms of their trousers, to cheat or mess with their men, to skulk in battle or sneak in quarters; in short, being now paid, they must do their duty and look as well as act like gentlemen. Do not abate them an ace, my dear general, but depend on every support of your friends here." [24] When he needed an agent in Congress, Washington often turned to Lynch. "Command me freely whenever you please," wrote the latter.[25] "I am happy to be at last able to write you that everything you directed me to get done is accomplished." [26]

In addition to Lynch and Richard Henry Lee, Washington used Benjamin Harrison as a spokesman and sort of personal agent in Congress. Harrison had attended many official meetings with Washington, had traveled with him frequently, and had visited at Mount Vernon. Writing to Joseph Reed, then in Philadelphia, concerning some desired arrangement, Washington said: "If you will hint the matter to Colonel Harrison, I dare venture to say that Congress will make it agreeable to you in every shape they can." [27] John Adams later described Harrison as Washington's "private, confidential correspondent." [28] Ardent in his support of aggressive action, the Virginian for many months shrank from the hazards of independence. At the First Congress he said he would have come on foot rather than stay away, and offered a toast: "A constitutional death to Lords Bute, Mansfield and North." [29] Later, his hesitation moved the irrepressible Charles Lee to liken him to the prince of Lilliput, "hobbling with one high shoe and one low one." [30]

The tie between Washington and Harrison caused a flurry of excitement in the summer of 1775. On July 21, Harrison wrote a letter to the general which a British officer, Captain Ascough of the *Swan,* intercepted in Rhode Island. It was sent to Admiral Graves, a bitter enemy of the Americans, who kept the original. General Gage received a copy. British agents published a version of it in a Boston paper. This printed "copy" contained a passage which put both Harrison and Washington in a murky light. As printed, the letter consisted of two sharply contrasting parts. The first, entirely matter-of-fact and businesslike, related routine actions of Congress pertaining to the army. The second, written in the manner of a skilled literary hireling and utterly foreign to the rest of the letter, purported to relate a sordid personal intrigue. There is every reason for thinking that the second part is a forgery which a British propaganda agent added in order to humiliate the two leaders. The copy sent to England by Gage does not contain the doubtful passage. Neither does a second copy in the Haldimand papers. A "copy" in the Admiralty files, which does include the passage, is not in the handwriting of Harrison. The incident suggests that British agents were informed of the official tie between Harrison and Washington and endeavored to exploit it in such a manner as to discredit the two men. Congress quickly expressed its contempt for the maneuver by sending Harrison with Franklin and Lynch to confer with Washington and the New England leaders at a very important conference in Cambridge.

iv

The factions in Congress aligned themselves in ways that placed Washington in an unassailable position. He could count on the moderates and the militants to approve his military proposals and actions that were essential to the winning of the war. The two groups, controlling every delegation in Congress, committed the country to a vigorous forward policy consonant with his views. He acknowledged his reliance on the two groups when he named the first vessels he acquired as the nucleus of an American fleet. The *Hancock*, the *Harrison,* and the *Lynch* paid tribute to the moderates; the *Franklin,* the *Lee,* and the *Warren* honored the militants.

The relations of Washington and Congress were determined by the military strategy which they adopted at the outset of the struggle. They decided against guerilla warfare in favor of the plan of keeping a large American force close by the main British army in America. One purpose, of course, was to prevent the British from dividing their army into bands capable of raiding at will in all the colonies. If the British should so divide their forces, in the face of a concentrated American army, Washington could overwhelm, one by one, their small detachments left to hold the most strategic points such as Boston, Philadelphia, and New York. Since it was essential that the American army be able to strike quickly, it followed that it must be mobile and maneuverable. It must therefore be well organized, effectively disciplined, and centrally controlled. But there was a danger inherent in such a powerful instrument. It might be used by a few strong men to establish a military despotism in the colonies.

By whom, then, should the army be controlled? To whom should it be responsible? It could not be operated efficiently by the thirteen separate colonial governments. It must be subject to one centralizing authority. There were only two sources of such authority—the army itself and the Continental Congress. To lodge supreme, unlimited authority in the army was to establish a military dictatorship. Practically everybody opposed that. The primary aim of the war was to perpetuate government of civilians, by civilians, and for civilians. To Washington, this aim was wholly acceptable. He came from a society dominated by men of large property who were determined to be masters of their estates. The spirit of freedom, independence, and self-reliance engendered by the southern plantations did not dispose their owners to submit tamely to an authority outside themselves. With Washington, the idea of civilian supremacy was bred in the bone. In addition, he aspired to gain, in the highest degree, the esteem of his countrymen. To achieve that he must respect their deepest convictions and their most cherished rights. Had he undertaken to establish an army dictatorship, his name and memory would have become symbols of evil, provocative of maledictions, forever. "To obtain the applause of deserving men," he wrote, "is a heartfelt satisfaction; to merit it is my highest wish."[31] "I am happy . . . to find and to hear from different quarters, that my reputation stands fair, that my conduct hitherto has given universal satisfaction."[32] After the evacuation of Boston, the authorities of Massachusetts conveyed to him their appreciation of the respect he had shown for the civil constitution of the colony. In replying to the assembly he said: "A regard to every provincial institution, where not incompatible with the common interest, I hold a principle of duty and of policy, and it shall ever form a part of my conduct."[33]

The decision to keep a large force intact presupposed the existence of a centralized authority, lest the army be shattered or neutralized by the conflicting claims and demands of a dozen provincial governments. Moreover, the commander in chief needed a recognized authority as the source of the power which he must assert over subordinate officers. Such a supreme, central authority at the top must be civilian in character, in order to shield the army from the hatred of the people. If they would respect its authority, the army would be exempted from the kind of internal opposition that might lead to civil war. A conflict of that sort, by deflecting the army from its main task, would assure the success of the British.

A centralized, civilian authority. Only Congress could provide it. The members recognized the fact when in June 1775 they created the army, issued the commissions to its general officers, provided the money for its needs, and adopted the rules and regulations for its government. In all this initial work Washington, while yet a delegate, made his personal contribution. Once he had assumed the command he had the strongest interest in magnifying the authority of Congress. His own authority, which must be extensive, would not possess a force greater than that of its source. Consequently, he strove to exalt the dignity and prestige of Congress. He manifested toward it a respectful subordination. He toiled laboriously to keep it well informed. He asserted its superiority and claimed freedom of action for its creature, the army. "No provincial Congress," he said, "can, with any propriety, interfere in the disposition of the troops on the continental establishment, much less control the orders of any general officer."[34] In his correspondence he carefully avoided statements derogatory to Congress or its members. "I have studiously avoided in all letters intended for . . . Congress every expression that could give pain or uneasiness; and shall observe the same rule with respect to private letters, further than appears absolutely necessary for the elucidation of facts."[35]

Much as Washington needed the sustaining authority of Congress, he needed also extensive powers of action. A force of several thousand men constituted a world in itself. It might not have to care for infants or educate children, but even so its activities would be legion, and its movements would affect a multitude of interests. It would have to buy supplies, engage workmen, put currency into circulation, construct buildings, provide sanitation, obtain wagon transportation, acquire ships, procure intelligence, deal with local governments, and supervise relations between soldiers and civilians. It must provide courts, religious services, and hospitals. The country as yet had no body of law to govern activities in such a large sphere. Congress, remote from the scene of operations, could not legislate quickly for emergencies. In such circumstances it was necessary to grant Washington considerable freedom of action and to allow him to exercise powers not precisely defined. "In cases of extreme necessity," he said, "nothing but decision can insure success."[36] General Gates had written to him in June 1775: "I must . . . entreat you not to leave the Congress until you are provided not only with all the powers, but all the means their power can bestow."[37]

Soon after Washington took command of the army he found that the confusion at camp, the uncertainties of the service, and the extended scale of operations presented a host of problems for which Congress had not made provision. New offices were needed; lesser officers must be appointed; special supplies must be obtained; the method of paying the troops should be improved. In dealing with such matters Washington usually received the full support of Congress. Either he made recommendations which it speedily approved, or he acted in advance on his own initiative, reporting his decisions for formal ratification, which was readily granted. So faithfully did Congress comply with his wishes as to technical matters pertaining to the organization and administration of the army that it was, in this regard, little more than a rubber stamp.

Other actions which Washington deemed essential to the safety or success of the army were of a much more comprehensive and significant nature, bearing directly on the general aims of the war. Under his decisive leadership the army could not refrain from exercising powers in a way that affected the central issue of 1775—independence versus conciliation. The majority in Congress thought that certain drastic measures would savor strongly of independence. Should the colonies enter into a permanent confederation? Should American ports be thrown open to the vessels of foreign nations? Should stern measures be employed to suppress the king's friends in America? Should the colonies be encouraged to set up new governments independent of Britain's authority? Should Congress seek assistance from foreign states? Should it establish a navy which would extend the war to the highways of the world?

Such questions the militants were prepared to answer in the affirmative. But the moderates and conciliationists hesitated. They were reluctant to authorize measures that implied a severance of the tie with Britain. The party division on such issues is illustrated by a motion of Richard Henry Lee that Congress order the suppression of the British postal service in the colonies. Three other militants—Samuel Adams, John Langdon, and Eliphalet Dyer—supported Lee. They defended the proposal as a means of lessening Britain's power. "Our enemies here," said Lee, "are corresponding for our ruin."[38] The moderates, headed by Willing and Deane, and the conciliationists, led by Duane and Robert R. Livingston, united to defeat the motion. They stated the view that the British postal service was not one of the grievances against which the colonies were resisting. To strike at an unoffending institution would violate the principle of a defensive war. Congress desired merely to restore the state of things existing before 1763, of which the royal mail was a part.

If Washington had voted on Lee's motion, the chances are a thousand to one that he would have supported it as a means of crippling the British army. In other instances he deemed that drastic actions were necessary to the safety or success of the American forces. He was compelled to move in a zone where the limits of his authority had not been precisely determined. With respect to all the great measures which tended toward independence he acted on his own initiative, in advance of written authorization from Congress. There is every reason to believe that he had entered into a tacit agreement with its members, the terms of which were as follows. He was free to act in emergencies in the light of his judgment and discretion. If he should do something for which Congress had not provided specific authorization, he was to report the action immediately to the president. If Congress should disapprove, he would be so notified, and the act would not be repeated. If Congress should ignore the act and neither approve nor disapprove, its silence was to be construed as consent. This arrangement gave him a flexible authority and allowed him to act with a *de facto* approval of Congress. It also exempted the members from making written endorsements of drastic measures that might be interpreted as support for independence. As early as June 25, 1775, he stated that he would not hesitate to order the seizure of a royal governor (Tryon of New York) "if the Continental Congress was not sitting."[39] Six months later General Charles Lee wrote to him: ". . . the Congress have given you authority to take any step . . . which you shall think necessary for the public service; but if they have not given you expressly and literally authority with respect to the city of New York, I am confident that any measure you think right to plan and put in execution will be approved of. I have the greatest reason to believe, from the most authentic intelligence, that the best members of Congress expect that you would take much upon yourself, as referring every matter of importance to them is defeating the project. . . . To you they look up for decision; by your conduct they are to be inspired by decision. In fact, your situation is such that the salvation of the whole depends on your striking, at certain crises, vigorous strokes, without previously communicating your intention."[40]

Such was the view of General Lee after he had been closely associated with Washington more than six months. During this time Washington had taken, independently, on his own authority, a number of decisive actions that could be considered as possible steps toward independence. Not one of them had been disavowed or repudiated by Congress.

VIII. The Generals

> . . . there is not a difficulty that you . . . very justly complain of . . . that I am not every day experiencing; but we must bear up against them, and make the best of mankind as they are, since we cannot have them as we wish.[1]
>
> — WASHINGTON TO SCHUYLER, DECEMBER 24, 1775

THE political climate of New York proved to be favorable to the moderate point of view. The strategic importance of the province, together with its feeble defenses, made certain that a British invasion and occupation would not be long delayed. That danger fostered attitudes of caution and restraint. The anxieties of the inhabitants infected the leaders also. A conflict of interests and loyalties came to a focus in the person of a moderate member of the Second Congress — Philip John Schuyler of Albany.

In June 1775 Congress placed him in command of the Continental army in New York, with the rank of major general. Since New York was designated at that time as inferior only to Boston as a theater of war, Schuyler was second in importance to Washington. Late in June, when Congress authorized an invasion of Canada, it left the decision for such an undertaking to Schuyler's discretion.

There is little evidence of contact between Schuyler and Washington prior to May 1775. Schuyler had not attended the First Continental Congress. The two men served on important committees in the Second Congress before they set out together from Philadelphia, late in June, to assume their respective commands. There is no doubt that the New Yorker was acceptable to the Virginian. Schuyler had served honorably in the northern campaigns during the French and Indian War. He was now the proper age — forty-one — not quite two years younger than the general. Having been the unanimous choice of the New York delegates in Congress, he harmonized the conflicting elements of the province. He shared the hope of the moderates — that vigorous military action would soon achieve conciliation on American terms. "Now or never," he wrote to Washington, "is the time for every virtuous American to exert himself in the cause of liberty and his country. . . . I can with a good conscience declare that I have devoted myself to the service of my country in the firmest resolution to sink or swim with it, unanxious how I quit the stage of life, provided that I leave to my posterity the happy reflection that their ancestor was an honest American."[2]

Undoubtedly, Schuyler owed his high place in the American hierarchy to his political importance in a pivotal colony, as an outstanding leader in the Albany area. Washington believed that the Americans must, at all costs, prevent a junction of British forces in Canada with those in New York City. To this end the insurgents must occupy and hold the Hudson valley. This they must do in cooperation with the civil authorities of the province, for all parties in Congress agreed that the army must not become an instrument for establishing a military despotism. However, the Revolutionary government of New York exhibited a marked disinclination for decisive action against the British. The provincial congress had instructed its delegates in Congress to work for "the restoration of harmony between Great Britain and the colonies."[3] When Washington and his entourage, en route to Boston, arrived at New York City late in June, the citizens gave him a cordial reception. But that very evening they welcomed the royal governor, William Tryon, who by a strange coincidence reached the city simultaneously with Washington. "We will not favor either the American general or the British governor": thus spake the men of caution. From the New York insurgent congress Washington received an address which, saying little about vigorous military exertion, proclaimed its "fondest wish" for an accommodation "with our mother country" and expressed its "fullest assurance" that at the end of "the glorious struggle for American liberty" the general would "cheerfully resign the important deposit" committed into his hands, and "resume the character of our worthiest citizen."[4] Seeking to keep the British quiet, the provincial congress permitted their warships stationed in the harbor to obtain provisions from the city.

In the face of this awkward situation Washington and Congress strove to control the vital Hudson valley. Upon whom could they depend for assistance? The area was carved into large estates which were owned by provincial magnates and worked by tenant farmers. Many of the great landed families favored the American cause: the Livingstons, the Van Cortlandts, the Van Rensselaers. In this group belonged Philip Schuyler. However, these lords of the manor did not always command the loyalty of their tenants. In fact there was bitter antagonism between the two. As recently as 1766 the tenants had revolted against the aristocratic land system and the high rents which it exacted. They wanted a type of tenure that would give them full, free, and independent ownership.

It was not to be expected that such tenants would rush to arms in a cause espoused by their landlords. Why should they fight for the privilege of paying rent? Thus it happened that the Hudson valley magnates could not bring many fighting men to the American camps. What was the alternative? Should Congress appeal directly to the tenants for support? If so, what inducements should it offer to them? Should it promise them the land they cultivated and thereby strike down the magnates? Such a course would convert the insurgent movement into a shattering revolutionary upheaval. In the middle colonies and the south many leading insurgents owned large estates that were cultivated by tenants, servants, or slaves. If Congress should encourage the tenants of New York to help themselves to the lands of their overlords, where would such a process of acquisition stop? Clearly, Congress could not sanction attacks on the property of men who adhered to its cause. If it did that, it would soon find itself without any adherents at all.

Thus the realities of war forced Congress into a partnership with the Hudson valley magnates which assigned to them the posts of leadership in the strategically vital area. Washington readily acquiesced in the necessity. A large landowner himself, who had endeavored to settle tenants on his Kanawha lands, he could scarcely find fault with the New York overlords. Although the experiences of the war made him a strong partisan of the yeoman class, at the same time he always recognized the great importance of leadership. In those times, a man of remarkable force, energy, and ability usually acquired wealth. Such men were needed by the American cause. Lacking at the start the backing of a strong government, it must look to citizens of fortune for many services. Skilled merchants were needed to obtain supplies; private loans were required by emergencies; rare and expensive articles must be contributed by individual owners.

The reliance on the New York magnates as the mainstay of the American cause in the Hudson valley involved Washington in a tangle of difficulties that taxed his abilities to the utmost. For the unfortunate fact was that those leaders, as exemplified by Schuyler, could not rally to the American standard an effective body of fighting men. For military operations on the northern frontier Washington and Schuyler were obliged to utilize New England troops. But, alas, the frontiersmen from the east were land-hungry democrats who detested landlord princes. The Green Mountain boys of Vermont were determined to take unto themselves a large tract of land claimed by New York. Such were the people whom Schuyler was called upon to command. They did not like him personally. Their individualism and sense of equality appeared to him as little better than insubordination. They did not respond to his appeals for order, regularity, and discipline. They told him that they ought to be commanded by a New England general. And what could he do? In opposing such sturdy foes he could expect little aid from the lukewarm insurgent government in New York City. He could not even provide his men with adequate supplies.

Sorely exasperated by his trials, Schuyler turned to Washington for relief. Letter after letter arrived from Albany at the Cambridge camp. The northern general was beset by a host of troubles. His health had given way and he had been forced to take to his bed.

Now he wished to resign. Congress should give him additional instructions. Supplies were inadequate, the men were not paid; their nonchalance and insubordination kept them on the verge of desertion or mutiny.

No general ever received more steadfast support than Washington's to Schuyler. The commander in chief endorsed and justified the New Yorker's official orders. A stream of praise, recognition, appreciation, and encouragement flowed from Cambridge to Albany. The northern general was urged not to resign. A kinship of misfortune was established as Washington alluded to his own trials, so much like those of his harassed partner. Congress was requested to send a delegation to the north—and complied. The general sustained Schuyler in his strife with the New Englanders and defended him against their charges that he was lukewarm or actually disloyal to the cause. All this attention Washington lavished upon an officer whose chief mission was to effect the conquest of Canada and who refused to lead his men in battle or even to leave his home base in New York.

Schuyler responded to such handsome treatment with obvious appreciation. Washington became "my dear general." "I am happy that your excellency approved of my conduct."[5] "I feel in the most sensible manner the favorable opinion you are pleased to entertain of me."[6] "I am fully convinced that your excellency intended me all possible justice."[7] Despite his manifold afflictions, Schuyler remained in command in the north and held the vital Hudson valley for the American cause.

ii

Five of the members of Congress who attended when it made the momentous decision for war left Philadelphia soon afterward to serve in the armies. Washington, Schuyler, and Brigadier General John Sullivan departed in June; Patrick Henry accepted an important post in August; Christopher Gadsden went home in January

1776 to command in South Carolina. The withdrawal of so many militant leaders tended to soften the temper of Congress and to increase the influence of the moderates and conciliationists. Since many of the most zealous men joined the army, it became the focus of the militant spirit. The officers were among the most forward and aggressive leaders, and once they had taken up arms they became the visible symbols of the "rebellion." They exposed themselves to the wrath of the enemy, standing as they did on the front line among those who might be accused of levying war against the king. Men who had made their choice between victory and the gallows were not likely to indulge in neutrality, moderation, or temporizing expedients. Thus the leaders who were most militant to begin with were placed in a situation that was certain to intensify their zeal. Most inclined toward independence at the start, they were most exposed to dangers that would force them to go the whole way.

When Washington arrived at Cambridge he found the army in a poorly organized state. It was a loose combination of companies from the four New England colonies. Each provincial contingent had its own officers. The whole was presided over by a commander in chief, General Artemas Ward of Massachusetts. A political leader, with virtually no military experience, Ward had succeeded in holding the diverse groups together largely by reason of his personal popularity with the men. In poor health, and lax as a disciplinarian, he presided over his raw recruits in a mild, easygoing manner. Even so, his troops won the decisive battle of Bunker Hill and succeeded in their main task — that of keeping the British army cooped up in Boston. He readily surrendered the command to Washington and took the second place as the top-ranking major general in the American army.

Washington organized the forces around Boston as a unit, grouping them into three divisions, each commanded by a major general who held his commission from Congress. By this action he moved far toward placing the army on a continental basis. The arrangement put most of the men under general officers from colonies other than their own. A division consisted of two brigades, each led by a brigadier general. Thus Washington's staff consisted of nine general officers — his council of war.

The ten generals formed the most active, militant, and aggressive group in the colonies. Seven were New Englanders conspicuous for their forwardness in the cause. Of these, only one, Major General Israel Putnam of Connecticut, had had extensive military experience — and that was not of the sort to qualify him to direct a large body of men in formal warfare. On the whole the New England commanders had risen to the top by reason of their ardor and their political activities. Brigadier General John Sullivan of New Hampshire, only thirty-five, was an eloquent Irish lawyer whose military experience was a minus quantity. Brigadier General Nathanael Greene, now thirty-three years old, son of an antiwar Quaker, had joined a newly formed Rhode Island company in 1773. The next year he bought a musket and began to study the art of war. This was his preparation when in May 1775 he was elected brigadier general of a nonexistent Rhode Island "army of observation." This he proceeded to organize. He then led his novices into Cambridge early in June. "He had had no military experience beyond service for six months as a private in a militia company."[8] Yet in spite of such handicaps, it was not long until Washington's secretary, Joseph Reed, wrote that the men under Greene's command were "the best disciplined and appointed in the whole American army."[9] Major General Ward's active service was limited to a subordinate part in one campaign in the French and Indian War — a fruitless assault on Ticonderoga in 1758. Brigadier General William Heath, a farmer in his thirty-ninth year, had done nothing in the way of active duty beyond drilling militia companies in time of peace.

What, then, were the qualifications of these generals? They were sturdy leaders who had come to the top as active, persistent opponents of British rule. In December 1774, Sullivan led a party of raiders who broke into the royal fort, William and Mary, at Portsmouth harbor and seized a hundred barrels of the king's powder. Governor Wentworth denounced this deed (the first armed attack of the Revolution on British forces) as an act of treason. During the Stamp

Act crisis, Artemas Ward so resolutely defied the crown that Governor Bernard withdrew his commission as colonel in the provincial militia. Acting thereafter with Samuel Adams, Ward stood at the head of the patriot party and passed every test required of a militant leader. As early as 1770, Heath, foreseeing the clash of arms, began the publication of articles under the signature, "A Military Countryman," which he continued until the war began. "In them he urged the importance of military discipline and skill in the use of arms, as the only means, under heaven, that could save the country from falling prey to any daring invader." [10]

From the provincial congress of Massachusetts, Heath and Ward accepted appointments as provincial generals, with the avowed purpose of nullifying two of the British punitive acts. They continued to serve after the news arrived that parliament had proclaimed the colony to be in a state of rebellion. Thus they became the first military leaders to be exposed to the charge of levying war against the king.

General Ward impressed an observing visitor at camp as "a calm, cool, thoughtful man"; General Putnam appeared to be "a rough, fiery genius." [11] Of the five senior generals named by Congress, only Putnam shared with Washington the honor of a unanimous election. The valor of the Connecticut commander was a byword in New England. A British scout, observing a militia company at Framingham, Massachusetts, early in 1775, heard one of its officers exhort his troops by quoting Caesar, Pompey, Putnam, "and all such great men." [12] "Old Put" was not only the oldest of the generals (he was fifty-seven in 1775) but also the most colorful. About his name clustered many legends that commemorated his daring and bravery. Washington used him as his deputy commander at Boston, placing him in charge of the second division in the center of the American lines. "I suppose," wrote Washington's secretary in March 1776, "old Putt was to command the detachment intended for Boston . . . as I do not know any officer but himself who could have been depended on for so hazardous a service." [13]

Putnam came by his courage honestly, for his father had been one of the few to stand out against the witchcraft hysteria in Salem Village, at the height of its persecuting fury. As a young man he moved to Pomfret, Connecticut, where he left his farm to fight in the French and Indian War. For nearly ten years he served, chiefly in scouting parties that experienced many wild adventures and dangers in the Ticonderoga area. He also took part in expeditions to Montreal, Havana, and Detroit. Returning to Pomfret after Pontiac's War, he was soon embroiled in the resistance to Britain, beginning with the Stamp Act controversy. When the clouds of war appeared, he emerged as the military leader "who encouraged the Connecticut people to gather together."[14] His reputation for bravery, his rugged character, his democratic manner, his dynamic energy, and his zeal for the American cause commended him to the yeomen of New England. His impetuosity and poor spelling exposed him to the ridicule of the enemy early in 1775, when he helped to arouse the countryside by sending on to New York a false report of a battle supposed to have been fought near Boston. Responding to the Lexington alarm, he rode a hundred miles in eighteen hours in order to be on hand to command the reinforcements from Connecticut. He urged the occupation of Bunker Hill which precipitated the decisive battle, in which he commanded in the field as an aide of Colonel William Prescott. It was said that he would lead where anyone would follow. Imparting some of his courage and zeal to his men, he stood out as the foremost morale builder in the army.

iii

If Putnam was the most daring of the American generals, Charles Lee was the most eccentric. Named "Boiling Water" by his friends, the Mohawk Indians, Lee combined in his strange nature the qualities of apostle of liberty, soldier of fortune, and prima donna. Undoubtedly he owed his high place in the Continental army to Washington. He was the only professional soldier available to the colonies who had served as a general in a reputable, organized army. Son of an English colonel, he had been educated to the profession of arms. An officer's commission had been acquired for him at the impressive age of fourteen. When twenty-four, he commanded a company of grenadiers.

Four years of campaigning in the French and Indian War familiarized him with much of North America. First he served at Louisburg; then at Halifax, Philadelphia, and New York. He was wounded at Ticonderoga in 1758, and took part in the conquest of Fort Niagara in 1759. Next he was a member of the first English party to cross Lake Erie and to push southward to Fort Duquesne. Thence he marched several hundred miles to Crown Point. In his last expedition he crossed Lake Ontario and reached Montreal. After its capture he returned to England in 1760, and was sent to fight the Spaniards in Portugal. There he distinguished himself by leading a commando raid against a Spanish outpost. This occurred in October 1762.

The ensuing peace did not suit the temperament of the young hero, whose restless nature had been stirred by so many years of excitement and adventure. His combative instincts drew him into political warfare in which he flayed the government for its efforts to tax the colonies. Having been prematurely promoted in the army, he now found the door to advancement closed. Seeking fortune or excitement elsewhere, he visited Poland and became a favorite of the king. Returning to England again he soon suffered a stroke of misfortune. His liberal views, expressed in sarcastic attacks on leading men, evidently estranged him from the court. His wartime chief, William Pitt, had deserted to the enemy. The king ignored his application for promotion while allowing him to wait many weeks in expectant hope. Finally he realized that he was out of favor at court and that his friends of the war years either had abandoned him or had lost influence. He again returned to Europe, an embittered man who deplored the decline of liberty in England. Now he served as a major general in the Polish army; next he joined the Russian army and fought against the Turks; then he traveled extensively in Europe. Finding his opponents strongly entrenched in power in England, he sailed for America, arriving at New York in November 1773. At once he was at home among friends whose enemies were his enemies.

He probably met Washington the first time at Williamsburg in May 1774, when both were there during the session of the House of Burgesses. It was an exciting time. The royal governor, Lord Dunmore, dissolved the house for its support of Boston, whereupon a group of the members, including Washington, issued a call for an extralegal convention to meet in August. Washington returned to Mount Vernon to work out the Fairfax program of revolutionary committees and military companies which the convention adopted. Lee went to Boston to confer with its militant leaders, who were then on the point of preparing for armed resistance. Rumors reached England that he had urged the Bostonians to take up arms. Gage reported that he had conspired "with the enemies of government" and that "his conduct was so offensive to his acquaintances in the [British] troops that none of them would associate with him."[15]

Lee probably met Washington again at Philadelphia during the First Continental Congress, where the former was described as "very busy amongst the delegates."[16] After its adjournment, Lee proceeded to Annapolis, there to attend a meeting of the Maryland convention which approved the measures of the First Congress. He encouraged the delegates "to adopt resolutions for putting the militia on a better footing, forming them into new companies and regiments, and supplying them with arms and ammunition. A plan for the new organization was furnished by him, and he personally superintended the arrangements for mustering the companies at Annapolis."[17] In this wise he labored in Maryland while Washington was fostering the new independent companies in Virginia. Lee arrived at Mount Vernon at the end of December 1774, and remained there six days. At his departure he borrowed £15 from Washington. He journeyed to Williamsburg to carry forward the work he had started at Annapolis. He then returned to Philadelphia for the meeting of the Second Congress. During its sessions he devoted much of his time to training the newly formed militia companies of Philadelphia.

John Adams tells us that Congress elected Lee the third-ranking general in deference to the "earnest desire" of General Washington and the wishes of "our best friends in the southern colonies." [18] Another observer reported that Congress made the appointment "more to please Washington" than from "any opinion or confidence they had in Mr. Lee." [19] Curiously, at the time of his election Lee was still receiving the half pay of an officer of the British army. This he renounced soon afterward.

Since Ward was ranked at the top of the major generals largely for reasons of courtesy, it is plain that Washington regarded Lee as his principal assistant. "He is the first officer in military knowledge and experience in the whole army," wrote the general in 1776. "He is zealously attached to the cause, honest and well meaning, but rather fickle and violent I fear in his temper. However, he possesses an uncommon share of good sense and spirit." [20] When one remembers the military training and experience of most of the newly appointed generals (Ward, Schuyler, Sullivan, Greene, Heath, Putnam), it is understandable why Washington favored the selection of Lee, despite his foibles and eccentricities. He had some contributions to offer which were not to be had elsewhere. Familiar with English politics and English political leaders, he was qualified to ascertain the meaning and intent of their measures. More important, he knew personally many of the British officers, including Burgoyne and Gage. He understood the British method of waging war. His knowledge of European courts and diplomacy far exceeded that of any other American officer. His familiarity with several foreign languages was valuable in a camp where such knowledge was extremely rare. He had the gift of expressing himself easily and forcefully in writing. In these respects he brought to the army abilities, experience, and information which Washington lacked. In addition he was sympathetic toward the Americans as a people and understood their methods of fighting. He had traveled widely over the country that was to be a principal scene of the war. He had succeeded in winning the good will of the Indians — to the extent of being adopted by the Mohawks. About the same age as Washington, he recognized that as an outsider he would have to serve under a native commander.

iv

Washington sponsored Lee after the two had conferred at length, so it is to be presumed that they agreed in their views of the military aspect of the war. Lee had stated his position in a widely circulated article, first printed in 1774. He called it *Strictures on a Pamphlet Entitled a "Friendly Address to All Reasonable Americans."* [21] In this essay Lee undertook to demolish the arguments of a New York clergyman, Dr. Myles Cooper, who had urged the colonists to submit, partly because they could not hope to withstand the military might of Britain. To this warning Lee replied by denying the effectiveness of the British army. He contended that it could put only fifteen thousand infantry in the field. Enlistments in England provided only the worst sort of recruits — men who either "desert upon every occasion" or "are not strong enough to carry packs." [22] In the last war the regulars "were defeated or baffled for three years successively in every part of the continent," whereas the colonial militiamen "were frequently crowned with success." [23] The yeomanry of America, he continued, "have infinite advantages over the peasantry of other countries; they are accustomed from their infancy to firearms; they are expert in the use of them; whereas the lower and middle people of England are, by the tyranny of certain laws, almost as ignorant in the use of a musket as they are of the ancient catapulta. The Americans are likewise, to a man, skilful in the management of the instruments necessary for all military works, such as spades, pickaxes, hatchets, etc." [24]

The conditions of warfare would be such that "it is impossible to calculate how many victories must be gained before these colonies could be subdued," whereas a single victory won by the colonies "must decide the contest in their favor."[25] Their present unpreparedness was not a serious handicap. To the argument that they lacked generals, Lee replied that Britain did not have any, either. He insisted that the colonists, by a modernized, simplified type of training, might become in a few months "a most formidable infantry." He then offered such a model. "Let one simple plan be adopted for the formation and subdivision of your battalions; let them be instructed only in so much of the manual exercise as to prevent confusion and accidents in loading and firing; let them be taught to form, to retreat, to advance, to change their front, to rally to their colors; let them be taught to reduce themselves from a line of fire to a line of impression, that is, from two deep to four, six or eight. This is all so easy and simple that it may be acquired in three months."[26]

For the American friends of the king, Lee had only scorn and contempt. "Dreadfully formidable they must be indeed."[27] New England all together would not send forth more than fifty loyalist recruits; New York not more than a dozen. Meanwhile, the colonies could expect to receive aid from foreign states. All the maritime powers of Europe would compete for their trade. "America (more particularly since the distractions in Poland have taken place) has been the great granary . . . of Europe."[28] When the Dutch provinces were fighting for their independence from Spain, their neighbors had willingly offered aid.

In his freedom from hidebound tradition and his willingness to adapt old methods to American conditions, Lee was as one with Washington. In view of the superior military experience, the aggressiveness, and the egotism of the English volunteer, what was his influence in the army? Was his the leading part? Or did Washington utilize his talents? A clue to the mystery appears in a highly important letter which Washington sent to General Gage in August 1775. Lee wrote the first draft. Washington used about a fifth of it without change, altered another fifth, and discarded the rest. To the part retained he added more than Lee's contribution, including the most important passage in the letter. The final draft differed drastically in tone and substance from the original version. This bit of evidence suggests that Washington was the "boss."

Horatio Gates, one of Lee's companions at camp, had also been an officer in the British army. Like Lee, Gates had served in the colonies during most of the French and Indian War. His propensity for liberty was strengthened by his long exposure to the invigorating climate of freedom in America. Like Lee he returned to England after the war, there to suffer frustration and disappointment at the hands of a venal court that was repelled by outspoken young officers who espoused the cause of liberty and America. Unlike Lee, however, Gates did not become a soldier of fortune and a restless globe-trotter. Instead, he moved to America, purchased a large farm in the Shenandoah Valley, and settled down to the placid life of a country gentleman. There we find him in July 1774. "I . . . stick steadily to the cultivation of my farm," he writes, "am intimate with few, read when I have time, and content myself with domestic comforts as my circumstances and fortune afford me. . . . Selfishness and sycophancy possess so generally the minds of men that I think the many are best avoided, and the few only who are liberal and sincere to be sought for and caressed."[29] At his modest retreat, Traveler's Rest, he enjoyed his release from the "anxious hope or fear that scorches the bosoms of all those that aspire to gain or dread to lose by that deceitful will o' the wisp, court favor." He had escaped "the malice of secret enemies" and the "treachery of pretended friends."[30]

In the summer of 1774 a change in Gates's attitude put an end to his repose and tranquillity. On July 1 he had written to Lee urging a visit to Traveler's Rest. He described his quiet life and manifested no interest in politics. He spoke of General Gage as "humane" and "honorable" and was inclined to think that the British general "has some secret medicine in his pocket to heal the wounds that threaten the life of American liberty."[31] Unaware that Lee was engaged in dangerous political activity and surprised that his friend tarried so long in Williamsburg, Gates urged him to become a farmer in the Shenandoah Valley.

After writing thus to Lee, Gates made a trip to Baltimore. Evidently he learned of things that changed his attitude completely. In a note to Lee of August 17 he had no good word for Gage. He (Gates) had discovered that Lee was engaged in some hazardous political activity and advised his friend to be cautious in the presence "of all such persons as may reasonably be suspected to watch your words and actions. . . . Be careful how you act, for be assured Gage knows you too well . . . not to be glad of any plausible pretense to prevent your good services in the public cause." Gates then announced a resolution. "I am ready," he said, "to risk my life to preserve the liberty of the western world." [32]

> On this condition would I build my fame,
> And emulate the Greek and Roman name;
> Think freedom's rights bought cheaply with my blood—
> And die with pleasure for my country's good.[33]

One may with good reason imagine that Lee showed the above letter to Washington, either at Philadelphia in the autumn of 1774, or when he visited Mount Vernon in December. There is no other evidence of a tie between Washington and Gates until the latter called at Mount Vernon early in May of 1775. Washington, in his uniform, was then on the point of departing, with Richard Henry Lee, to attend the Second Congress. John Adams attributed the appointment of Gates as adjutant general in the American army to "the earnest desire of General Washington" and the "extreme attachment" of many southern delegates.[34] Since there is no evidence of a kinship of Gates with many southerners, it is likely that Washington's influence carried the most weight.

What did Gates have to offer to the Continental army? In military knowledge and experience he ranked second only to General Lee. Perhaps his chief asset was a human quality which endeared him to the enlisted men. Democratic and friendly in manner, kindly and humane, a good mixer with a ready smile, he radiated a genial warmth and a sense of ruddy health and robust confidence. Appropriately, he was soon assigned to the recruiting service. Making the welfare of the individual soldier his special care, he took pains to provide the men adequately with shelter, food, and clothing, and to comfort their relatives at home. Although nearly five years older than Washington, he co-operated willingly with the general, without sinking to the level of a sycophant. A genuine friend of liberty, he was zealously devoted to the cause.

v

The initial zeal of most of the army leaders was soon enhanced by an action of General Gage which branded them as criminals fit for the gallows. Gage had issued his first proclamation against the "rebels" in June, before Congress had fully established the army and before the general officers had been elected. He had confined his condemnations to the people of Massachusetts and had named only John Hancock and Samuel Adams as so culpable as to be unworthy of pardons. What, then, was the status, in British law, of Washington and his fellow officers as commanders of the Continental army? Gage told them in the summer of 1775.

On August 11 of that year Washington wrote an extremely important letter to Gage. He noted that "officers engaged in the cause of liberty and their country" had fallen into Gage's hands, "by the fortunes of war." Such officers, continued the letter, "have been thrown indiscriminately into a common jail, appropriate for felons." No consideration "has been had for those of the most respectable rank, when languishing with wounds and sickness." Some "have been even amputated in this unworthy situation." Washington then insisted that the captured officers be treated as prisoners of war, with proper attention to the "claims of rank"—not as common criminals. He notified Gage that British prisoners of the American army would be treated "exactly by the rule you shall observe toward . . . ours. . . ."[35]

Gage replied on August 13. Denying the charge of cruel treatment of prisoners, he said that British mercy had moved him to overlook "the criminal in the captive." He next alluded to the American prisoners, "whose lives by the law of the land are destined to the cord. . . ." Admitting that American officers had been kept indiscriminately in hospitals, he announced that he acknowledged no rank "that is not derived from the king." [36]

In his second letter Washington began by implying that Gage and his associates might "best deserve the appellation of rebels" and punishment by the "cord." In defense of the rank of American officers he said: "I cannot conceive one more honorable than that which flows from the uncorrupted choice of a brave and free people." To Gage's threats about the "cord," Washington replied that the king's friends in the colonies ("those execrable parricides whose counsels and aid have deluged their country with blood") had hitherto "been protected from the fury of a justly enraged people." [37]

Gage did not answer Washington's second letter. The correspondence ended in such a way as to expose American officers to the British allegation that they were not prisoners of war, entitled to honorable treatment according to rank, but common criminals "whose lives by the law of the land are destined to the cord. . . ."

In his second letter to Gage, Washington sounded a note that was to reverberate across the continent and to shake the world. When justifying the rank of American officers he said that "the uncorrupted choice of a brave and free people" is "the purest source and original fountain of all power." For the first time in his career he stated boldly a faith in popular sovereignty and announced his identification with and his reliance upon the common people of America. On August 19, 1775, he served notice that the Continental army was dedicated to the cause of popular government. Above an authority derived from the king, he placed a greater authority, newly created by the people. In doing this he did not state an idle theory or an empty formula. He recognized an existing fact. The people of America had aroused themselves to action and he had emerged as the leader. Of the state of opinion in May 1775 General Gage remarked: "From what can be learned it is not found that one province is in a better situation than another. The people called friends of government are few in all . . . the opposition party numerous, active, and violent."[38] General Schuyler, after he had reviewed his troops at Ticonderoga, wrote to Washington: "The officers and men are all good looking people, and decent in their deportment, and I really believe they will make good soldiers as soon as I can get the better of this nonchalance of theirs. Bravery I believe they are far from wanting."[39]

All over the land local committees had come into being and stood ready to act in co-operation with the army. In sponsoring the Fairfax Resolves and the Continental Association, Washington had been instrumental in creating the network of local agencies that arose in the winter of 1774–1775. They were composed in the main of loyal and militant adherents of the cause — plain, ordinary folk who were willing to work and hazard their lives without hope of immediate reward. When Washington took the field, committees of safety had absorbed the functions of local government. To them he turned for a dozen services that the new army was obliged to obtain from civilian sources. Did he seek information about the surrounding country? A local committee could supply it. Did he need to engage workmen, enlist sailors, acquire vessels? Did he need messengers to carry dispatches? Did he seek the aid of men skilled in procuring supplies? Did he need an artisan with a specialized skill? Did he need a safe place to which prisoners might be sent? Did he need assistance in apprehending deserters? Did he seek news of the enemy's movements? For such aids and many more he found the local committees of safety indispensable — almost as necessary to the success of the cause as the army itself. With their members he established close and friendly contacts, treating them with the utmost courtesy and respect. He invested them with the prestige of his approval, and strengthened them with the weight and authority of Congress and the army. What a stir it caused in a locality when word arrived that the stately general — the symbol of America — requested its assistance! How the committee members hurried into action and with what deference they addressed him in reply!

He had not been long at his post before tributes began to roll into camp. Three officers of his old Fairfax company wrote: "We are to inform you, sir, by desire of the company, that if at any time you shall judge it expedient to join the troops at Cambridge, or march elsewhere, they will cheerfully do it."[40] His overseer, informing him of British ships near Alexandria and of preparations to move his property from Mount Vernon, said: "Everybody tells me that, if they could have notice, they would immediately come and defend your property as long as they had life."[41] At Portsmouth, New Hampshire, the committee of safety wrote: "When we consider ourselves as the objects of your attention, and the alacrity with which you have, as it were, flown to our relief . . . we are filled with the deepest sense of gratitude."[42] A young slave poet, Phillis Wheatley, composed aspiring verses in his honor. The freeholders of a new settlement in Massachusetts voted to name it "Washington," and instructed Edmund Quincy to wait on the general "with the compliments of the town and acquaint him therewith."[43] The evacuation of Boston sent a chorus in his praise echoing through the land.

The assistance and appreciation Washington received from the common folk seem to have had a humanizing effect on his austere nature. The events which exalted him in reputation also brought him into a closer association with plain and lowly people. Only as his part in the Revolution unfolded did his greatness appear. His early career, before 1774, has not revealed him, to many students, as an especially attractive man. The strength and fortitude, the industry and ability, the energy and stamina were all evident. But there was something lacking—some human quality—some sense of affiliation with the fortunes of mankind. His relations with his mother had not been happy. The influence of children—his own—was denied to him. His reserve and awkwardness of expression, in both speech and writing, did not invite familiarities or equip him for the easy exchange of conversational pleasantries. He had devoted himself largely to the acquisition of an estate, and his business success placed him in a conventional society in which he was not wholly at home. In his relations with obscure people he stood apart—a master, an employer, a landlord. As an officer in the French and Indian War he had gone to the frontier as an outsider, and had directed men whose personal fate was not closely interwoven with his own. His youth at that time made it difficult for him to establish friendly ties, appropriate to his premature authority, with the older men under his command.

How different from all this was his situation as commander in chief during the first year of the war! He had assumed the leadership of a popular movement. In so doing he had exposed himself to the worst possible fate, in the event of failure. Conviction and personal necessity now joined to urge him forward to victory. Upon whom was he to depend? Principally, on the ordinary people of America. Many men of fortune hesitated and faltered. There were trimmers, waverers, hedgers, straddlers. The ugly specter of profiteering raised its head, once the financing of the war had changed from voluntary contributions to regular disbursements by Congress and the army. In the face of multiplying difficulties, he received an unwavering support from many ordinary people. Could he fail to appreciate their courage and self-denial? Could he fail to respond to the popular acclaim? He would indeed have had a heart of stone if he had not been moved by the support of humble people, at a time when he was marked as a condemned man — when timid souls withheld wholehearted assistance in order to keep in good standing with the enemy. The ice of his reserve thawed in the warmth of popular approval and support. An element of sympathy, compassion, understanding — a sense of identification with the people — now tempered his austere nature. Those traditional oppressors of the people — monarchy and aristocracy — had branded him a criminal. He responded with the assertion that the people were "the purest source and original fountain of all power." He did not express his kinship with them in a blatant manner; rather it suffused his actions and utterances. Replying to the congratulations extended by Congress on the occasion of the evacuation of Boston, he wrote to President Hancock: "I beg you to assure them, that it will ever be my highest ambition to approve myself a faithful servant of the public; and that to be in any degree instrumental in procuring to my American brethren a restitution of their just rights and privileges will constitute my chief happiness. . . . They were indeed at first 'a band of undisciplined husbandmen' but it is (under God) to their bravery and attention to their duty that I am indebted for that success which has procured me the only reward I wish to receive—the affection and esteem of my countrymen."[44]

IX. Washington Acts

> I have never entertained an idea of an accommodation since I heard of the measures which were adopted in consequence of the Bunker's Hill fight.[1]
>
> — WASHINGTON TO JOSEPH REED, FEBRUARY 10, 1776

SOON after Washington took command of the army he acted in a way that carried the war to the enemy on many fronts. The reports he received from England, signifying that the ministry would meet the American resistance with superior force, convinced him that his army must make a maximum effort. It must do everything that its enemy might do. It must act as if it were the instrument of a sovereign state.

The first fruit of Washington's initiative was the expedition which he sent out in September to effect the conquest of Canada. By the end of July he had received reports of the British response to the news of Lexington and Concord. The information convinced him that the ministry would not change its plans. He noted that the news of the battle made little impression in England. His secretary remarked: "Stocks fell only 1½ per cent, which they often do on the slightest alarm. A ministry never dreads a fall till it gets to 8 per cent."[2]

After receiving this news, Washington wrote to General Gage on August 11 relative to the treatment of American prisoners. Gage replied by calling them criminals. In his rejoinder of August 19 Washington claimed that his authority, derived from the people, was superior to an authority derived from the king. Gage then charged that Washington was striving for independence.

In his letter of August 11 Washington had implied that Gage was a servant of the ministry — not of the king — and that the American resistance was not directed against the symbol of British authority. To this assumption Gage replied: "Till I read your insinuations in regard to ministers, I conceived that I had acted under the king, whose wishes . . . as well as those of his ministers . . . have been to see this unhappy breach forever closed. But unfortunately . . . those who . . . influence the councils of America have views very distant from accommodation."[3]

Having received Washington's letter proclaiming popular sovereignty, Gage wrote to Dartmouth, August 20, as follows: "The designs of the leaders of the rebellion are plain. . . . A plan was laid in this province and adjusted with some of the same stamp in others for a total independence, whilst they . . . pretended to be aggrieved and discontented only on account of taxation. . . . They would still deceive and lull the mother country into the belief that nothing is meant against the nation, and that their quarrel is only with the ministers, but it is hoped the nation will see through the fallacy and deceit. It matters not who holds the helm of state; the stroke is leveled at the British nation, on whose ruins they hope to build their so much vaunted American empire, and to rise like a phoenix out of the ashes of the mother country."[4]

In this setting, Washington projected the Quebec expedition, with the object of bringing Canada into "an indissoluble union" with the thirteen colonies. He first announced his purpose on August 20, the day after he sent his popular sovereignty letter to Gage. Soon afterward he wrote: "The acquisition of Canada is of immeasurable importance to the cause we are engaged in."[5] "To whomsoever it belongs," he elaborated, "in their favor probably will the balance turn. If it is in ours, success I think will most certainly crown our virtuous struggles. If it is in theirs, the contest at best will be doubtful, hazardous and bloody." Again he asserted the aim of holding Canada permanently, describing it as "the only link wanting in the great continental chain of union."[6]

Washington projected the Canada expedition independently of General Schuyler and in such a way as to prod the New Yorker into a co-operating action. Congress, on July 27, had decreed that an invasion of Canada should be ordered by Schuyler: "Resolved that if General Schuyler finds it practicable, and that it will not be disagreeable to the Canadians, he do immediately take possession of St. John's, Montreal, and any other parts of the country. . . ."[7] Congress had thus authorized him to set the time for an invasion. His importance, coupled with the ticklish political situation in New York, made it impracticable for Washington to attempt to dictate to him. The squire of the Potomac could not very well lord it over the squire of the Hudson.

What was the situation in northern New York when Washington announced his plan for an expedition to Quebec? He had recently received two letters from Schuyler, who was then at Ticonderoga. They told that he was engaged in building boats, "to carry me across the lake [Champlain]." He thought that one vessel, which was on the stocks, would transport three hundred men. "Another is putting up today."[8] Provisions at Ticonderoga were so scarce that he dared not order a thousand of his soldiers to come on from Albany, lest they starve. He had heard of a recent movement of British troops from Boston to Canada. "If so, I fear we shall not be able to penetrate into Canada, or even attack St. John's with success."[9] He was waiting for orders to move to Fort St. John. From whom he expected such orders is not clear, since Congress had explicitly directed that he "do immediately take possession of St. John's."

Washington deemed it imperative to invade Canada at once. He believed that Britain needed it in order to conquer the thirteen colonies and would therefore reinforce it in the spring. Something must be done to animate Schuyler. Washington proposed that Benedict Arnold should lead an independent expedition that would ascend the Kennebec, cross the mountainous wilderness to the headwaters of the Chaudière, and proceed down that stream to Quebec. This dangerous and difficult route had only one advantage: it would enable Arnold's men to pass from Cambridge to Canada without setting foot in Schuyler's territory and without subjecting them to his delaying tactics. The force would consist of New Hampshire militiamen—those sturdy rivals of Schuyler and his New York friends.

Washington informed Schuyler of the plan in a letter which reached the latter in Albany. At once the New Yorker sprang to action. He was glad to learn of Washington's decision and wished "only that the thought had struck you sooner." He would at once send to Canada his army of seventeen hundred men ("far short of what I would wish"). "I move immediately, weak and ill appointed as we were."[10] With Arnold on the march, Schuyler could not afford to remain idle and risk the conquest and later domination of Canada by New York's rivals. Moreover, Arnold's party, advancing on Quebec, would prevent the British governor of Canada from opposing an expedition sent by Schuyler that would move on Montreal by way of Lake Champlain and the Sorel (Richelieu) River.

When he told Schuyler of the plan, Washington wrote that "the final determination is deferred until I hear from you. . . . Not a moment's time is to be lost."[11] From Washington's letter it appeared that the Arnold expedition would proceed, regardless of Schuyler's reply. The troops were "not considered as composing a part of the continental army . . . so that it will not be proper for me to give orders respecting them."[12]

After receiving Schuyler's approval, Washington prepared an address to the inhabitants of Canada which urged them to unite with the thirteen colonies "in an indissoluble union."[13] A British official, reading this plea, would surely have called it a declaration of independence, since it said that the new confederation, created for the purpose of undermining Britain's authority, was to endure forever. To prevent such a union was now a fixed aim of British policy.

What part did Congress play in the genesis of the Arnold expedition? It was notified after the event. "I am now to inform the Hon. Congress," wrote Washington on September 21, "that . . . I have detached Colonel Arnold with one thousand men to penetrate into Canada by way of the Kennebec River, and if possible to make himself master of Quebec."[14] He also sent to Congress a copy of his

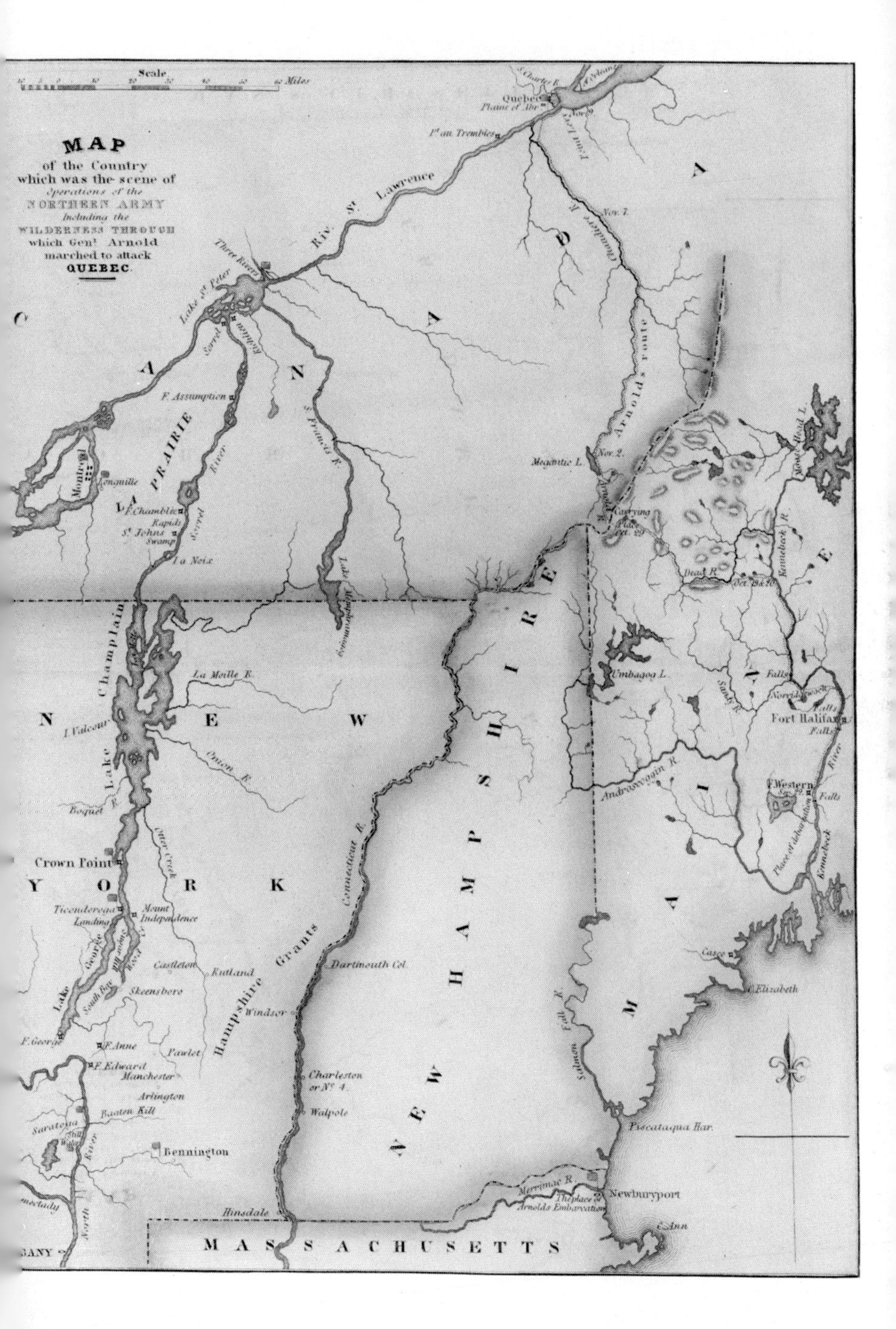

Scene of Operations of the Army in the North

address to the Canadians which invited them to join "with us in an indissoluble union." He then added: ". . . I hope the Congress will have a clear view of the motives, plan, and intended execution of the enterprise, and that I shall be so happy as to meet with their approbation in it."[15] Congress signified its approval on October 5, when it authorized him to seize two English munition ships en route to Quebec.

On November 18, Schuyler at Ticonderoga received the news that his deputy commander, Brigadier General Richard Montgomery, had taken Montreal. For many weeks the tide of hope at the Cambridge camp ran high. But, alas, in mid-January 1776, Washington learned that the American forces had suffered a disastrous defeat at Quebec and that "the brave and worthy Montgomery" had fallen in the battle. Washington did not delay for one moment. He summoned a council of leaders, who immediately recommended that three New England colonies each raise a regiment to march at once to reinforce the Canada expedition. After calling upon the three colonies to supply the required troops, Washington informed Congress of his action. "If the measure contravenes any resolution of theirs," he wrote to President Hancock, "they will please to recommend the levying and marching of the regiments as soon as possible, and do me the justice to believe that my intentions were good, if my judgment erred."[16] To Joseph Reed, then in Philadelphia, he explained that it appeared unwise to wait for an authorization from Congress. It was unsafe to delay until "after several days' debate . . . when in the meantime all might be lost. The urgency of the case, therefore, must apologize to Congress for my adoption of this measure."[17]

Washington need not have worried about the attitude of Congress. As soon as it learned of the Quebec disaster it authorized him to select a general to succeed Montgomery. On January 29 it formally approved his emergency measures, thereby endorsing his hope that "our affairs may still be retrieved in Canada, before the king's troops can get reinforced." "I consider," he explained, "that the important period is now arrived when the Canadians and consequently their Indians must take their side. Should any indecisive operations of ours, therefore, give the bias against us, it is much easier to foresee than to rectify the dreadful consequences which must inevitably follow from it."[18]

ii

The management of the army near Boston compelled Washington to assume responsibilities and to take, on his own initiative, a number of actions more appropriate to an independent state than to dependent provinces. Since the British army exercised all the powers of a sovereign nation, it followed that Washington and his troops must act with equal freedom. Neither the status of dependency nor the psychology of inferiority could equip the Americans to fight effectively against a major foe.

About the middle of September Washington received additional news from Britain, when a letter from Thomas Hutchinson fell into his hands. Written at London on June 2, it described the response of British officials to the first reports of Lexington and Concord. Hutchinson said that he saw "nothing but ruin and misery . . . to follow, the general voice here being for a greater force to be sent to America."[19] Washington now realized that the war would be a protracted one — that his troops must be prepared to fight for some time, and in any part of the colonies. Consequently, they must be effectively organized and disciplined, under long-term enlistments. As things stood in September, the army suffered from two handicaps that threatened to be fatal. The men were enlisted to serve no longer than December 31, 1775. Arrangements, therefore, must be made during October and November for recruiting a new army. Secondly, Washington deemed it urgent to improve and strengthen the discipline of the men. To that end it would be necessary to increase the power and authority of the officers. Congress had adopted in June a rather extensive army code, but it proved to be ineffectual. Although it designated as offenses the various kinds of misconduct that appear in an army, it did not prescribe penalties and punishments. When Washington arrived at Cambridge he found the army operating under a code of its own. The officers and men refused to subscribe to the Congress code, fearing that if they did so they would commit themselves "to a longer service than that for which they engaged under their several provincial establishments."[20] Washington did not insist upon enforcing the Congress code. As long as the troops were not likely to be exposed to combat, the problem of discipline was not serious. But foreseeing a long hard war, he decided that an adequate code should be prepared at once. It would then be accepted by the officers and men when they enlisted in the new army, and thereafter everything would be on a proper military footing.

The urgency of the army's plight moved Congress to send a committee of three of its members to confer with the general. They arrived at the Cambridge camp in mid-October, and were joined by civilian representatives of the four New England colonies. The occasion enabled Washington to present a number of proposals covering all the ills that afflicted the army. He occupied a commanding position at the conference. The members sent by Congress—Franklin, Harrison, and Lynch—were among his most steadfast supporters in that body. He alone represented the army. Having helped to draft the original army code of Congress, and possessing the fullest information on existing conditions, he could speak with the utmost authority. The representative of Rhode Island, Governor Nicholas Cooke, and one spokesman for New Hampshire, General John Sullivan, were particularly well disposed and friendly. The backing of the Congress committee gave him a deciding influence, since Congress was now providing the money for the maintenance of the army.

The occasion permitted him to present his views on all the problems that had arisen during his command, and for which Congress had not provided adequate solutions. Now it was necessary to arrange for the enlistment of a new army and to draft a code of rules that would enable the officers to weld it into a disciplined force.

Washington submitted about fifty subjects for the consideration of the conferees. They acted swiftly and functioned like a well oiled machine. Their decisions, for the most part, ratified his recommendations. On thirteen topics they either put a final stamp of approval on things he had done without authorization, or directed him to do things that he wanted to do. On twenty-seven questions the conference made recommendations that were to be acted on by Congress. Six of his questions involved issues of such importance that they were merely referred to Congress, without recommendation.

Within two weeks after Lynch, Harrison, and Franklin returned to Philadelphia, Lynch wrote to the general: "I am happy to inform you that Congress has agreed to every recommendation of the committee."[21] Clearly, Washington's views had prevailed. The new measures provided that the army before Boston should consist of 20,373 officers and men. The other recommendations, for the most part, stiffened the army code by defining the penalties and punishments that were to be inflicted on officers or men convicted by courts-martial. Up to now the courts-martial had declined to define or fix punishments in important cases; they refused to exercise an authority that Congress had failed to exercise. The new code of November corrected this failing. To illustrate: it decreed that a sentinel found guilty of sleeping on duty should be punished with twenty to thirty-nine lashes.

The new code contained two articles of far-reaching importance. The first reads as follows: "All persons convicted of holding a treacherous correspondence with, or giving intelligence to the enemy, shall suffer death, or such other punishment as a general court-martial shall think proper."[22] This article was probably the result of the detection of the first spy of the Revolution. In July Congress established a hospital and placed it in charge of Dr. Benjamin Church — a Boston physician who had for some time been a member of the inner circle of patriot leadership in Massachusetts. He was also a paid informer for General Gage. Late in September, Washington obtained a suspicious letter, written in cipher and intended for the British. A searching investigation disclosed that

Dr. Church was its author. At a full council of war, held October 4, Church acknowledged the fact and "explained his intention in writing the said letter as calculated to impress the enemy with a strong idea of our strength and situation in order to prevent an attack at a time when the continental army was in great want of ammunition."[23] Washington then asked the council "whether it did not appear that Dr. Church had carried on a criminal correspondence with the enemy"—to which the members unanimously answered in the affirmative. The question was then proposed and discussed, "what were the proper steps to be taken with respect to him?" The generals concluded that, in view of the "enormity of the crime" and "the very inadequate punishment" provided by the existing army code, the case "should be referred to the General Congress for their direction."[24]

The Cambridge conference recommended, on October 21, that convicted spies and informers be put to death. Congress so enacted on November 7. At the same time it ordered that Church be "confined in some secure jail." Before the news of this action reached Massachusetts the assembly there considered the case. It noted that Church had been convicted of a "traitorous" act and that the army court-martial lacked the authority to inflict "condign punishment." It then resolved that he be "secured" and that "such further measures with respect to him may be pursued as . . . the laws of this colony will justify."[25]

The case presented an issue with which the authorities of Massachusetts were reluctant to grapple. The offense was treason—giving aid to the enemy. Treason against whom? Obviously, against either the colony of Massachusetts or the United Colonies. Treason was a crime against a sovereign. If one could commit treason against Massachusetts, was it not a sovereign, independent state? The assembly implied that Church was guilty of treason but it shrank from imposing the punishment that was deemed appropriate to the crime. The convicted traitor was to be treated according to "the laws of this colony." As long as Massachusetts was a British colony, the only treason its law could recognize was treason against the king. Was an act of assistance to the king an act of treason against him? In failing to inflict the "condign punishment" for treason, the Massachusetts assembly drew back from the decisive step. It admitted that Massachusetts was still a British colony.

The action of Congress was more drastic. By authorizing the army to put convicted traitors and spies to death, it defined treachery and informing as high crimes against the United Colonies. Was not the union, then, an independent, sovereign nation? The two crimes against it—treachery and informing—consisted, not of giving aid to the enemies of the king, but of giving aid to the agents of the king. The onetime sovereign had become an enemy; a new sovereign had taken his place. For all practical purposes Congress adopted a declaration of independence on November 7. The resolve it approved that day originated in the army headquarters at Cambridge. It was submitted by Washington to the Congress committee, adopted by it on October 21, and then transmitted to Congress for final ratification.

A second resolve adopted by Congress on November 7 was a twin brother of the spy resolve. It authorized an army court-martial to inflict the death penalty on officers or enlisted men convicted of taking part in a mutiny or sedition. Congress thus exercised a supreme lawmaking power when it designated high crimes and ordered its agent and creature, the army, to inflict the ultimate punishment. The crime in question was that of acting in a manner beneficial to the king. The mutiny-and-sedition resolve originated in the army headquarters at Cambridge. It was submitted by Washington to the Congress committee, adopted by it on October 21, and then transmitted to Congress for final ratification.

iii

Early in October 1775 Washington received reports of new British plans for a vigorous prosecution of the war. Later, he said that these reports convinced him that conciliation was no longer attainable. The ministry made its decision on the basis of papers sent by Gage which described the battle of Bunker Hill. It also had before it reports of the creation of the Continental army and the appointment of Washington as commander in chief.

The new plan, as transmitted by Dartmouth to Gage, authorized the use of the Indians in warfare against the colonists and proposed to ship a large assortment of presents for the Iroquois. Dartmouth informed Gage on August 2: "It being his majesty's intention that we should have, if possible, in North America early in the next spring an army of at least twenty thousand men, exclusive of Canadians and Indians, the proper steps are now taking for such arrangements."[26]

Intelligence sent by American agents in London tallied with the instructions in official letters to Gage. The king's forces were to occupy New York, Albany, Ticonderoga, and Crown Point. Canadians, the Iroquois, and British regulars from Quebec would meet a major British force moving northward from New York City and establish a British power line from Manhattan to the St. Lawrence. Raiding parties would then drive into western New England, ravage the countryside, divert American forces from Boston, and deprive them of their inland supplies. Southward, British warships were to destroy the coastwise trade of the colonies, in order to dry up another source of supply. The grand result would be the division, demoralization, and destruction of the main American army.

Early in November Washington received a copy of the royal Proclamation of Rebellion—an ominous edict issued by the king on August 23. It declared that "many of our subjects . . . led by dangerous and ill designing men [of whom Washington was obviously the first] . . . have at length proceeded to open and avowed rebellion by arraying themselves in a hostile manner . . . traitorously preparing, ordering, and levying war against us. . . ." Announcing the royal determination "to bring the traitors to justice," the Proclamation called upon all the king's subjects to "disclose and make known all treasons and traitorous conspiracies . . . in order to bring to condign punishment the authors, perpetrators, and abettors of such traitorous designs." [27]

The Proclamation of Rebellion was issued two days after the agents of Congress presented to the king its humble petition of July 8. Not only did the king contemptuously refuse to receive the petition; he replied by branding its authors as traitors. Not alone the battle of Bunker Hill, but also — and more important — the warlike measures of Congress provoked the British actions of August 1775. On the twenty-ninth, Dartmouth directed the lords of the admiralty to seize American ships. He stated that the inhabitants of twelve colonies had "traitorously combined together for the general purpose of resisting the authority of this kingdom" and had "in a hostile manner, arrayed themselves in arms, and committed acts of open and actual rebellion." [28] The colonies thus named were all those, and only those, that had participated in the Second Congress. A month later Dartmouth wrote: "The last advices from North America are the fullest evidence of an open and declared war on the part of the twelve associated colonies, and there is no room left for any other consideration but that of proceeding against them in all respects, with the utmost vigor, as the open and avowed enemies of the state." [29] A final move in the unfolding of the new policy came in December, when Lord George Germain sent instructions to the British general in command of a projected expedition against South Carolina. He was directed to issue a proclamation offering pardons to "rebels" who would lay down their arms. But such pardons were not to be granted to "the principal instigators and abettors of the present rebellion." [30]

One interesting part of the new British plan of operations was the recall of Gage to England and the appointment of Sir William Howe as commander in chief in the thirteen colonies. Since the ministry evidently adopted the strategic plan worked out by Gage, the question arises: Why was he not permitted to execute it in the field? The most plausible answer is that the ministry hoped to win the war by a mixture of stratagem and force, rather than by a sole reliance on its armed might. Gage had become an embittered enemy of the Americans, and they in turn detested him. Had he been left in the supreme command, the result doubtless would have been a spasm of fierce, savage warfare. It certainly was not to the interest of the ministry to lay waste the colonies and thereby to destroy what it was trying to preserve. Sir William Howe, as commander in chief, could wage another type of war. His name did not arouse angry passions or bitter memories among the colonists. In fact he was widely known as their friend. He had once declared that he would not serve against them. The people of Boston had erected a statue to commemorate his popular brother, who had fallen at Ticonderoga in 1758. It would be one of the duties of Sir William to offer pardons to misguided insurgents and to rally the king's friends in America to the royal standard. The Proclamation of Rebellion provided an inducement for wavering men to seek the king's mercy. By a judicious mixture of force, threat, and clemency, a large body of the insurgents might be detached from the American cause. The most militant among them would then be isolated and could be conquered with ease.

However much such a strategy might feed the hopes of the conciliationists, it could not appeal to the moderates or the militants. In the first place, it betrayed a weakness on the part of Britain — the disinclination of the ministry to wage a relentless, destructive war. In the second place, it left the responsible leaders exposed to the penalties for treason. For both reasons the militants were encouraged to redouble their efforts. In Washington's case, a British attempt to win over a large part of his following, if successful, would have delivered him helpless into the hands of his enemies. However, such considerations were secondary. The major weakness of the policy of promising pardons through a friendly general was the failure of the ministry to offer concessions on the underlying issues of the war. The policy therefore assumed either that the colonists lacked conviction in the stand they had taken, or that they would quail before the punishments in store for them if they did not submit. But the leaders had already made their decision. They had counted the cost before they took up arms. They believed that their most essential rights were at stake. Having decided to risk their lives in order to defend those rights, there was no reason why a verbal threat should cause them to surrender abjectly — cause them to acknowledge themselves to be criminals in need of pardons, and to do this without gaining a single thing for which they were fighting.

In its answer to the Proclamation of Rebellion, Congress followed a course which Washington had marked out in August. When General Gage had threatened to treat American prisoners as criminals, Washington had replied: "If your officers, our prisoners, receive a treatment from me different from what I wish to show them, they and you will remember the occasion of it." [31] At the same time he claimed for himself a source of authority superior to that of Gage, and thereby placed Congress above the king. Nearly four months later Congress adopted Washington's policy as its own. By a resolve of December 6 it declared that "whatever punishment shall be inflicted upon any persons in the power of our enemies for favoring, aiding, or abetting the cause of American liberty, shall be retaliated in the same kind, and the same degree, upon those who shall favor, aid, or abet the system of ministerial oppression." [32] In this manner Congress matched the king's proclamation against rebels with a parallel proclamation against oppressors. What the king could do, Congress could do. Like Washington, Congress asserted the superiority of the source from which it drew its power, for it issued its proclamation "in the name of the people of these United Colonies" and by virtue of an authority derived from them, "according to the purest maxims of representation." [33] In his letter to Gage of August 19, Washington had justified his rank as derived from the people — "the purest source and original fountain of all power."

iv

Once Washington had closed his mind to the idea of conciliation, the army under his leadership girded itself for decisive action. It now became the fountain from which the sentiment in favor of independence spread throughout the land. On October 13 Washington wrote a letter to Richard Henry Lee. It does not survive, but something of its tenor may be inferred from Lee's reply. "I assure you," he told the general, "that no man living approves the vigorous measures you mention more than myself. Great bodies, you know, move slow; and it is as sure that the most palpable and glorious events may be delayed, and the best causes finally lost, by slow, timid, and indecisive councils. We must be content, however, to take human nature as we find it, and endeavor to draw good out of evil." [34]

On October 26 Washington issued an important general order to the troops. "The times and the importance of the great cause we are engaged in," it reads, "allow no room for hesitation and delay. When . . . a brutal, savage enemy (more so than was ever yet found in a civilized nation) are threatening us . . . with destruction from foreign troops, it little becomes the character of a soldier to shrink from danger. . . ." [35] Soon afterward he wrote that recent British actions afforded "evident proof of the diabolical designs of administration to prosecute, with unrelenting fury, the most cruel and savage war that ever a civilized nation engaged in." [36] He also made clear that he did not expect assistance from the people of Britain. "It has long been my political creed," he informed Joseph Reed, "that the ministry durst not have gone on as they did, but under the firmest persuasion that the people were with them." [37]

General Charles Lee used his caustic pen frequently to convey to Congress the militant attitude of the army. His correspondents included John Adams, Richard Henry Lee, Edward Rutledge, Robert Morris, and Benjamin Rush. After receiving the reports of the ministry's new war plans, Lee wrote at once to John Adams: "Now is the time to show your firmness. If the least timidity is displayed we are all ruined. . . . You ought to begin by confiscating . . . the estates of all the notorious enemies to American liberty. . . . Afterward you should invite all the maritime powers of the world into your ports." [38] Soon followed a letter that made a blistering attack on George III. It stated that reluctant men "begin to suspect that the king is as bad as the worst of his ministry. To have advanced such a proposition last year would have been thought treason and impiety. Next year — if you will have patience — king and tyrant will be a synonymous term. . . . I am even sanguine enough to flatter myself that nurses will soon frighten their naughty children, if they do not cease crying, [by warning them] that the king will fetch 'em away." [39]

Nor did Lee shrink from giving advice concerning the management of Congress. He advised Benjamin Rush that the cautious members should be led gently along the path to independence by easy stages. "Would you," he asked the Philadelphia physician, "venture to prescribe at once a wholesome, solid, nutritious diet to a stomach weakened and contaminated by a flimsy, windy, and noxious course of feeding? It is the same in politics." [40]

The cautious members to whom Lee alluded were two moderates, Benjamin Harrison and Thomas Lynch, who visited Cambridge in October. The occasion gave General Horatio Gates an opportunity to express his views. According to Lee, Gates ("who is as mad an enthusiast as Colonel Rumbald") frightened the southerners "out of their wits." [41] This happened about October 20. On the twenty-third General Nathanael Greene wrote in favor of independence to a Rhode Island delegate in Congress, Samuel Ward. The colonies, said Greene, now had no other alternative except subjugation. Without independence, they could not expect to get aid from France. As an enemy of Britain, France "acts upon a true plan of policy in refusing to intermeddle until she is satisfied that there is no hope of accommodation. Should France undertake to furnish us with powder and other articles, and the breach with Great Britain and the colonies be afterward made up, she would incur the hostility of her rival without reaping any solid advantage." [42]

General Sullivan, writing to John Adams, asked why Congress had not declared independence. Did the members think, he asked, that a declaration would cause the British to "throw their shot and shells with more force than at present"? Did Congress believe that the royal Proclamation of Rebellion would be more severe "if we had openly declared war"? Could the king's agents "have treated our prisoners worse if we were in open and avowed rebellion than they now do"? [43] Sullivan then urged Adams to use his talents "to destroy that spirit of moderation which has almost ruined, and, if not speedily rooted out, will prove the final overthrow of America. That spirit gave them possession of Boston, lost us all our arms and ammunition, and now causes our brothers who have fallen into their hands to be treated like rebels." [44]

v

In moving to its appointed goal of independence, the revolutionary movement resembled an imperfectly organized expedition made up of loosely connected groups that advanced at different rates of speed. Washington, the generals, and the army were the riders who opened the road and went ahead to secure the forward positions. At a comfortable distance behind followed the slow-moving Congress, comparable to a heavily loaded coach. Attending it were the thirteen provincial governments—some in advance of Congress and not far behind the army; some dragging along at the rear of the procession, often in danger of falling into the hands of the enemy. At one point in the journey the army was compelled to acquire boats and to put out to sea.

Washington, acting on his own authority and assuming full responsibility, took the initiative in creating an American navy. Many weeks before Congress could bring itself to act on the subject he drove ahead and acquired a small fleet which he used as a weapon of the army. The vessels were commerce raiders, which sallied forth to intercept ships en route to Boston with supplies for the British army. "Finding the ministerial troops resolved to keep themselves close within their lines," he explained, "and that it was judged impracticable to get at them, I have fitted out six armed vessels, with design to pick up some of their store ships and transports."[45]

Washington's action touched the basic issue on which the militants in Congress differed from the moderates and the conciliationists. To cautious men, commerce raiding by American warships seemed to carry the war beyond its proper scope. British trade on the high seas was not a grievance of the colonies; therefore it was improper for them to strike at it with armed force. The plan was denounced as a "most wild, visionary, mad project." "It was an infant taking a mad bull by its horns."[46] Apparently, many well-to-do merchants feared that Britain would retaliate by bombarding American port towns and by seizing all American merchant ships. Washington's plan contained an element of privateering, for it assigned to the seamen one third of the booty that might be taken by the raiders. The critics of this arrangement objected that "it would ruin the character and corrupt the morals of all our seamen. It would make them selfish, piratical, mercenary, bent wholly upon plunder."[47]

To Washington the business was simple. It was an effective military device, essential to victory. His commission vested him "with every power and authority to act . . . for the good and welfare of the service."[48] It did not make sense to fight against formidable foes and at the same time to sit idly by while their supply ships were busy furnishing them with the sinews of war.

On September 2 he appointed the captain of the first vessel of his fleet-to-be. A prize was taken five days later. By October 20 the little navy consisted of six vessels. It was a government fleet, engaged for continuous service, manned by detachments from the army, and financed by Continental funds. It acted under orders issued by the general, and the army's treasury received two thirds of the booty. In one five-day period early in November the commanders reported six captures. Washington named a certain Stephen Moylan to supervise the operations. Moylan then appointed agents in the principal ports, who were ordered to hire and equip new vessels, to provision those in service, and to receive and dispose of the prizes.

Washington informed Congress of his new venture in a letter

which reached Philadelphia October 13. The members approved at once by authorizing that an armed vessel be fitted out to cruise for three months in order to intercept "such transports as may be laden with warlike stores and other supplies for our enemies."[49] When Lynch, Harrison, and Franklin visited Cambridge they were informed of the six-vessel fleet and were then asked: "Will this be agreeable to Congress?"[50] They approved the scheme and promised to recommend it to Congress. On November 25 the final authorization was granted. By a resolve of that day Congress declared that "the captures heretofore made by vessels fitted out at the continental charge were justifiable, and that the distribution of the captors' share of the prizes by General Washington be confirmed."[51] Three days later Congress adopted rules for the "Navy of the United Colonies"—legislation comparable to that of June 1775 which established the Continental army.

Washington's initiative in building the first American fleet seems to have broken the opposition in Congress to the creation of a navy. Although his six vessels were in one sense a Continental unit, they were restricted in their activities. They could operate only in the waters adjacent to New England. Congress found it impossible to repudiate his action because it was essential to victory. Since his fleet represented the thirteen colonies, it offered the British a pretext for retaliation against all. But six little vessels could not protect every port on the continent. Hence it became necessary for Congress to establish a truly Continental navy capable of defending the colonies as a whole.

The creation of the navy carried the resistance another step toward independence. The American army was not wholly an innovation. The colonies had always provided for their defense on land. They had always had their militia companies; they had fought many wars by themselves. A Continental army confirmed an old custom. But a navy was another matter. Never had the colonies provided for their defense by sea. That had been the task of Britain. A navy was an appurtenance of a sovereign. Could Congress provide one without severing one of the strongest ties that bound them to the parent state? More than any other force the British navy held the empire together. For the colonists to reject it and to replace it with one of their own was to cut themselves loose from old moorings and to set out on a new course.

vi

From time to time the American leaders were plagued by British maneuvers for a negotiated peace. Having accurately appraised the intentions of the ministry, Washington viewed such gestures with a cold eye. He realized that they might appeal to the less resolute patriots who sought an easy way out of the struggle, thereby inducing a soft attitude that would enfeeble the will to resist. Since the ministry did not announce officially any peace terms except unconditional surrender, Washington correctly judged that Britain's military effort was the decisive fact, and that vague peace proposals were merely a military weapon, designed to undermine American morale. When such a peace feeler raised its head early in 1776, he killed it with one blow.

The principal in the transaction was a British peer, Lord Drummond. He arrived in Philadelphia about the first of January. When some of the patriots of the city proposed to arrest him, certain members of Congress vouched for him and he was allowed to remain at large. His mysterious mission generated many rumors. Some of the knowing ones said that he was an agent of the ministry bringing a peace overture; others thought that he had come to ascertain "the whole scope, design, and views of Congress. . . . Certain it is he has had private conversations with several characters of the first distinction among us."[52]

Foremost among the members of Congress who received the confidence of the visiting lord was Thomas Lynch of South Carolina, the stalwart friend of Washington. Drummond disclosed to Lynch the inwardness of his mission. Alleging that he had had many conversations with the ministers, he displayed a paper "approved by each of them" which he was certain would be supported by the two houses of parliament. The terms it offered were generous in the extreme. Britain would renounce the power of taxing the colonies and grant to them full control over their internal affairs. The charters were "to be held sacred, that of Boston to be restored." Britain might collect taxes on American trade but the revenue so derived was to be paid to the colony in which it was collected, to be used as the provincial legislature might direct. Lynch was assured that the ministry "wanted nothing but a show of revenue to hold up to parliament, as they are afraid to propose reconciliation without saving what the stiff old Englishmen call the honor of the nation."[53] The terms, said Lynch, were such as he would dictate if he had the ministers at his feet.

If Lord North and his colleagues intended to offer such terms, it is difficult to understand why they were busily seeking to place an army of twenty thousand men in the thirteen colonies. An official offer of the Drummond terms, published in January 1776, would undoubtedly have brought the war to a speedy end. All the public acts of the ministry pointed in the opposite direction. Consequently, the most realistic leaders in Congress viewed the Drummond mission as a snare intended to throw the colonies off their guard.

Early in February Lynch sent a curious letter to Washington, to whom he had previously transmitted a summary of the Drummond proposal. The South Carolinian now forwarded to Washington a letter written by Drummond and addressed to General Robertson, a member of Howe's staff in Boston. Drummond had asked Lynch to have Washington send the letter through the British lines to Robertson. In this letter to Robertson, Drummond described his activities in Philadelphia. "From all the conversation I had at Philadelphia . . . with those gentlemen," wrote Drummond, ". . . I have every reason to think them . . . seriously disposed toward reconciliation." Drummond then told Robertson of his plan. It was that of sending a deputation from Congress to London for a conference with the ministers. To arrange this Drummond asked Robertson to obtain a British passport and send it to Drummond, through

Washington. "Such passport must be left blank, for filling up names. . . ."[54]

Washington was thus asked to act as an intermediary between a British agent in Philadelphia and a British general in Boston, with the purpose of arranging a mission to London of unnamed members of Congress who were to negotiate a peace.

Washington did not forward the Drummond letter to General Robertson; instead he sent it to Congress. Writing to President Hancock, February 14, he observed that he had "never heard of his lordship's being invested with power to treat with Congress upon the subject of our grievances, nor of his having laid any propositions before them for an accommodation. . . ." Washington then said that Drummond's letter "has embarrassed me much, and I am not without suspicion of its meaning more than the generous purposes it professes." As to a negotiation such as Drummond proposed, Washington said emphatically that it was a mode "which I hope will never be thought of." Drummond's conduct he deplored as "premature and officious, and leading to consequences of a fatal and injurious nature to the rights of this country."[55]

On March 6, President Hancock replied to Washington: "The Congress highly approve your care and attention in stopping Lord Drummond's letter, and entirely concur with you in sentiment with regard to his lordship's officious and unwarrantable zeal."[56]

Thus ended a divertive maneuver that had created quite a little stir at Philadelphia during January and February of 1776.

X. More Action

> . . . the period is arrived when nothing less than the most decisive and vigorous measures should be pursued. Our enemies from the other side of the Atlantic will be sufficiently numerous. It highly concerns us to have as few internal ones as possible.[1]
>
> —WASHINGTON TO CHARLES LEE, JANUARY 23, 1776

THE view has long prevailed that Massachusetts led the colonies in promoting independence. Yet its provincial congress never directed its delegates at Philadelphia to propose or even to vote for separation. As late as mid-April 1776, John Adams, writing home to a friend, took notice of a report that "sighs for independence" were universal in the colony. He then asked why the provincial authorities did not publicly declare themselves in favor of the decisive step. The southern colonies, he added, "say you are afraid."[2]

The reluctance of Massachusetts mirrored the diffidence that prevailed in most of the colonies. When Congress adopted its first statement of war aims, late in May 1775, it laid bare the condition that was to make the decision for independence so difficult to attain. According to that statement, the colonies were striving to preserve their provincial institutions and to retain control over their "internal police."[3] They did not propose to obliterate local distinctions or to fuse all the American people into one mass. In November 1775 John Adams described the force of provincialism, observing that "an instantaneous alteration of the character of a colony and . . . [of] those sentiments which its inhabitants imbibed with their mother's milk and which has grown with their growth, and strengthened with their strength, cannot be made without a miracle."[4]

Since the colonists were fighting to avoid domination by an external power, it followed that all important decisions should be made by themselves. By far the most important decision was that of transforming a colony into a state. Only its people could make it. The act of independence could not proceed from a simple majority vote in Congress; it must flow from thirteen separate actions taken in the thirteen provincial capitals. However, all thirteen decisions must be made together. All the colonies must move en bloc into statehood. Otherwise, the confederation would consist partly of colonies and partly of states. Success in the war required that the union be preserved; hence if some colonies were to become independent, so must the others.

Congress provided the agency through which the colonies might act in unison. However, the delegates could not presume to act on such a vital issue as independence merely on the basis of their personal inclinations. Some of the delegations consisted of only two members. It was out of the question for a very few men, alone, to commit a colony to independence. Each delegation, therefore, sought instructions from a larger body, such as a provincial congress or assembly.

It was a grim responsibility that the members of those bodies were called upon to assume. Each colony had its quota of friends of the king who would surely reveal the names of men so audacious as to vote to deprive the sovereign of a part of his dominions. That would be what the British government regarded as the unpardonable crime. The members of a provincial congress could not be certain that if they took the fatal step they would be supported by the other colonies. They might be left alone, on an island of treason. They were, for the most part, ordinary citizens of very modest means. They had behind them no organizations except hastily formed revolutionary bodies that might disintegrate overnight. After a political contest has turned into a war, it is a rare civilian who, in the face of the armed might and punitive power of the enemy, will act boldly against him, without some covering support from military forces on his side. Once Britain had undertaken to use its army to apprehend American leaders, they needed the protection of a comparable force. After July 1775 such a force was available. It was the Continental army, under the leadership of Washington. One of its main functions, prior to July 1776, was to unify the country politically by providing military security to civilian leaders who were called upon to make the perilous decision for independence.

ii

The relationship between Congress and the provincial governments manifested itself early in June 1775. The insurgents of Massachusetts had virtually overthrown their government that was based on British authority and had replaced it with one of their own devising. Since it appeared unlikely that the old government would soon be restored, the status of the new one was of pressing interest. The colony needed a respected authority; otherwise it might sink into anarchy. The presence of the army magnified the need; without an established civil power a military despotism might arise. If the leaders should create new institutions and place them on a permanent footing they would reject finally the authority of Britain. For prudential reasons they were not prepared to take, alone, such a decisive step. So they referred the subject to Philadelphia.

In a letter of May 16 they appealed to Congress for advice. They deplored that the colony "was denied the exercise of civil government" according to its charter and reported that they trembled "at having an army . . . established here without a civil power to provide for and control" it. They then expressed the hope that Congress would favor them with its "most explicit advice respecting the taking up and exercising the powers of civil government." In closing, they promised that they would either submit to any general plan that Congress might adopt, or undertake "to establish such a form of government here" as would promote both the advantage of the colony and "the union and interest of all America."[5]

This appeal placed before Congress the main issue of independence. Had the members formed a general plan of civil government for all the colonies, they would have moved far toward casting off the authority of Britain. Had they instructed Massachusetts to act according to its own light, they would have endorsed in advance any radical measure that the province might have seen fit to adopt. Neither the conciliationists nor the moderates in Congress were ready at this time to commit themselves to any public action that savored strongly of independence. In consequence, the advice which Congress offered to the province on June 9 did not propose anything very drastic. Congress merely recommended that the people should improvise, for temporary use, a government similar to the one that had existed under the royal charter of 1691. According to the official view of Congress, Britain had unlawfully attempted to alter the legitimate government. The province was instructed, not to devise new institutions looking toward an independent status, but to resist Britain's innovations in order to preserve the old ways. The people, therefore, were justified in exercising, temporarily, the powers of government "until a governor of his majesty's appointment will consent to govern the colony according to its charter."[6]

Thus the program of Congress of June 1775 assumed that the colonies would continue to be dependencies of Britain. The aim was to restore the empire as it had existed in the past—not to set the colonies afloat as independent states. This program had a deterring effect on the local leaders who manned the provincial governments. It imposed a veto on decisive actions by individual colonies. It said that the aim of all the colonies was the preservation of the tie with Britain. It followed, then, that if the leaders of a colony should adopt, unilaterally, a measure looking toward independence, they would act in defiance of the other members of the union.

As the war progressed, the June program of Congress proved to be inadequate. In opposing an army that was supported by a powerful government, Washington soon realized the need of American governments that could act with freedom and energy. Obliged to fight against a sovereign force, he found it necessary to encourage the governments on his side to act like sovereigns, too.

Whenever Congress considered the status of the provincial governments, it encountered a related question: what should be done with the king's friends in America? Their activities raised issues akin to independence. To proscribe them was to brand them as disloyal. Disloyal to whom? Certainly not to the king.

During the first months of the war the American leaders asserted that they were fighting against the ministry — not against the king. The distinction between king and ministry had an important bearing on independence. By 1775 most of the colonists believed that they were united to Britain only through the king. He had issued the charters upon which their provincial governments rested. Technically, they owed allegiance to him as a person. As long as they insisted that they were opposing only his ministers, they could say that their allegiance to Britain was not involved in the resistance. According to the theory, the king was not personally responsible for the war. He had been led astray by his advisers. It was the early aim of the American leaders to drive the evil ministers from the presence of the throne and to replace them with new advisers who would lead the sovereign in the right path.

From this idea it followed that a severe attack on the king would strike at the only bond of union between the colonies and Britain. If the colonists should proclaim that they were fighting against the king, or refer to the British army as the king's troops, or denounce George III as a tyrant, they would direct their attacks at him and thereby reject the only British authority over them that they had recognized.

So also the use of the word "Tory" had an overtone of independence. In English politics the Tories were the friends of the king, who magnified his power and prerogative. To refer to the enemies of the American cause as Tories was to indentify them with the king and thereby to assert that he was the main target of the resistance. Such an attack could lead only to a renunciation of the allegiance which the colonists had previously acknowledged.

Soon after General Gage had condemned the American officers as criminals, Washington started a campaign against the Tories, with the aim of rendering them harmless. As the head of the army he could not evade the issue of allegiance. It did not make sense to ask soldiers to profess loyalty to an enemy against whom they were fighting. Americans could not be expected to die for the cause without feeling a sense of attachment to America as a separate country. Washington acted on the theory that loyalty to Britain was disloyalty to America, that a new allegiance had replaced the old, and that a new sovereign — the American people — had superseded the king.

iii

After Washington's arrival at Cambridge early in July, his headquarters served as the political capital of the four New England colonies. By the end of December each of them had committed itself to independence. Each did this while co-operating with the general. He encouraged the local leaders by giving them the sense that the whole union stood behind them. Whenever he interfered in the domestic politics of a colony, he acted with its civil authorities and his council of generals, seven of whom were New Englanders. The co-operation between the army and the New England governments proved to be so effective, as a means of promoting independence, that it was later extended to other parts of the union — first to the four colonies of the south; then to the five of the middle area.

Dramatic events that occurred in mid-October directed Washington's thoughts to the province of New Hampshire. On October 16 four British warships appeared at the town of Falmouth on the coast of Maine — a town described by General Howe as distinguished for its opposition to the British government. In an address to the inhabitants, the British captain condemned them as "guilty of the most unpardonable rebellion" and warned that he had come to "execute a just punishment." In a parley with the local leaders he demanded that they deliver "four gentlemen of the town as hostages."[7] When this ultimatum was rejected, the captain ordered an attack. The bombardment began at about half past nine in the morning of October 18 and continued until dark. General Howe reported that about five hundred houses and fourteen ships were burned and that several other vessels were captured and destroyed, all "without any loss on our part." [8]

A report of the disaster arrived at Washington's headquarters on October 23. He notified Congress immediately, denouncing the attack as "an outrage exceeding in barbarity and cruelty every hostile act practised among civilized nations." [9]

On the day Falmouth went up in flames, the delegates of New Hampshire presented to Congress a request from their provincial congress. The northern colony solicited advice with respect to the establishment of a new government. Congress referred the request to a committee that was considering it when, on November 1, Washington's letter conveying the news of Falmouth arrived in Philadelphia. The next day Franklin, Harrison, and Lynch returned from the Cambridge conference. These events seem to have spurred Congress to action, for on November 3 it adopted a resolve reported by the committee on the New Hampshire petition. It advised the authorities of the province to call together representatives of the people for the purpose of establishing such a form of government as would best serve their needs "during the continuance of the present dispute between Great Britain and the colonies." [10]

This resolve went much farther than the earlier resolve of June 9 for Massachusetts. In its advice to the Bay Colony Congress had emphasized the king's authority as the basis of colonial government. Now in November Congress directed New Hampshire to adopt any kind of government the people wanted and to act in such a way that it would come directly from them. Only one feature of the new policy softened the suggestion of independence: the idea of limiting the government to the duration of the conflict. Concerning this point the delegates of New Hampshire explained: "To ease the minds of some few persons who were fearful of independence, we thought it advisable not to oppose that part too much, for once we have taken any sort of government, nothing but negotiation with Great Britain can alter it." [11]

By authorizing New Hampshire to replace a royal government

with one to be created by the people, Congress for the first time asserted the idea of popular sovereignty. In so doing it endorsed Washington's view, expressed in his letter of August 19 to General Gage, that a popular election was "the purest source and original fountain of all power."

When Washington learned of the attack on Falmouth he also received a report that the British sea raiders would strike next at Portsmouth, New Hampshire. Thither he sent General Sullivan with instructions to prepare its defenses. From Cambridge also went a party of riflemen whom Washington thought might be used to advantage "should the enemy attempt to set fire to the town."[12] Sullivan found the local defenses inadequate and immediately set the people to work improving them. He reported on October 29 that within two or three days all would be ready. The committee of safety of the province wrote to him that it was "deeply impressed with gratitude to General Washington for his early attention and kindness to the colony in sending you with some forces" and expressed the hope that "the same generous disposition will induce him to continue his assistance while our danger remains."[13]

Sullivan ran into one set of enemies who annoyed him considerably. Writing to Washington on October 29 he said: "That infernal crew of Tories . . . walk the streets here with impunity and will with a sneer tell the people . . . that all our liberty poles will soon be converted into gallows. . . . Some . . . have now turned upon me and are flying from one street to another, proclaiming that you gave me no authority . . . or did anything more than send me here to see the town reduced to ashes." "I entreat your excellency," he continued, "to give some directions what to do with these persons, as I am fully convinced that if an engagement were to happen they would with their own hands set fire to the town, expecting a reward from the ministry for such hellish services." He concluded: "Sir, I shall wait your directions respecting these villains and see that they are strictly complied with."[14]

Sullivan's letter prompted Washington to formulate the first official policy against the Tories. He replied with a letter of November 5 and a set of instructions dated November 7. In these papers he referred to recent British offenses, such as the destruction of seaport towns and the demand that American leaders be delivered as hostages to British authorities. He noted that General Howe had prohibited the inhabitants of Boston from leaving the town without permission and had ordered them to take up arms under British officers. Such measures, he continued, "ought to be opposed by every means in our power."[15] He then directed Sullivan to seize all officers of the crown who were acting as "enemies of their country" and to detain them "as hostages for the security of those towns which our ministerial enemies threaten to invade."[16]

While enjoying the protection of Washington and the army the New Hampshire leaders received from Congress the resolve of November 3. Immediately they arranged for the election of a constitutional convention. Shortly before the old provincial congress expired it adopted the following resolve: ". . . that the thanks of this house be given to his excellency, General Washington, for his early care and notice taken of this colony in sending General Sullivan and other assistance to us when in great fear and distress."[17] Obviously, Washington's action had encouraged the people to cast off the king's government in order to replace it with one of their own.

In the late autumn of 1775 the towns elected delegates to attend the convention. They met at Exeter in December and drew up the first constitution of the Revolutionary era. It did not provide specifically for independence, since its authors declared that they had "never sought to throw off" their dependence on Great Britain and that they would rejoice in such a reconciliation "as shall be approved by the Continental Congress." The new government was to continue "during the present unhappy and unnatural contest."[18] Such avowals did not satisfy the partisans of Britain. At Portsmouth, a meeting of more than two hundred freeholders denounced the constitution as an act of independence.

From the struggle in New Hampshire emerged one of the strong leaders of the war, the *de facto* governor, Meshech Weare. As a dependable collaborator of Washington he did his part to maintain cordial relations between New Hampshire and the army. When Washington, in January 1776, asked the province to send additional troops to Canada, its government, under the leadership of Weare, complied with dispatch. "You may depend upon it, sir," he wrote to the general, "we shall not fail to do our utmost to forward this reinforcement."[19] The protection of the army at Cambridge continued to give heart to the New Hampshire patriots. Writing to Washington on March 12, Weare informed him that "we do . . . gratefully acknowledge the goodness of your intentions, that upon the first discovery and notice given that any of the troops from Boston, on leaving that place, might appear on the coast to attempt a landing, you would come or send immediately to our assistance."[20]

iv

At Lebanon, Connecticut, Washington found another pillar of the cause in the person of Governor Jonathan Trumbull. By November the two men had established a close and friendly working relationship. Their effective co-operation helped to make the colony one of the main bastions of the union. They collaborated in devising a program which, when adopted by the Connecticut legislature, appealed to Washington as a model which he recommended to the other colonies. Protected by Massachusetts in the east and by New York in the west, Connecticut enjoyed an unusual measure of security from attack. The blessing of relative safety permitted its leaders to act with a degree of boldness that was not vouchsafed to colonies more exposed to the blows of the enemy.

In mid-November Washington forwarded to Governor Trumbull a modified copy of the instructions which directed General Sullivan to subdue the Tories of New Hampshire. After reciting the wrongs committed by Britain, the copy for Connecticut denounced "the most tyrannical and cruel system . . . that ever disgraced the most despotical reign. . . ." Thus Washington now leveled the attack directly at the king. The order then continued: "I therefore desire that you will delay no time in causing the seizure of every officer of government . . . who have given proofs of their unfriendly disposition to the cause we are engaged in, and hold them as hostages for the security of those towns now threatened with invasion." Furthermore, the measures of "the most despotical reign . . . ought to be opposed by every means in our power." [21] Washington sent these instructions in company with a letter in which he urged the Connecticut governor to give thought to the Tories. It "is now very apparent," he wrote, "that we have nothing to depend on in the present contest, but our own strength, care, firmness, and union." Coming to the heart of the matter he asked: "Why should persons who are preying upon the vitals of their country be suffered to stalk at large, whilst we know they will do us every mischief in their power?" The letter closed with the plea: "These, sir, are points I beg to submit to your serious consideration." [22]

One may imagine the stir caused by these momentous communications, weighted with the authority of the Continental Congress, the army, and the general, when they were read by Governor Trumbull and his co-workers at the little town of Lebanon. The October session of the Connecticut legislature had done nothing of a startling or drastic nature. Evidently, the dispatches from Washington gave a strong impetus to action. At any rate, the December session of the legislature adopted a far-reaching program in line with his suggestions. It was the first systematic body of law directed against the Tories. One act named a variety of offenses: espionage, supplying the British forces, enlistment therein or encouraging others to enlist, piloting British vessels, or doing anything to aid the war effort of the enemy. The penalties were severe: forfeiture of one's estate and imprisonment up to three years. Such persons as should place themselves under the protection of British forces or who should assist in giving effect to British measures were to suffer loss of their estates. Another act authorized Washington "to administer an oath and to swear any person or persons to the truth of matters relative to the public service." [23]

This legislation pushed Connecticut far toward independence. It asserted that the inhabitants owed allegiance to Congress and the colony. To serve the crown was now a crime, punishable by the loss of one's whole estate. Washington received the news with jubilation. Immediately he sent a summary of the laws to Governor Nicholas Cooke of Rhode Island, with a strong recommendation that that colony should follow its neighbor's example. "The situation of our affairs," he wrote, "seems to call for regulations like these, and I should think the other colonies ought to adopt similar ones." Admitting that at another time they "would seem extraordinary," he insisted that they had "now become absolutely necessary for preserving our country against the strides of tyranny." [24]

The close accord between Washington and Trumbull also comes to light in the response of Connecticut to the setback of the Canada expedition at Quebec. The news arrived at Lebanon before Trumbull received any word on the subject from Washington. As soon as the governor learned of the disaster he secured arrangements for raising a Connecticut regiment to hasten to Quebec. "It seemed necessary that no time be lost," he explained.[25] By an odd coincidence Trumbull reported this action to Cambridge on the very day that Washington's council of war decided to ask Connecticut to raise a regiment of volunteers to serve in Canada.

V

Rhode Island made its commitment to independence on November 6, 1775, when its assembly adopted a sweeping law which defined certain forms of aid to Britain as treason and prescribed the death penalty as punishment for the crime. Within a short time a radical change of opinion had occurred in the colony. Late in August the assembly had resolved that it ardently wished "to see the former friendship . . . between these colonies and Great Britain restored." [26] On September 14 the governor, Nicholas Cooke, wrote optimistically of political happenings in Britain and Ireland which, he thought, would soon "compel the ministry to depart from their favorite plan of establishing arbitrary government in America."[27]

Governor Cooke, who represented Rhode Island at the Cambridge conference in October, was present when it approved the recommendation to the effect that captured spies should be put to death. He had barely left Cambridge when the news of the burning of Falmouth arrived. Immediately General Greene informed him of the event. In an urgent letter of October 24 Greene reported that British naval officers in America had recently received orders to burn all seaport towns that would not disarm themselves and give hostages for their good behavior. He feared particularly an attack on Newport. "Death and destruction," he lamented, "seem to mark their footsteps."[28] On November 2 Washington sent to Cooke a copy of the proceedings of the Cambridge conference. Included therein was the resolve against spies, bearing now the approval of the Congress committee, the general, and the army.

Such was the setting at Providence when on November 6 the assembly made its fateful decision. Its act of that date did not express a desire for conciliation. It accused the king's ministers of pursuing a plan for subjecting America "to an absolute, unconditional state of slavery."[29] They had now proceeded "to the burning of our towns, and spreading desolation and slaughter as far as it hath been in their power." Thc law then defined three acts as treason: corresponding with the enemy, supplying his armed forces, and serving as a pilot on any of his vessels. A person "so offending shall suffer the pains of death, as in cases of felony, and shall forfeit his lands, goods, and chattels to the colony."[30] Thus the defiant assembly asserted that the inhabitants owed allegiance to the United Colonies and to Rhode Island and that treason consisted of giving aid to the agents of the crown.

In mid-November Washington wrote to Governor Cooke suggesting the seizure of all active Tories in Rhode Island. Cooke replied at once that "the defenseless, precarious situation of the town of Newport induced the assembly to postpone the measure until the inhabitants of that town are more generally removed."[31]

A British armed vessel in the harbor was terrorizing them with threats of bombardment in retaliation to hostile acts. Emboldened by this protection, the king's friends asserted themselves, defied the insurgent authorities, and made the town "an asylum for such as are disaffected to American liberty."[32]

About the middle of December Governor Cooke learned that ten vessels had recently sailed from Boston. Fearing that they might strike at Rhode Island, he asked Washington to send thither a detachment from the army. The Rhode Islanders, he said, would welcome General Lee as a resident commander and hoped that he might come at once to put Newport in a good state of defense. Washington immediately ordered Lee to go, but sent with him only a party of riflemen — not the full regiment solicited by Cooke. The Rhode Island tour of General Lee lasted ten days. He did little to improve the defenses of Newport but he staged a colorful drama at the expense of the local Tories.

By this time Lee was the most fiery advocate of independence in America. Long since he had brushed aside the fiction of an innocent king and a guilty ministry. During the past four months he had repeatedly denounced George III as a tyrant. Early in October he offered a program for militant action on all fronts. He would seize all the royal governors, all British officials, and the leading Tories, confiscate their estates, and hold them as hostages in the hinterland. "Great Britain," he said, "is so sunk in corruption and stupidity that she is no longer fit to be the presiding power. . . . We must be independent or slaves."[33]

At Newport, Lee — as he tells us — "took the liberty, without any authority but the conviction of the necessity, to administer a very strong oath to some of the leading Tories."[34] Meeting refusals from two British customhouse officers and another loyalist, he sent them under guard to the patriot stronghold of Providence.

In devising his oath General Lee made a declaration of independence. He required the signers to swear allegiance to the Continental Congress and to Rhode Island and to withhold aid from the "wicked instruments of ministerial tyranny commonly called the king's troops and navy."[35] In line with the Rhode Island law of November 6, his oath branded as "treasons" the crimes of espionage and of supplying the British forces with provisions. However, he did more than attempt to enforce a Rhode Island law, for the act of November 6 did not apply to Newport. He took the liberty of extending it to that town, by his personal fiat. And he offered another innovation. His oath obliged the signers to pledge that they would bear arms in defense of American liberty.

The three recalcitrants who refused to sign told him that "no provocation on the part of the court could prevail upon them to act with the continent." "To take up arms against their sovereign," they said, was "too monstrous an impiety."[36]

Whether Washington knew of Lee's intention to administer the oath does not appear. It is evident, however, that the commander in chief expected that Lee would do something at Newport to render the Tories harmless. When he transmitted a copy of the oath to Congress, Washington sent it with a letter of December 31 in which he said: "General Lee is just returned from his excursion to Rhode Island. . . . He has endeavored all in his power to make friends of those who were our enemies. You have enclosed a specimen of his abilities in that way for your perusal. I am of opinion that if the same plan was pursued through every province, it would have a very good effect."[37]

The Lee oath (which defined espionage as treason) gave effect to the resolve against spies which Congress had adopted on November 7. Lee added a new offense to the Continental list of treasons — that of supplying the armed forces of the enemy. His chief innovation — the pledge to bear arms in defense of American liberty — implied that the people now owed allegiance to the union and to their respective colonies.

vi

At the close of 1775 the movement for independence received a strong stimulus from an action of the provincial congress of Massachusetts. About December 20 that body again elected delegates to the Continental Congress. Among those chosen was a young, energetic merchant of Marblehead, a protégé of Samuel Adams — Elbridge Gerry. Until this time the Massachusetts delegation was controlled by three members (John Hancock, Robert Treat Paine, and Thomas Cushing) who co-operated with the moderate party and who shied away from measures that were flavored with the pungent seasoning of independence. Only Samuel Adams and John Adams were consistent militants. Hancock's position as president of Congress restrained him from bold courses when the majority was reluctant to move fast. Benjamin Harrison, a leader of the moderate group, described Hancock as "noble, disinterested, and generous to a very great degree." [38]

Another Massachusetts delegate, Thomas Cushing, exhibited a timidity that estranged him from the two Adamses. Speaking of his minority position in the Bay Colony delegation, John Adams wrote in November 1775: ". . . it is very hard to be linked and yoked externally with people who have either no opinions or opposite opinions, and to be plagued with the opposition of our own colony to the most necessary measures." [39] Samuel Adams spoke disparagingly of Cushing as a man who was entitled to his convictions — if he could form any.

In electing Gerry, Massachusetts made its decision in favor of independence. After he replaced Cushing in Congress early in February 1776, three of the most stalwart militants in America controlled the Massachusetts delegation and cast its vote consistently for the most resolute measures. Gerry was not an inch behind the two Adamses in his devotion to independence. Moreover, his election had a profound effect on Congress as a whole. As long as Massachusetts, under the direction of Paine, Hancock, and Cushing, acted with the moderates, the smaller New England colonies were deprived of leadership and were as voices crying in the wilderness. After the Adams partnership gained control, with the arrival of Gerry, Massachusetts provided able, forceful leadership to a united New England. The four votes of the area in Congress—nearly one third of the total—could now be counted on for any measure pointing toward independence. This powerful bloc attracted other militants. Georgia, already favorably disposed, made the fifth. Only two other delegations were needed for a majority. The solid New England phalanx greatly strengthened the militants, such as Richard Henry Lee, in the Virginia delegation. Virginia's example in turn exerted a powerful influence in the south. Thus the election of Gerry acted as a lever to shift Congress as a whole onto the side of independence.

The records of the time tell us that Gerry made the first proposal that Washington be appointed commander in chief. One of the last things the general did in Philadelphia before he set out for Cambridge was to obtain a letter of introduction to Gerry from Samuel Adams. "Our patriotic General Washington," wrote Adams, "will deliver this letter to you."[40] Gerry, in the fall and winter of 1775, was a very influential member of the Massachusetts House of Representatives. Washington was compelled to deal with the House on a variety of subjects. Gerry was the liaison between the two. Ordinarily he was appointed to the committees that conferred with the general. His confidence in Washington was not lessened by the association. "It is happy," he wrote in December, "to find a man independent in his fortune, of good sense and true patriotism filling a public office."[41] On one vital issue Gerry sided with Washington against Samuel Adams. When the legislature of Massachusetts had before it a bill to govern the militia, Adams wished to keep the men under the supreme command of provincial officers. Gerry urged that whenever the militia should serve in conjunction with the Continental army, it should be placed under the command of Washington.

Gerry strove to maintain friendly relations between the general and the civil authorities of Massachusetts. It appears that Washington was victimized for a time by clever enemies who intercepted some of his letters and inserted in them forged passages that reflected harshly on the New Englanders. Such letters probably turned up in Philadelphia and were used to inflame the southerners against the New Englanders and to embitter the latter toward Washington. It was inevitable that a certain amount of friction should arise when an outsider, imbued with a Continental point of view, attempted to modify some of the customary practices of a people who were jealously attached to their local liberties. In this ticklish situation Gerry acted as a conciliator. By the end of 1775 the mist of suspicion had been dispelled, and reasonable harmony prevailed between the general and the leaders of Massachusetts.

In the meantime Gerry and Washington had collaborated in an effort to secure from the Massachusetts congress an act which virtually committed the colony to independence. In October 1775 Washington deemed it urgent that vessels supplying the British army should be seized. To this end he established his little fleet of six armed commerce raiders. But the resources of the army were not sufficient for operations on the necessary scale. Consequently he proposed that his little fleet be supplemented by vessels of private citizens. He thought that such privateers should be strictly regulated by law. If an individual shipowner were to be free, on his own authority alone, to go out and capture ships, there would be no assurance that a raider would not seize vessels belonging to Americans or to friendly countries. Hence it was necessary that some government should provide a legal framework in which such activities would be conducted. Some government must grant the requisite authority, in the form of letters of marque and reprisal, and establish courts to determine whether captures were indeed taken from the enemy.

But, alas, as soon as the subject was mentioned up rose the troublesome specter of independence. Only sovereigns issued letters of marque; only independent states established prize courts. Thomas Cushing said in October that it would not do to urge Congress to take such a bold step. The reluctance in Philadelphia had the effect of passing the explosive issue to the provincial governments. Some colony must rush in where Congress feared to tread.

At the Cambridge conference, Washington and the other participants considered the question: "Should not the fitting out of privateers by individuals be done under some authority, and accidental captures be subject to some regulations to prevent piracies?" The Congress committee replied on October 22 that the legislature of Massachusetts "ought properly to take cognizance of all armed vessels fitted out in this province and that commissions should be granted in such cases."[42] In this manner Washington and a committee speaking for the majority in Congress authorized Massachusetts to act like a sovereign in the realm of privateering.

Armed with this recommendation, Gerry presented to the Massachusetts legislature a bill which became law on November 10. He had written to Samuel Adams on October 9: "My attention is directed to fitting out privateers, which I hope will make them swarm here." In this letter Gerry offered another suggestion looking to independence. Referring to reports that the ministry planned to engage foreign mercenaries, he said: "If foreign force is employed against us, we may be greatly puzzled, unless we endeavor at the same thing."[43]

The act of November 10, of which Gerry was the author, directed the executive officials of Massachusetts to commission privateers and to establish prize courts. Washington at once sent a copy of the law to Philadelphia. Congress approved it on November 25 by authorizing the colonies to establish prize courts and to enlarge the powers of those in existence.

Opponents of Gerry's law had criticized it as inconsistent with the royal charter and therefore as an act leading to independence. To meet such objections Gerry wrote an ingenious preamble. It stated that, by the royal charter, the crown had authorized the provincial council, in emergencies, to wage war at sea against every such person as should attempt "the destruction, invasion, detriment, or annoyance" of the province.[44] The crown, said Gerry, had authorized war against itself. He later noted that when this preamble was printed in London, it was regarded as a "curiosity." The law was the first of its kind. John Adams called it "one of the boldest, most dangerous, and most important . . . measures in the history of the new world."[45] A well informed contemporary described it as a spirited act, "contemplated by few." In view of such testimony, and of the radical nature of the law,[46] it is reasonable to infer that Washington's actions, both in establishing his little fleet and in securing the recommendation of the Congress committee on October 22, helped to overcome the fears of cautious legislators who shrank from a sharp break with the past.

On January 18, 1776, the Massachusetts legislature adopted a new set of instructions to guide its delegates in Congress. Not a word was said about conciliation. The five delegates were now authorized to do whatever they thought necessary "to establish the right and liberty of the American colonies on a basis permanent and secure."[47] Since a majority of the delegation—the two Adamses and Gerry—held extremely advanced views, the instructions amounted to a mandate for independence.

XI. A Setback

> I am not fond of stretching my powers; and if the Congress will say, "Thus far and no farther you shall go," I will promise not to offend whilst I continue in their service.[1]
>
> — WASHINGTON TO JOSEPH REED, MARCH 3, 1776

NEW YEAR's day, 1776. After more than eight months of the excitements of war, the port of New York remained neglected. It was the orphan of the American cause. Congress, it is true, had made generous provision, on paper, for its defense, and had entrusted the execution to General Schuyler. The impressive commander had visited the city early in July of 1775. Satisfying himself that urgent action was not needed, he had repaired to Albany. Soon he was too immersed in the details of the Canada expedition to give much thought to the provincial metropolis. Washington devoted himself to Boston and to the problems of New England and Canada, leaving the strategic port on the Hudson to the care of the provincial authorities of New York. They did not bestir themselves. The shore line areas of Manhattan, Long Island, Staten Island, and the lower mainland lay exposed to British warships that plied the waters adjacent to the port. Such potential marauders could batter down buildings at will, or set fire to the town without hindrance. The danger induced a prudential caution on the part of the patriots. They displayed a marked aversion to hostile measures, and even failed to place the city in a strong defensive posture. The British governor, William Tryon, remained at large and encouraged the king's friends to assert themselves. The royal ships supplied them with arms, while rumors foretold that a large British force would soon occupy the area.

Washington's initial reception at New York in June 1775 had not been a happy one. The provincial congress had politely expressed its wish that he would soon retire to civilian life. When, early in October, he learned of Britain's plans for a vigorous prosecution of the war, his thoughts naturally turned to the environs of Manhattan. He then approached Congress with a query. If the British should attempt to occupy the town, he asked, should a part of his army be sent thither, or should the province be defended by itself and its neighbors, or should he await directions from Congress? It is probable that he viewed Lee's expedition to Rhode Island as a dress rehearsal for a similar but much more important action in New York.

On January 5 Lee submitted to Washington a spirited letter. He said that he was so fearful that the enemy would occupy New York that he could not sleep. "You have it in your power," he continued, "to prevent this dreadful event." He assumed that Congress had "given you authority to take any steps in that place . . . which you shall think necessary for the public service." But even if the power had not been expressly granted, "any measure you think right to plan and put in execution will be approved of." The "best members of Congress expect that you would take much upon yourself." To refer every matter to them, Lee thought, would be to defeat the project. "To you they look up for decision. By your conduct they are inspired with decision. . . . New York must be secured, but it never will . . . be secured by direct order of Congress. They find themselves awkwardly situated on this head. You must step in to their relief." Washington's situation, added Lee, "is such that the salvation of the whole depends on your striking, at certain crises, vigorous strokes, without previously communicating your intention."[2]

The inventive Lee then suggested that he be sent to Connecticut to enlist a body of volunteers. He would lead them to New York in order to secure the city and to suppress a "dangerous banditti of Tories who have appeared on Long Island. . . . Not to crush these serpents, before their rattles are grown, would be ruinous."[3]

One of the "best members of Congress," John Adams, happened

to be in the vicinity of Cambridge at this time. Washington asked his opinion of the merits of Lee's plan. Adams replied with startling alacrity. On January 6 he wrote to Washington endorsing the project. He thought that the enterprise "would not be attended with much difficulty." The Connecticut people, "who are very ready upon such occasions," along with "the friends of liberty in New York," might "easily accomplish the work." The city, the province, and the Hudson he regarded as the nexus of the southern and northern colonies and as "a kind of a key to the whole continent." Of Washington's authority to act, Adams had not the slightest doubt. "Your commission," he pointed out, "constitutes you commander of all forces now raised or to be raised . . . for the defense of American liberty, and for repelling every hostile invasion thereof; and [you] are vested with full power and authority to act as you shall think fit for the good and welfare of the service. . . . That New York is within your command . . . cannot bear a question."[4]

The armed Tories of Long Island, continued Adams, who were supplying the king's forces, "were guilty of a hostile invasion of American liberty." He added: "If in the city a body of Tories are waiting only for a force to protect them, to declare themselves on the side of our enemies, it is high time that city was secured."[5]

On January 7 Washington informed Governor Trumbull of the plan and solicited his aid in the recruitment of volunteers in Connecticut. "Every necessary expense attending their march will be borne by the public."[6] On the day following Washington issued the official instructions to General Lee. They directed him to proceed to New York, "with such volunteers as are willing to join you"—there "to put that city into the best posture of defense which the season and circumstances will admit of." Lee was also ordered to disarm all "justly suspected" Tories on Long Island and elsewhere, and if necessary to secure them.[7]

What was the meaning of the proposed expedition? Both Washington and Lee now favored independence. Lee's views on the subject were undoubtedly well known in Congress, for he had expressed them strongly in letters sent to Philadelphia as early as October.

Writing to Robert Morris on January 3, he described his activity in Rhode Island and then said: "I hope it will be approved of by our sovereign, for such now must the Congress be esteemed. The king's speech absolutely destroys all hope of reunion." [8] The oath which Lee administered at Newport asserted the theory that Americans owed their allegiance to a new sovereign — the union — and that an act of loyalty to Britain was a heinous offense. Washington clearly endorsed Lee's conduct in administering the oath in Rhode Island. In December 1775 he wrote: "I think . . . that it is high time a test act was prepared and every man called upon to declare himself." A letter from Washington's acting secretary, early in January, makes it clear that the main purpose of Lee's mission to Newport was that of suppressing the Tories. On December 31, Washington sent a copy of the Lee oath to Congress. And in his instructions to Lee of January 8 he gave Lee a blanket authority. Certainly Lee was likely to use his favorite device — the loyalty oath. The instructions stated: "In all other matters relative to the execution of the general plan . . . your own judgment (as it is impossible with propriety to give particular direction), and the advice of those whom you have reasons to believe are hearty in the cause, must direct, keeping always in view the declared intentions of Congress." [9]

Among those who were "hearty in the cause" was a New York militant, Captain Isaac Sears. Lee later used him in New York to apprehend the Tories and to administer the oath. Sears was at Cambridge with Washington early in January, when the plans for the expedition were adopted. He set it in motion by going to Connecticut, in advance of Lee, to recruit volunteers. Lee wrote to Washington on February 14: "You must pardon me . . . for a liberty I have taken. You know that Sears was to collect our volunteers in Connecticut; but he thought he could not succeed unless he had some nominal office and rank. I accordingly, most imprudently by virtue of the power deputed by you to me (which power you never deputed), appointed him adjutant-general with rank of lieutenant-colonel for the expedition. It can have no bad consequences; the man was much tickled and it added spurs to his head.

He is a creature of much spirit and public virtue, and ought to have his back clapped."[10]

Lee had advised bold action, without an advance communication of plans. That is what happened. He arrived at the border of New York before Congress learned of the expedition. In the meantime, it had adopted a policy at odds with that of the generals. On January 2 it directed the colonies, individually, to disarm and arrest the most dangerous Tories. To accomplish this, a colony might ask for a detachment of the army, but such a force was to be under the local officials. Washington, in projecting the expedition, did not obtain permission from the New York authorities. Nor did he place Lee in subordination to them. He merely sent them a letter, to be delivered by Lee, notifying them of the plan and urging them to "give every assistance in their power."[11] The expedition set out before Washington learned of the Congress resolve of January 2. Lee began his march to New York before Congress had received Washington's official report on Lee's activities in Rhode Island.

ii

A stroke of misfortune hit Lee while he was en route to New York. Washington had initiated the project in the atmosphere of optimism that prevailed at camp after the receipt of the reports of the early successes of the Canada expedition. Montreal had been taken and Quebec was expected soon to fall. But unhappily about mid-January the news of the defeat at Quebec reached the Manhattan area. It arrived in company with reports that a British squadron was headed for New York. Disaster seemed to stare the port in the face, and fear gripped the more timid among the citizens. Lee was in Connecticut at the time. The New York provincial committee of safety, having received confidential advices of his destination, sent him an agitated letter.

Described by Lee as "woefully hysterical," this letter protested that the New York authorities had received no information of the expedition from either Congress, Washington, or Lee. The committee politely asked for a statement of Lee's plans. It described the preparations for defense then under way in New York. It was true that they were not yet matured, but any rash action on Lee's part would throw everything into confusion. "Deeply interested in the preservation of the metropolis," and attentive to the wishes of the people of the city, "who expect our prudent care of their lives and property," the committee stated its desire to refrain from provoking hostilities with the British warships in the harbor. The letter closed by asking Lee to halt in western Connecticut until he could enter into an "explanation" with the committee.[12]

Lee now found himself in an embarrassing situation. He had learned of the Congress resolve of January 2 which gave to the civil authorities of a colony the power to decide whether a detachment of the army should operate within its territory. The New York committee of safety had told him to stay out. His instructions from Washington ordered him to abide by the declared intentions of Congress. What was he to do? Should he submit to the New York committee and return ignominiously to Cambridge? Should he go ahead on his own responsibility, thereby defying Congress, Washington, and New York? He acted with extraordinary swiftness, and in a manner worthy of his genius. He dispatched posthaste four letters—one to Congress, one to Robert Morris, one to the New York committee of safety, and one to Washington.

He informed Congress that he had "collected a body of about twelve hundred men from Connecticut, whose zeal and ardor . . . cannot be sufficiently praised." With this force he was "marching directly to New York to execute the different purposes" for which he was detached. Sending to Congress the "woefully hysterical" letter from the New York committee, he observed that "these gentlemen probably are not apprised of the danger hanging over their heads." He then announced his intention to move. "I shall proceed with one division . . . to that city. A moment's delay may be fatal." The reinforcing of the city, he said, should not be vetoed by British threats. "If they are to prescribe what number of troops . . . are to enter the city, all I can say is that New York must be considered as the ministry's place and not the continent's."

Lee devoted most of this letter to the Tories, whom he described as "so riveted in their opinions that . . . should an angel descend from heaven with his golden trumpet and ring in their ears that their conduct was criminal he would be disregarded." Alluding to the oath he had administered in Rhode Island, he promised to repeat the performance in New York. "It will be a sort of criterion by which you will be able to distinguish the desperate fanatics from those who are reclaimable." He then offered a copious criticism of the anti-Tory policy of Congress and proposed a sweeping new one of his own. Stating that he had at hand a force capable of "purging" New York and its environs of "traitors," he announced that he would "expect with impatience the determination of the Congress," and that he hoped to receive their orders "before or immediately on my arrival." And then he exploded a bombshell. This very instant he had received word that the British fleet had sailed, and he found it necessary to go to New York at once and occupy the city.[13]

Robert Morris at the time was a member of Congress. In a letter to him, Lee described the recent oath incident in Rhode Island and unfolded the plan for similar activity in New York. Sounding an ominous warning, he said that the complacency of the New York provincial congress might ruin the American cause. "New York will be one day or the other the ministry's. They play fast and loose with you in such a manner as to give you an air of extreme ridicule." Fearful that his letter to Congress might be regarded as "presumptuous," he asked Morris to be one of his advocates, "if it is taken in this light." The audacious general also took the occasion to favor Morris with another strong plea for independence.[14]

To the New York committee of safety Lee offered soothing assurances. It was not his intention to provoke hostilities with British warships in the harbor. He intended only to put the city in a state of defense and to transact certain other business of such a delicate nature that he would reveal it to the committee orally. Discounting British threats to destroy New York he disclosed one of his main ideas about the strategy of the war. "The destruction of the seaport towns," he said, "would . . . be a severer stroke to the ministry . . . than to the inhabitants themselves. The seaport towns are the only holds they have on America. They are considered as pledges of servitude. The menacing [of] destruction to them may be of admirable use, but the real destruction of them must extinguish all hopes of success." And for the presumed menace he proposed a stern antidote, warning that if the British should "make a pretext of my presence to fire on the town, the first house set in flames by their guns shall be the funeral pile of some of their best friends." In deference to the "request" of the committee, he announced that he would leave most of his men on the western frontier of Connecticut and enter New York with "a force just strong enough to secure it against any designs of the enemy, until it shall please the Continental Congress to take measures for its permanent security."[15]

Writing to Washington, Lee declared his determination to advance. He disparaged the placing of Continental troops under provincial authorities as "fraught with difficulties and evil." He expected to receive the orders of Congress before or immediately on his arrival at New York; otherwise he could "not venture to march into the province." Of the attitude there he said: "The Whigs, I mean the stout ones, are . . . very desirous that a body of troops should be stationed in their city. The timid ones are averse, merely from the spirit of procrastination which is characteristic of timidity." Tom Paine's *Common Sense* now made its initial appearance in the correspondence of the generals. "I never saw," wrote Lee, "such a masterly, irresistible performance." "It will . . . in concurrence with the transcendent folly and wickedness of the ministry, give the *coup de grace* to Great Britain. In short, I own myself convinced by the arguments of the necessity of separation."[16]

Having announced to Congress, to the New York committee of safety, and to Washington his resolution to advance at once to New York, Lee—as he said—suffered an attack of gout which prostrated him until he learned of the response of Congress to his manifestoes. It was a timely stroke of illness, for it enabled him to maintain a lofty position without acting against the orders of all the authorities to whom he was subordinate. Did he intend to dash to New York, as he promised to do in his letter to Congress? Or was that letter (to use one of his favorite expressions) a *brutum fulmen* — a harmless thunderbolt? While at Stamford he notified Congress on January 22 that he intended to advance at once. Two days later (still at Stamford) he sent the same message to Washington, without mentioning that he had been suddenly afflicted with the gout. At any rate, his maneuvers saved the expedition, preserved his dignity and prestige, and enabled him to avoid an open violation of the orders and instructions of his superiors.

iii

Lee's explosive letter was read in Congress on January 26. It caused a furore, signifying as it did that the irrepressible general was on his way to New York, if indeed he was not already there. Presumably, he was acting in direct defiance of the orders of Congress and against the wishes of the civil authorities of New York. What should be done? Behind Lee stood Washington. Should Congress condemn the expedition, repudiate and discredit the two leading generals, and thereby strike a blow at the army? Should it condone an open violation of its authority? Thomas Nelson, a delegate from Virginia, described the uproar in Congress that was set off by Lee's audacity. Nelson wrote to Jefferson: "The letter . . . being read, a violent debate arose, on one side as to the impropriety of an armed force from one province entering another without permission of the civil authority of that province, or without express orders of Congress. It was alleged that this was setting up the military above the civil. On the other side was urged the absolute necessity of securing that province, the loss of which would cut off all communication between the northern and southern colonies and which if effected would ruin America."[17]

The debate ended in a temporary victory for Washington and

Lee. Congress did not reprimand the generals. It merely appointed a committee of three of its members to go to New York to consult with Lee. Indirectly, this action approved the declared intention of Lee, for it put a stamp of approval on his presumed presence in New York. It assumed that his task there was so urgent, right, and important that he could not properly be summoned to wait upon Congress at Philadelphia. Moreover, the majority of the committee consisted of two steadfast friends of Washington, who could be depended upon to sustain him to the limit. Thomas Lynch and Benjamin Harrison, who received the new assignment, had proved their loyalty to the general by the wholehearted support they had given him at the Cambridge conference in the preceding October. When President Hancock notified Lee of the appointment of the committee he said: "I have only to add my best wishes . . . that success may attend your important exertions."[18] Lee had expected that he would not be permitted to enter New York. After he learned of the action of Congress he wrote to Washington: "I consider it as a piece of the greatest good fortune that Congress have detached a committee to this place; otherwise I must have made a most ridiculous figure, besides bringing upon myself the enmity of the whole province."[19]

Lee's victory seems to have alleviated his gout sufficiently to permit his being carried on a litter from Stamford to New York. He entered the city in triumph on February 4, and immediately conferred with the Congress committee and the New York leaders. At this time he prepared a plan for the defense of the area which Washington used later to guide the operations of the main army when it arrived the following April. Lee believed that the security of New York depended on Long Island, which, he assumed, the British would endeavor to control. He proposed to establish at Brooklyn a fortified camp of four thousand men, and to cut off the western end of Long Island from Long Island Sound by erecting shore batteries at Hell Gate. He thought that the town of New York could not be protected against bombardment by British warships; therefore his plan called for protected "lodgments" for two thousand men on Manhattan and for earthworks and barricades within the city. On the Hudson, the pass in the highlands was to be guarded by a battalion. He persuaded the New York leaders to provide, on paper, a large body of troops for these tasks. But skeptical of the response, he obtained promises of men from Connecticut, Pennsylvania, and New Jersey.

Nor did he neglect the Tories on Long Island. Thither he sent his energetic aide, Colonel Isaac Sears, the New York militant and popular leader. About the middle of March Sears reported: "It is a duty that I owe to my commander to acquaint him of my proceedings in executing the order he gave me. Yesterday afternoon I arrived at Newtown and tendered the oath to four of the grate Tories, which they swallowed as hard as if it was a four pound shot that they were trying to git down. On this day at 11 o'clock I came here [Jamaica], whare I sent out scouting parties, and have ben able to ketch but five Tories, and they of the first rank, which swallowed the oath. The houses are so scatering it is impossible to ketch many without hosses to rid after them. But I shall exert myself to ketch the great part of the ringleadors and beleve I shell effect it, but not less than five days from this time. I can assure your honor they are a set of villins in this country, and beleve the better half of them are wateing for suport and intend to take up arms against us. And it is my oppinion nothing else will do but removeing the ringleadors to a place of securety."[20]

Lee's appraisal of the threat of the British to bombard New York proved to be sound. They intended to occupy and use the town later. A British captain ingeniously explained that Lee's purpose was to provoke the warships to destroy a town which the rebels hated for its loyalty to the king, adding that the ships would not gratify him by executing his plan. Satisfied that the British would not retaliate, Lee prohibited all communication with the vessel which Governor Tryon used as the headquarters of British and Tory operations in the area.

In his manifold activities Lee relied upon the rank and file of the people. "To do them justice," he wrote to Washington, "the whole show a wonderful alacrity; and, in removing the cannon, men and boys of all ages worked with greatest zeal and pleasure. I really believe that the generality here are as well affected as any on the continent."[21] Of the cautious leaders, however, he had a different opinion. Once he complained of "the accursed provincial congress." The committee of the Continental Congress shared his view, finding the conduct of the New Yorkers "timid and trimming to the greatest degree."[22] Earlier, Lynch reported that they had done nothing in the way of defense preparations. "The apathy that holds Congress in fetters is more forceable here."[23]

For a time Lee outmaneuvered his opponents in New York, but his success did not last. His forcing tactics aroused resentments. By putting himself in direct communication with Congress he divorced himself from Washington, thereby enabling his enemies to strike at him directly, without involving the commander in chief. Three actions of Congress virtually repudiated his manipulations of the expedition. First, it countermanded an order which directed that a battalion of Pennsylvanians should join him at New York. This reversal knocked out an important part of his plan. Congress explained that the British invasion of which he was so fearful had not materialized. On February 17 he was relieved of his command in New York and ordered to Canada. In giving this order Congress betrayed a skepticism of his gout. When asked in advance by Robert Morris concerning his attitude toward the Canada command, Lee had mentioned his gout as the only deterrent. Having made provision for his removal from New York, Congress again placed the city and its environs under the command of General Schuyler, thereby restoring the arrangement that had existed before the intervention of Lee.

Most important, Congress on March 9 adopted a resolve which flatly repudiated his experiments with the loyalty oath. The resolve stated "that no oath, by way of test, be imposed upon, exacted, or required of any inhabitant of these colonies by any military officers."[24] The New York delegates in Congress had objected to Lee's coercive measures, asserting that the exacting of an oath was an act within the power of the civil authority alone. The rebuke saddened the impetuous general. He grieved that his "conduct in administering an oath to the disaffected in Long Island should have brought down such a thundering stigma" upon his head. "I myself," he continued, "saw . . . the irregularity of the proceeding. . . . I confess that I expected a reprimand but flattered myself that it might have been conveyed to me in a less severe manner than a public resolve." Such a public censure, he added, "sinks deep in my spirits, and I sincerely wish that a natural warmth of temper and . . . an immoderate zeal for the rights and safety of this country may never hurry me a second time into any measure which may so justly merit reprehension." [25]

iv

When Washington learned of the fate of the expedition, he accepted his share of the responsibility. Although he had not expressly authorized Lee to administer the loyalty oath, he had given an implied approval so strong as to amount to an order. He had dispatched Lee to New York before Congress received his report on the initial experiment in Rhode Island. For this assumption of authority he had the blessing of John Adams, who had helped to draft his commission as commander in chief.

There is reason to believe that a party in Congress was acting in concert with the generals to provide an authorization for the New York venture. On January 3 Congress ordered a Connecticut regiment under Colonel David Waterbury to march to Long Island for the purpose of disarming the Tories there. As soon as Governor Trumbull learned from Washington of the projected expedition, he appointed Colonel Waterbury to one of the regiments that were to accompany Lee. Something strange happened, however, for on January 10 Congress withdrew its permission for Waterbury's regiment to enter Long Island. Washington commented on the change in a letter to Lee of January 23. "I . . . am exceeding sorry to hear that Congress countermanded the embarkation of the two regiments intended against the Tories on Long Island."[26] He then indicated that the resolve of January 3 had provided the authority for the Lee expedition. "As Congress seem to have altered their views in this instance, and the men who went with you from Connecticut are upon a very different footing from what I expected, it will be right to give Congress the earliest notice of your proceedings and to disband your troops as soon as you think circumstances will admit of it."[27]

On January 29 President Hancock, writing in his official capacity, informed Washington that "the Congress highly approve your sending General Lee to New York as a measure judicious and necessary."[28]

Upon learning that Lee intended to go into New York, despite the opposition of the provincial authorities, Washington sent him a letter reaffirming the original instructions: ". . . you will see the necessity of being decisive and expeditious in your operations . . . the Tories should be disarmed immediately . . . you can seize upon the persons of some of the principals . . . happy should I be if the governor could be one of them. . . . I very much approve your conduct." At the same time Washington directed Lee to obey Congress. "I sincerely wish," he wrote, "that the letter you expect from Congress may empower you to act conformable to your own and my sentiments on this occasion. If they should order differently we must submit, as they doubtless will have good reasons for what they may determine on."[29]

After Lee established direct contact with Congress, he left Washington pretty much in the dark. When the general finally demanded a report, Lee sent a letter which summarized the fate of the expedition. Congress, he said, had not yet taken the least step for the security of New York. "The instant I leave it . . . the provincial congress and inhabitants will relapse into their former hysterics; the men-of-war and Mr. Tryon will return to their old station at the wharves, and the first regiments who arrive from England will take quiet possession of the town and Long Island. I have written letters till

I am tired on the subject to Congress, but have received no answer." The Congress committee with which he had conferred, Lee continued, had agreed that five thousand men were needed at New York. The committee had departed and no notice had been taken of its recommendations. "Great and extensive works were resolved upon and we have scarcely sufficient numbers to mark out the ground, much less to throw up the works." He then spoke of his ban on the intercourse between the city and the ship of Governor Tryon as "a measure which has thrown the mayor, council, and Tories into agonies. The . . . rage for paying court to this great man is inconceivable. They cannot be weaned from him. We must put wormwood in his paps or they will cry to suck, as they are in their second childhood."[30]

Joseph Reed, Washington's observer and reporter at Philadelphia, notified him of criticisms of the Lee expedition that were current there at the end of February. The critics were particularly irked by the cost of employing the Connecticut men in the Continental service. Washington had placed them on the army payroll without authorization from Congress. Replying to Reed (in a letter undoubtedly intended to be seen by many of the delegates) Washington defended himself and justified the expedition. "If I have done wrong," he concluded, "those members of Congress, who think the matter ought to have been left to them, must consider my proceedings as an error of judgment. . . . It is . . . worthy of consideration that in cases of extreme necessity (as the present), nothing but decision can insure success. . . . However, I am not fond of stretching my powers; and if Congress will say, 'Thus far and no farther you shall go,' I will promise not to offend whilst I continue in their service."[31] The episode ended by Reed's assuring Washington that his statement had given perfect satisfaction to Congress.

The contrast between the success of the generals in New England and their failure in New York is striking. They went to Massachusetts as welcome, invited guests; Lee went to New York as an unwanted outsider. In New England they commanded local troops; Lee had to impose Connecticut men on the reluctant New Yorkers.

At Cambridge they were assisted by seven New England generals and had the support of like-minded civil authorities; Lee had to act alone at New York, in opposition to the provincial officials. Washington had the full support of Congress in his New England activities; Lee at New York found himself so placed that he either had to quit or threaten to act against the will of his superiors.

The expedition had two incidental effects. It taught Washington much about the politics of New York. The knowledge was useful to him later when he was stationed in the province with the main army. Secondly, he took over the plan which Lee worked out for the defense of the Manhattan area.

Did the episode show that the New Yorkers as a whole were hostile to the American cause? Lee testified that the generality of the people were as loyal as any other Americans. The main charge against them pertained to their refusal to prepare elaborate defenses. In that refusal they were probably sensible. Lee's defense plan contained a fatal defect. It was most unlikely that the British would invade New York except with a large force. Lee proposed to base the defense of the city on western Long Island and to establish there an armed camp of three or four thousand men. But there was nothing to prevent the arrival at Long Island of a larger British force directly from the Atlantic Ocean. There was nothing to prevent the landing of such a force on Long Island and the subsequent encirclement or expulsion of the sort of camp which Lee proposed. The situation in New York was such that it could be defended only by a very large force. Even the whole American army proved to be unequal to the task. Since the New Yorkers were right in thinking that limited defensive gestures were useless, their refusal to make them did not in itself denote indifference to the American cause.

XII. Congress Bestirs Itself

> The Congress are proceeding in their military preparations. . . . I believe a majority of them would cut the knot tomorrow, but [they] must have the concurrence of the people.[1]
>
> — JOSEPH REED TO MR. PETTIT, MARCH 1776

AT the end of 1775 Washington received reports which verified his appraisal of the intentions of the British government. Dispatches from London included copies of the speech which George III had read to parliament on October 26. The king had declared that all the thirteen colonies were engaged in open rebellion, levying war for the purpose of establishing an independent state. He had pledged that vigorous measures would be employed to crush the revolt, including the use of foreign troops. Washington's experience of British politics had taught him that the policies announced by the king in a speech to parliament would soon be enacted into law. The most recent acts of the court, such as the royal Proclamation of Rebellion and the initial preparations for war, lacked as yet the sanction of law. The king's speech gave assurance that parliament's approval would soon be forthcoming. Washington responded by ordering the Lee expedition to proceed to New York. The king's speech also prompted him to begin a letter writing campaign in behalf of independence. For such a project he had available an able collaborator, his military secretary, Joseph Reed, who spent the winter of 1775–1776 in Philadelphia.

Reed was close to the leaders of both Pennsylvania and Congress. His contacts with Benjamin Harrison, Thomas Lynch, Robert Morris, Richard Henry Lee, and President Hancock enabled him to get before Congress certain information and proposals which Washington conveyed to him privately when the occasion did not admit of a direct, formal communication to the members as a whole. Reed was one of the sponsors of Tom Paine and the publication of *Common Sense.* By an astonishing coincidence, that powerful plea for independence made its appearance in Philadelphia on the same day that Washington at Cambridge issued the first orders for General Lee to advance to New York. Since the Lee expedition was based on the principle of independence, it asserted in action the idea which Paine expressed in glowing words of exhortation.

The letter writing campaign opened on January 2 with a letter to Reed from Washington's acting secretary, Stephen Moylan. "Look at the king's speech," he exclaimed, "it is enclosed in this or in the general's letter to you." Referring to the king's charge that the colonies were seeking independence, Moylan asked if Congress would not now declare that it had done "what his most gracious majesty insists on." Would not the members "strain every nerve to accomplish it? . . . Are there remaining any hopes of a desirable alternative?" Urging that Congress act like a sovereign by inviting foreign states to trade with America, Moylan asserted that "the king's speech is the key to open all ports."[2] He also suggested that Congress play the part of the supreme authority of an independent state by sending diplomatic agents to foreign powers.

Washington at this time directed the attention of Congress to the king. In a letter of January 4 he enclosed a copy of the king's speech, which he described as "full of rancor and resentment against us." He emphasized the importance of the king, referring to the "royal will" and to measures "authorized and sanctioned by the name of his majesty."[3] By emphasizing the role of the king, Washington suggested that he was the enemy of America. If so, the colonists no longer owed him allegiance.

The next letter to Reed, dated January 14, forwarded a report "just arrived" of the response of parliament to the king's speech. The two houses had endorsed it, "with assurances of standing by his majesty with lives and fortunes." Other advices from England revealed that "we have nothing to expect but the most vigorous exertions of administration, who have a dead majority upon all questions."[4] Nine days later Washington referred to the British forces as "our enemies" and as "the king's troops."[5] Presumably, the colonies were no longer resisting the ministry; they were fighting directly against the king. He therefore appeared as the author of America's grievances. He must be defeated, repudiated, and cast aside. The colonies must become independent states.

"Shall we never leave off debating, and boldly declare independence?" Thus queried Stephen Moylan on January 30. "The bulk of the people," he insisted, "will not be against it. . . . Can it be supposed that a reconciliation will take place after the loss of blood, cities and treasure already suffered?"[6] Washington again endorsed Moylan's extreme views in a parallel letter to Reed. On January 31 he spoke of "the sound doctrine and unanswerable reasoning contained in the pamphlet, *Common Sense*."[7]

The campaign reached its high point in a letter of February 10, in which Washington asserted that he had favored independence since early in the preceding October. To George III, whom he called a tyrant, and to his "diabolical ministry," he would now declare, "in words as clear as the sun in its meridian brightness," that "we are determined to shake off all connections with a state so unjust and unnatural. . . ."[8]

Despite the strong expression of Washington's pro-independence views, both in writing and in action, he continued to command the full support of Congress in matters pertaining to the army. The delegates attended promptly to his requests and almost invariably adopted his recommendations, usually without alteration. The moderates and militants (who together controlled every delegation in Congress) stood by him faithfully. The continuing approval of his course was indirectly an endorsement of independence. At the least it foreshadowed the final outcome. Only once did Congress administer a rebuke — in the affair of the Lee expedition to New York.

ii

The removal of General Lee from his command in New York marked the high point of the influence of the conciliationists in Congress. For over eight months, from June 1775 to March 1776, the delegates had done little except to provide for the army — and then talk. During these months the moderates had generally lined up with the conciliationists in opposition to radical proposals. Neither group had yet abandoned the hope that armed resistance would render the king's friends odious in Britain, overturn the ministry, and procure far-reaching concessions. Until the end of 1775 the most drastic measures of Britain had been proclaimed by the ministry alone. Parliament, the supreme authority, had declared only Massachusetts to be in a state of rebellion, and that had not been done by a statute, but by a resolution that did not prescribe a penalty. The ministry had made the preparations for war, but it had done so without a declaration of war. Only two important laws touching America had been passed during most of the year 1775 — the laws prohibiting certain branches of the trade of New England and of five other colonies. But those acts did not apply to Delaware, North Carolina, Georgia, and New York; hence they did not strike at the union as a whole or impute guilt to Congress. The conciliationists and the moderates could comfort themselves, until March 1776, with the illusion that the American resistance, as conducted by Congress, had not been condemned by British law.

In February Thomas Lynch noted the extreme apathy of the delegates. It was the lull before the storm. John Adams was absent from Congress between December 9 and February 9, and the important Massachusetts delegation was then in the hands of the moderate members. The absence of Jefferson and Richard Henry Lee at this time softened the Virginia delegation. With two of the major colonies on the moderate side, the militant group suffered from a deficiency of leadership.

Suddenly, an abrupt change of opinion occurred. It came at the end of February. The influence of the conciliationists evaporated. Most of the moderates moved into the militant camp. The Congress that in February shrank from bold actions now proceeded to adopt strong measures in rapid succession. By the end of March a majority of the delegations was probably prepared to go the whole way. Had independence required only a majority vote, it might have come early in the spring of 1776.

Electrifying news from England caused the revolution in the attitude of Congress. On February 27 the members listened to the reading of a newly arrived act of parliament that had become law on December 22. It gave statutory force to the whole program of the ministry. It imposed on the trade of the thirteen colonies an inclusive embargo. It prohibited all vessels — British, foreign, American — from trading with any port or place within the American union. It decreed the seizure and confiscation of all American ships and their cargoes. It was a Boston Port Bill applied to all the colonies.

And it was more. It gave legal effect to the royal Proclamation of Rebellion of August 1775. It defined the American resistance as rebellion and treason. It provided for a method of granting pardons. Pardons for what? For the crime of treason. And who was guilty of this crime? The alleged criminals were the members of Congress and their agents. Many persons, the act said, "have assembled together an armed force, engaged his majesty's troops, and attacked his forts, have usurped the powers of government, and prohibited commerce with this kingdom."[9] All these actions of Congress were declared to have produced "rebellious and treasonable commotions."[10]

At last the answer had come. Britain would crush the revolt, with all the force at its disposal. The only terms offered were unconditional surrender. Individuals, it is true, might seek salvation by acknowledging themselves to be guilty of a high crime and by throwing themselves on the king's mercy. That was all. Twenty-five thousand troops were coming soon to enforce Britain's will. They would be aided by a sweeping, all-embracing ban on American trade.

The hopes of the moderates were blasted. Armed resistance had not caused the rulers of Britain to give in to the demands of the colonies. The apathy of Congress was replaced by a spirit of decision and resolution. John Adams and Elbridge Gerry had arrived recently to reinforce Samuel Adams in the pivotal Massachusetts delegation. John Hancock left the moderate group to join them. Massachusetts now spoke with a clear, strong voice. It provided the leadership needed to bring all the New England colonies into a solid militant bloc. Richard Henry Lee returned to Congress early in March. His colleague, Benjamin Harrison, forsook the moderates, thereby placing the powerful Virginia delegation squarely in the militant camp. The North Carolina and South Carolina delegations also abandoned the moderate position at this time. Georgia had already joined the militant group; hence a solid south came into being, ready to act with the New England militants. The south and New England, with their eight votes, could carry any measure except one requiring unanimous action (such as a declaration of independence) or one that affected the internal affairs of the middle colonies.

Congress moved to an advanced position on March 20. That day it issued an invitation to the Canadians to join the American union and urged them to form a government of the type that was common to the thirteen colonies. Since Congress at this time asserted that the union was to be permanent, the invitation to the Canadians proposed that they reject forever the sovereignty of Britain. They were invited to create a new government that would be based solely on their own authority. Such a government was not to exist merely during "the continuance of the present dispute." It was to be permanent.

In extending this invitation, Congress confirmed a position that Washington had taken early in September 1775, when, in an address to the Canadians, he had urged them to join the thirteen colonies "in an indissoluble union" in order that all Americans might enjoy "the blessings of a free government."

iii

It is highly probable that at the end of March a majority of each delegation in Congress—with one exception—approved of independence in principle. Yet more than three months elapsed before the Declaration was adopted. The delay was occasioned by doubts and hesitation in four important delegations—those of Maryland, Pennsylvania, New Jersey, and New York. Certain deterrents restrained the representatives of those colonies. As a group they did not oppose the idea of separation per se. They contended that the proper time for the historic step had not yet arrived. Better to wait a little longer, it was said, until certain obstacles to success had been removed. Conditions as yet unfavorable might change for the better if Congress would act with patience and restraint.

Some of the delegates believed that the British government had not finally closed the door against negotiations that might produce a settlement agreeable to the colonies. The Prohibitory Act had made provision for sending British agents to America for the purpose of granting pardons to repentant insurgents. Presumably, such agents were to treat with the authorities of colonies or localities. The act, by ignoring Congress, implied that its members were too disloyal to be recognized as negotiating agents. Once the king's representatives had satisfied themselves of the loyalty of any colony, district, or locality, they might declare it to be at peace with his majesty, whereupon it would no longer be subject to the Prohibitory Act.

In itself the act offered nothing whatsoever to Congress. But an incident soon occurred which led some of the members to hope that Congress might be accepted by the ministry as an equal partner in dignified negotiations. In March there arrived in Philadelphia one William Temple, who professed to bring confidential news from the London agent of Congress, Dr. Arthur Lee. Temple produced an alleged letter from Lee to Hancock that was "fastened somehow in the buttons of his coat."[11] It introduced Temple as a "true friend of America" whose intelligence could be trusted. The story which he told was that the ministry had decided to give in to the colonies, and had persuaded the king of the necessity of yielding. "The haughty monarch relented."[12] According to Temple, a party of negotiators, headed by Lord Howe and General Amherst, had sailed for Virginia. They would propose harsh terms but would not persist. They would eventually approach Congress and consent in the end to everything the colonists might ask for.

Here, then, was another gleam of hope—another pretext for delaying the final act of separation. Let us await the coming of the commissioners, said the cautious men, and hear what proposition they have to offer. To the realistic militants the tale of Mr. Temple was a fantasy. If the ministry intended to give in to the colonies why should it go to the vast expense of sending twenty or thirty thousand troops to America?

Even before the engaging Mr. Temple arrived at Philadelphia, Washington had started an offensive against the prospective negotiators. He viewed the plan as a maneuver of the ministry to win popular support in Britain. He pointed out that if the Americans should reject the overture, they could be pictured to the British public "as a people that will not hearken to any propositions of peace."[13] If the ministry intended to satisfy the colonists with adequate concessions it must repeal the oppressive laws of which they complained. "Was there ever anything more absurd," he asked, "than to repeal the very acts which have introduced all this confusion and bloodshed, and at the same time enact a law to restrain all intercourse with the colonies for opposing them? The drift and design are obvious; but is it possible that any sensible nation upon earth can be imposed upon by such a cobweb scheme or gauze covering?"[14] He insisted that a bona fide peace mission must be invested with "full and ample powers to treat with Congress." Otherwise, the emissaries would "come over with insidious intentions to distract, divide, and create as much confusion as possible."[15] After receiving the report that British negotiators were en route to Virginia he wrote a strong letter to his brother, John Augustine, in which he described the plan as a device to divide the colonies and to delude "weak minds among us" who "wish for peace without attending to the conditions."[16] That he intended this letter to be read by the leaders of Virginia is most likely.

The promise of a negotiation exerted an attraction sufficient to keep it before Congress for two months. Joseph Reed wrote to Washington on March 15: "To tell the truth . . . I am infinitely more afraid of these [British] commissioners than their generals and armies. If their propositions are plausible and behavior artful, I am apprehensive they will divide us. There is so much suspicion in Congress and so much party on this subject that very little more fuel is required to kindle the flame."[17]

Washington offered the antidote to the plan which eventually deprived it of its sting. Writing to Congress on March 24, he observed that the negotiators might soon arrive. If they should come to Boston, he would "be under much embarrassment respecting the manner of receiving them." He therefore sought directions from Congress concerning "the line of conduct to be pursued."[18] Should they be considered as ambassadors of a foreign power and given passports to go to Philadelphia? Or ought they to be restrained in any way? He would anxiously await the orders of Congress and comply with them literally.

Congress did not act until May 6. It then resolved: "That General Washington be informed that Congress suppose, if commissioners are intended to be sent from Great Britain to treat of peace, that the practice usual in such cases will be observed by making previous application for the necessary passports or safe conduct, and on such application being made, Congress will then direct the proper measures for the reception of such commissioners."[19]

Obviously, Congress accepted Washington's suggestion that British emissaries should be treated as agents of a foreign power and that in so doing the American authorities should act as agents of an independent state.

iv

Another deterrent to independence was the uncertainty of obtaining aid from foreign countries. Two related questions repeatedly came before Congress. Should the colonies open their ports to the vessels, products, and merchants of foreign lands? Should they try to form diplomatic ties with the European courts and seek to enter into commercial treaties and military alliances?

If Congress should open the ports of America to all foreign commerce, it would nullify the British navigation acts which forbade foreign merchants and vessels to trade with the colonies. In Europe, nearly everyone believed that the right to exclude foreigners from the commerce of one's colonies was the essence of the imperial power. If a parent state did not have that right, its title to its colonies was meaningless. If Congress should cast aside the sacred navigation acts, it would strike at Britain's authority as drastically as if it should order the beheading of the king.

Similarly, if Congress should undertake to negotiate with a foreign court it must assume the attributes of a sovereign nation. It must present itself to the world as the equal of the great British government.

The strongest pressure for opening American ports and for creating an American diplomacy came from the army. Ammunition and arms must be brought into the colonies by foreign merchants, in foreign vessels, from foreign ports. The meager funds of the union required that such goods should be purchased abroad on credit. The risks were so great that private merchants might not hazard large loans. A government was better able to oblige. Foreign trade would need the protection of a navy, and a foreign fleet would assist immeasurably the operations of the American army. Foreign troops might become necessary to American success, especially if Britain should hire a large force of mercenaries in Europe.

Before a country like France would grant substantial aid it must be assured that the Americans were determined to be independent.

If the French should give such assistance they would surely incur the hostility of Britain. Suppose that Congress, having received French aid, should make peace with Britain. A reconciliation would strengthen the British Empire — and immediately after the French had intensified Britain's hostility toward themselves. France had but two essential interests in helping the Americans: to weaken Britain and to strengthen itself. The French could weaken Britain by depriving it of its colonies. They could strengthen themselves by diverting the trade of America from Britain to France. Both aims required that the thirteen colonies should become independent states.

John Adams battled valiantly in Congress to open American ports to foreign trade. But he was skeptical of approaching France for a commercial treaty or a military alliance. He feared that Congress could not convince the French that they would benefit from either. "Would not our proposals and agents," he asked, "be treated with contempt? And if our proposals were made and rejected, would not this sink the spirits of our own people, elevate our enemies, and disgrace us in Europe?"[20] Robert Morris believed that the colonies could win the war without foreign allies. He feared that to court France while the colonies were weak might force them into a new bondage. Once they had won the war all nations would seek their trade and they could bargain with the maximum advantage.

Other members of Congress feared that France, a colonial power and a monarchy, would not assist rebellious subjects who were intent upon destroying an empire in order to create a republic. At the least, an appeal to France was uncertain as to its outcome. Before Congress could prudently take the final step, France should give a binding promise of assistance. If the colonies, in the hope of getting outside aid, should declare independence before obtaining a firm commitment from the French court, they would place themselves at its mercy and be obliged to accept its terms. Let France offer in advance an ironclad guarantee of aid, under favorable conditions; then the colonies might embrace independence with the assurance that it would yield its promised fruit. What disaster might befall the American cause if the colonies should act rashly in order to obtain foreign aid and then fail to get it! Better delay the fateful decision until a promise had become a certainty.

v

Congress had first moved into the foreign sphere on July 15, 1775, when it authorized the importation of war materials into the colonies and permitted the exportation of colonial produce in payment. This resolve breached the British navigation acts, for it permitted the importation of foreign goods, from foreign ports, in foreign vessels. However, it satisfied the moderates and conciliationists because it was a defensive military measure, of limited duration. It did not repudiate the navigation acts in principle, and Congress continued to abide by them in the main.

Two months later Congress moved again. On September 19 it established a "Secret Committee." At the outset, this committee consisted of seven members, most of whom were merchants. Its main task was that of securing war materials from foreign sources. Hence it provided an agency for executing the resolve of July 15. Since its purpose was limited to supplying the colonies with the sinews of war (in order to force Britain to preserve the empire by granting concessions) it did not point directly toward independence.

Shortly after the Secret Committee was set up, Congress received copies of the royal Proclamation of Rebellion. The delegates responded by creating, on November 29, a "Committee of Secret Correspondence." Consisting of five members, this committee was dominated by the moderates and conciliationists. Charged with the duty of corresponding "with our friends in Great Britain, Ireland, and other parts of the world," it undertook to ascertain the attitude of the French court toward the colonies.[21] It appointed Dr. Arthur Lee its agent in London and set in motion an embryonic intelligence service. It evolved into a miniature foreign office, just as the first committee, of September 19, became a rudimentary commerce department. The work of the two committees overlapped, but they were held together by two members who served on both—Benjamin Franklin and Robert Morris.

The initial arrangements of Congress for a supply of arms and powder did not meet the needs of the army. In the autumn of 1775 its shortage of firearms was acute. The deficiency prompted Washington to initiate the negotiations that led to the establishment of direct commercial relations with France. He had stated the needs of the army on October 19 at the Cambridge conference, but obtained from the Congress committee only a recommendation to the various assemblies that they should import all the firearms that could be procured. The assemblies failed to fulfill the expectation. Suddenly a stroke of good fortune favored the general. About December 13 there arrived at headquarters two French merchants, Messieurs Penet and Pliarne. They wished to supply the colonies with shipments of arms and ammunition directly from France. They had landed at Rhode Island and had been directed to Cambridge by Governor Cooke. Washington received them cordially, approved their plan, and sent them at once to Philadelphia, making the arrangements for the journey, paying their traveling expenses, and arming them with a letter to President Hancock. "I beg leave to recommend them and the important business they come upon," the letter said.[22]

En route the two travelers paused to pay their respects, by the post, to the general. "Our first obligation," they wrote, "is to return our thanks for the gracious reception which we have received from your excellency." And would the general, they added, tendering a gift, "prevail upon madam, your lady, to accept of some of the fruits of our colonies," as well as an offering of liqueurs and fifty small loaves of sugar.[23]

On December 30 the visitors appeared before Congress with their letter of introduction and were referred to the Secret Committee. Soon it was rumored that they contemplated an extensive trade. A member of Congress reported that they represented a company at Paris, and that they offered "to supply the continent from France with all sorts of goods and military stores." [24] They suggested that American ships might trade with France, and offered to send French vessels to America. About January 11 they informed Washington of their dealings with the Secret Committee. They proposed "to establish between America and France a branch of trade sufficient to supply all the wants of the new empire." [25] However, they had not yet come to terms with the Secret Committee.

After the departure of Penet and Pliarne, Washington wrote to all the nearby governments, calling upon them to provide the army with firearms. The responses were totally negative. In this correspondence he made it clear that he could not depend upon supplies from Congress or its Secret Committee. While the negotiations with Penet and Pliarne were proceeding in Philadelphia he wrote gloomy letters to Congress and Joseph Reed. The colonial governments could not help the army. "How to get furnished I know not. . . . The reflection on my situation and that of the army produces many an uneasy hour when all around me are wrapped in sleep. . . . I have often thought how much happier I should have been, if, instead of accepting a command under such circumstances, I had taken my musket on my shoulder and entered the ranks, or . . . had retired to the backcountry and lived in a wigwam." [26]

His letter to Hancock on the firearms crisis was read in Congress January 25. Evidently it produced the desired effect. Two days later, Congress appropriated £40,000 for the purchase of foreign goods and authorized the sale of American produce, to that value, "in some foreign European market." It also empowered the Secret Committee "to contract with proper persons for importing said goods and for exporting produce to pay for the same." [27] In the following November, Penet and Pliarne, writing at Nantes, informed the Secret Committee that they had purchased lead, powder, muskets, linen, and other goods to the value of £30,000 or £40,000.

Washington's intervention, through Messieurs Penet and Pliarne, seems to have overcome the opposition in Congress to action in the foreign field. During the February lull, Congress marked time, pending the receipt of authentic news of the Prohibitory Act. Rumors of its terms had arrived in Philadelphia ahead of the printed copies. Immediately after it was read in Congress, the two secret committees entered into arrangements to send Silas Deane to Paris on a twofold mission. This decision launched Congress on the sea of independent diplomacy. The Secret (or Commerce) Committee engaged Deane as a merchant and instructed him to buy supplies in France, authorizing him to draw on deposits which the Committee would make with three European bankers. The Committee of Secret Correspondence (Foreign Affairs) directed Deane to obtain an audience with the French foreign minister, Vergennes, at which Deane was to ask France for a loan and suggest that France might supplant Britain in the trade of the thirteen colonies. If France should provide credits for the purchase of supplies, a valuable cargo might be assembled that could be convoyed to America by two or three French ships of war. Deane was further advised that, if he found Vergennes friendly and was given a second interview, he should seek to discover the attitude of France on the great question. If the colonies "should be forced to form themselves into an independent state" would France "acknowledge them as such, receive their ambassadors, enter into any treaty or alliance with them, for commerce or defense, or both?"[28]

Two moderates (Harrison and Robert Morris), two conciliationists (Dickinson and Jay), and one militant (Franklin) composed the Correspondence Committee. Their instructions to Deane reflected the state of opinion in Congress. The decision to approach a foreign court was suggestive of the conduct of an independent state. However, the terms of the instructions gave the conciliationists a talking point. They could now argue: we must delay the final step until we learn whether France will agree to support us as an independent country. It was most unlikely that the French court would give such positive assurances before Congress had declared independence. Hence the proposal to put off the declaration until France had acted favorably threatened to postpone it indefinitely.

Did Washington contribute anything to the Deane mission? In the general's papers is a letter dated November 20, which contains the essential idea of the plan under which Deane acted. The author of the letter, "A Friend to America," proposed that Congress should send agents to France and Spain to buy powder, flints, and lead. Such agents were to get in touch with the ministers of the two countries and purchase the supplies, with the assistance of their governments. On January 2, Washington's amanuensis, Stephen Moylan, proposed that he be sent to Spain "with full and ample powers from the United States of America."[29] This highly important letter to Joseph Reed was undoubtedly intended to be passed around among members of Congress. That it stated Washington's views is most probable. It has a special meaning because, among the surviving records of the time, it is the earliest paper in which appears the phrase: "The United States of America." Independence undiluted. It is incredible that Moylan—a man who owed his place to Washington, who enjoyed the general's favor, and who sat at his right elbow—would have written such a letter to Washington's official secretary and principal link with Congress unless it stated views acceptable to the chief.

Silas Deane did not begin his journey from Philadelphia to France until April 3. During March three events occurred which further strengthened the militants and enabled them to carry through Congress two measures that practically severed the tie with Britain. For one thing, there arrived at Philadelphia a ship from France and Holland with large quantities of powder, arms, and saltpeter. The promise of foreign aid had become a reality. About March 12 Congress received reports that gave strong assurances of future aid from France. These dispatches told the story of an attempt by Britain to recruit a large number of mercenary troops in Russia. The plan at one time promised success but in the end it was vetoed by the empress. One reason for the failure was the attitude of the French ambassador at Moscow. He had informed the Russians that France did not intend to intervene in a dispute that was limited to Britain and its colonies but that France could not stand aside if Britain should employ foreign troops. Other reports received by Congress at this time stated that Britain had engaged four thousand Hanoverians and six thousand Hessians. Presumably, the employment of such mercenaries would offend the French and force them to assist the colonies. The militants in Congress could now press for independence with the argument that French aid was a foregone conclusion.

On March 25 Congress listened to the reading of a letter from Washington which announced the evacuation of Boston. This first major victory of the American army bathed the continent in a pleasant glow of confidence and satisfaction. Tributes to the general flowed in from all parts of the colonies. Congress voted to honor him with a gold medal. The Boston victory erected a pedestal upon which his friends placed him — the new American hero, the symbol of the American union. The proud British army had retreated in humiliation. Would not the court of France now be convinced that Britain's cause in America was doomed? The triumph, wrote General Schuyler, "cannot fail of the utmost salutary effects with the powers of Europe." [30]

As a matter of fact, the intention of the British to leave Boston was known in Congress as early as March 15. Joseph Reed on that day replied to a letter he had just received, by express, from Washington. "It is certain," he said, "that enterprize and success give a brilliance and luster which cannot be unacceptable to a good mind." [31] Animated by the happy tidings Congress on March 23 again clothed itself in the robes of sovereignty and acted the part of an independent authority. It adopted a resolve which invited the colonists to equip privateers, authorized them to seize British vessels, and provided for the creation of admiralty courts for the purpose of determining the status of prizes. Congress thus assumed a place among the sovereigns of the earth when it undertook to commission privateers and to erect courts to ascertain the legality of their captures and seizures.

When it enacted its privateering resolve of March 23, Congress finished a task that Washington had begun early in the preceding September. His little fleet of commerce raiders, which he created on his own initiative and authority, had done the work of privateers long before Congress was ready to invest the business with its full approval. Early in November he urged Congress to establish courts to determine the legality of captured ships. "Should not a court be established by authority of Congress," he wrote at this time, "to take cognizance of the prizes made by the continental vessels?"[32] In letter after letter he pleaded for action. Four and a half months after he began his campaign Congress capitulated. Its resolve of March 23, prompted in part by the evacuation of Boston, gave him a final endorsement and vindication.

The curtain rose on the last act of the foreign drama on April 6. Congress then voted to sweep aside the British acts of trade and navigation and to free the colonies entirely from their long commercial bondage to Britain. It now authorized the importation into America, directly from foreign countries, of non-British goods of every description. It also opened American ports to foreign ships and foreign merchants. Since Congress continued the boycott of British goods, it created a new American commercial system, separate from and hostile to that of the British imperium. And finally: "Resolved, That no slaves be imported into any of the thirteen United Colonies."[33]

When Silas Deane sailed for Paris he went as a *de facto* agent of Congress on its first diplomatic mission. The hope of securing aid from France now seemed certain of realization. In dispatching an agent to a foreign court, in authorizing privateers, in providing for prize courts, and in opening American ports to the goods, vessels, and merchants of the non-British world, Congress had gone about as far as it could go toward independence, short of a formal declaration. After it created the army in June 1775, every step it took led in one direction. At the end of the day's business on April 6, the distance to the final goal was short.

XIII. The Militants and the South

If the Virginians are wise, that arch-traitor to the rights of humanity, Lord Dunmore, should be instantly crushed, if it takes the force of the whole colony to do it.[1]

—WASHINGTON TO JOSEPH REED, DECEMBER 15, 1775

DURING March and early April Congress adopted several measures that were heavily weighted in favor of independence. But the militant leaders could not yet win approval for an outright act of separation, which required a unanimous vote of all the colonies. Many of the delegates said that they could not commit their constituents without mandates from home. Most of the provincial governments were reluctant to act. A colony that put itself far out in front might not be supported by the others. The local authorities therefore preferred that Congress should lead the way.

A few of the provincial governments had directed their delegates to oppose separation. Such instructions favored the men of caution. The final step, they said, must be delayed until all the delegations were instructed to take it. Thus the provincial governments were again called upon to act. But they were inclined to look to Philadelphia for leadership.

This chain of hesitation and delay forced the militants to take a hand in the local politics of several colonies. Although the militant majority in Congress could not impose independence upon a colony, there were some things that could be done. Congress could adopt resolves that would put the weight of the union behind the militants in the provincial capitals. It could urge the local authorities to act against the Tories. It could provide military support and security for the men who must make the fateful decision. By such means it could dispirit the opposition, invigorate the friends of independence, and encourage the provincial governments to direct their delegates to vote for separation.

In the spring of 1776 the militant leaders in Congress conducted two campaigns within the colonies—one in the south and one in the middle area.

Virginia, the Carolinas, and Georgia formed a distinctive section. Before 1774 each of those colonies had had a royal government presided over by a British governor and a council appointed by the king. The whole area rose spontaneously in opposition to the British measures which provoked the revolt. At first the leaders used the elected assemblies as agencies for common action. A series of quarrels between the governors and the assemblies ensued. In each colony the contest prompted the governor to dismiss the assembly and to attempt to rule without it. The people then sent delegates to a provincial congress which met in defiance of the governor, acted as a legislature, and set up a central executive body called the council of safety. The strife between these extralegal agencies and the royal officials soon led to open conflict. Lacking popular support, each of the governors found it necessary to retire from his capital and to take refuge on a British warship stationed off the coast of the colony. Lord Dunmore escaped from Williamsburg in June 1775, and Governor Josiah Martin of North Carolina fled from New Bern in July. The governor of South Carolina, Lord William Campbell, left Charleston in September, and Sir James Wright of Georgia made his getaway from Savannah in February 1776.

At the beginning of the war the British government decided not to send a large army to the south. Its plans of operations for that area were somewhat involved. Each of the royal governors was given the protection of a small flotilla, which became his military headquarters and political capital. From these bases the governors undertook to rally the king's friends to the royal standard and to arm them for battle. Reports were spread that large British forces would soon arrive and subdue the insurgents. All the while, the ships of the royal navy patrolled the waters of the coastal area, threatening destruction by bombardment to the towns and plantations of the insurgents.

Although Britain's power in the south was limited, it was not wholly to be despised. The menace of the king's ships restrained many prudent men from urging or even supporting such an extreme anti-British measure as independence. Inland, where the people were beyond the reach of the warships, they could afford to take a more positive stand. This situation tended to divide the people according to wealth. The rich planters and merchants, with extensive properties on or near the coast, were often reluctant to advertise a militant opposition to Britain. The poorer people, more protected, were more responsive to extreme measures. As the leaders of the exposed areas hesitated, the militants turned to the rank and file for support. If cautious men of the coastal area would not provide adequate support for the war, then the common people would have to take charge of the provincial governments. If they did so, they might introduce many reforms that would imperil the seacoast aristocracy. It was a trying situation. The wealthy planters and merchants did not wish to surrender abjectly to Britain's demands. They could not always afford the luxury of truculent utterances or deeds that might bring the wrath of the British navy down on their towns or plantations. If they should withdraw from the contest, they would deliver the provincial governments into the hands of their local adversaries and expose themselves to leveling reforms.

Late in 1775 opinion in the south was inflamed by efforts of the king's agents to incite slaves to revolt against masters who supported the American cause. Early in December Congress received startling news from Virginia. It impressed Samuel Adams as so important that he hastily relayed it in one of his rare letters to his friends in Massachusetts. Lord Dunmore had put together an armed force of regulars and volunteers, the latter consisting of "the inhabitants of Norfolk, a town inhabited by Scotch Tories, and such weak and timid people" as he could enlist. He had issued a proclamation (November 7) which called upon the Virginians "to resort to the king's standard or be deemed traitors." In addition, the proclamation offered freedom to slaves who would take leave of "rebel" masters and join his army. It also announced Dunmore's determination to execute martial law, "thereby tearing up the foundation of civil authority in that colony."[2]

In response to this proclamation, Congress on December 4 advised the patriot authorities of Virginia to call "a full and free representation of the people" in order to set up a government that would be capable of promoting the peace and security of the province. Such a government should endure until the end of the "present dispute."[3]

The British incitement of slave revolts had been foreshadowed in 1775 in Dr. Samuel Johnson's official tract, *Taxation no Tyranny*. The scheme was a military expedient. The proffered freedom was extended only to slaves who would enlist in Dunmore's army and whose masters were engaged in the American resistance. The rulers of Britain had not the slightest interest in emancipation on humanitarian grounds. It was their fixed policy to protect the African slave trade and to defeat all efforts of the colonists to limit or abolish it. The outstanding southern militants opposed not only the slave trade but slavery as well. Patrick Henry and Richard Henry Lee condemned both. In the first draft of the Declaration of Independence, Jefferson included a strong indictment of the traffic. Two years earlier Washington and George Mason had incorporated a similar denunciation in the Fairfax Resolves. "We take this opportunity," they said in Resolve 17, "of declaring our most earnest wishes to see an entire stop forever put to such a wicked, cruel, and unnatural trade."[4] To southern militants who condemned both slavery and the slave trade it was not convincing when British rulers, who defended both, used emancipation as a means of exposing slaves to death, in order to incite them to kill Americans who were fighting in a good cause.

On March 23, Congress adopted a full statement of the grievances which were driving the colonies toward independence. Among the eight major offenses listed was that of "instigating Negroes to murder their masters."[5]

ii

The militant campaign in the south for independence appears to have originated, at least in part, at the army headquarters in Cambridge. As soon as Washington learned of Dunmore's proclamation he urged that something should be done to protect the Virginia insurgents. On December 14 he wrote to President Hancock: "I make no doubt . . . that the Congress will take every necessary measure to dispossess Lord Dunmore of his hold on Virginia."[6] A day later, in a letter to Joseph Reed, he urged that Dunmore be immediately crushed: ". . . otherwise, like a snowball in rolling his army will get size, some through fear, some through promises, and some from inclination joining his standard. But that which renders the measure indispensably necessary is the Negroes. For if he gets formidable, numbers will be tempted to join, who will be afraid to do it without."[7] On December 18 he sent Hancock a number of intercepted letters which, he said, exposed Lord Dunmore's schemes, adding that ". . . the fate of America depends a good deal on his being obliged to evacuate Norfolk this winter."[8] To Richard Henry Lee he exclaimed: "If, my dear sir, that man is not crushed before spring, he will become the most formidable enemy America has. . . . I do not think that forcing his lordship on shipboard is sufficient; nothing less than depriving him of life or liberty will secure peace to Virginia, as motives of resentment actuate his conduct to a degree equal to the total destruction of the colony."[9]

An important plan for operations in the south was devised by General Charles Lee, at a time when he was working closely with Washington. In mid-December Lee observed that everything was going smoothly in New England and that Virginia had become "the chief object of attention."[10] He outlined a comprehensive program for the south in which Virginia figured prominently. He proposed to seize Lord Dunmore, to arrest all British agents and all Tories, to confiscate their estates ("or at least to lay them under heavy contributions to the public"), to hold them as hostages "for their treatment of those of our party," and to establish two flying camps — one to be stationed near Williamsburg and one at Alexandria. Such flying camps should be commanded by officers who had the reputation "of being able to inspire the people with confidence." He also urged that Charleston, South Carolina, "should be well secured."[11]

The militant plan for the south had evidently been matured by the end of February 1776. On the day the British Prohibitory Act was read in Congress, Edward Rutledge moved that General Lee be appointed to command in the south. On March 1, Congress canceled its order which assigned Lee to duty in Canada and placed him in command of a newly created southern department of the army, which comprised Virginia, the Carolinas, and Georgia. Congress gave Lee as assistants four brigadier generals — all militants. To South Carolina it assigned John Armstrong; to North Carolina, James Moore; to Virginia, Robert Howe and Andrew Lewis.

General Lee had sent his plan for the south to Richard Henry Lee. About the time the latter must have received it, he left Philadelphia and returned to Virginia. While there he wrote to Samuel Adams, suggesting that Congress assign "a good general officer" to Virginia. Evidently the Virginia Lee had General Lee in mind when he thus addressed the senior Adams, for his letter said that Dunmore's ships "are not furnished with a single carrot."[12] In his letter to Richard Henry Lee of December 12, General Lee (transmitting his plan for the south) had urged the Virginians to see to it that the British warships were not furnished "with a single carrot."[13]

When Congress ordered General Lee to the southern colonies, it voted to send thither, as its highest representative, a man who was likely to broadcast his pleas for independence. It endorsed his view that the army should do certain things that would embolden the patriots and dispirit their enemies. It virtually authorized him to conduct in the south a crusade for independence, with its official benediction. His views were well known. Late in January he had written to Robert Morris: "You seem to wonder that I should join in the hue and cry for independence. I wrote on this subject in too great a haste to Mr. Rutledge and did not explain myself fully. . . . But it appears from the inexorable, bloody disposition of the king, the corruption of the parliament, and the pusilanimity of the people that you must infallibly be forced into it. I think the sooner it is done the better. . . ."[14] Writing again to Morris on February 21, Lee said that he considered reconciliation with Britain to be as chimerical "as a scheme of incorporation with the Afgan Tartars or any of the interior nations of Asia." He then urged that Congress immediately enter into a treaty with France. The separation from Britain, he thought, had already occurred; all schemes of reunion had become "idle and most dangerous dreams."[15]

The militant majority in Congress undoubtedly intended that General Lee should use the army in the south to silence the Tories. His views on that subject were no secret. The *Pennsylvania Evening Post* printed, in its issue of February 6, a letter from New York reporting Lee's activities there. It reads: "Lee says he will send word on board the [British] men of war, that if they set a house on fire, in consequence of his coming, he will chain one hundred of their friends together by the neck, and make the house their funeral pile." Writing to Washington on March 15, Joseph Reed stated one of the reasons for Lee's appointment. "We have everything to fear from the southward," Reed explained. "A cursed spirit of disaffection has appeared in the back parts of North and South Carolina which, if not subdued before the forces arrive from England, will prove a most formidable piece of business, especially when connected with the host of Negroes in the lower part of the country. Instead of painting their strength and power of resistance in ostentatious terms, as is the fashion of some folks, the gentlemen of that country acknowledge their weakness and dread the consequences."[16]

The new military plan for the south satisfied Washington. It gave effect to his policy of holding together the democratic and conservative wings of the Revolutionary party. The radicalism of the resistance had placed many popular leaders in high military posts. Patrick Henry had become the commander of Virginia's forces; Christopher Gadsden of South Carolina's. Both were distasteful to many men of fortune. The new military plan of Congress appealed to the southern militants because it promised independence. A concession was also offered to the conservatives. The creation of the southern department of the army had the effect of ousting Henry and Gadsden from their commands. General Armstrong replaced Gadsden; General Lewis superseded Henry. Washington approved of the changes. He said he thought that the Virginians "made a capital mistake when they took Henry out of the senate to place him in the field."[17] Of General Andrew Lewis he wrote: "I have always looked upon him as a man of spirit and a good officer; his experience is equal to anyone we have."[18]

Early in March General Lee visited Philadelphia on his way south. How different was the treatment he received from that he had suffered while in New York! The general who had been rebuffed was now greeted with respectful attention. His plans for the defense of the Manhattan area, which Congress had previously ignored, were made the basis of its official program for New York. However, on March 9 it adopted its rule which forbade a military officer to administer an oath to civilians. Undoubtedly, Congress intended that Lee, while in the south, should not employ methods of coercion against civilians, unless instructed to do so by the provincial authorities.

As Lee prepared to move against the southern Tories, Congress provided him with additional support. By a resolve of March 14 it urged each colony to disarm all its notorious enemies and all inhabitants who refused to fight against the British army and navy. The arms thus seized were to be delivered to the Continental army, to the provincial militias, or to approved bands of insurgents. This resolve did not treat the Tories entirely as enemies, for it directed that the arms to be taken from them should be paid for. However, it implied that an American owed a primary allegiance and loyalty to the union and to his colony. It pointed to the king as an enemy, and undertook to prevent his adherents from giving him aid and comfort. Washington had begun his campaign against the Tories early in November 1775. In March, Congress arrived at one of the positions he had taken four months earlier.

XIV. Action in the South

. . . we hesitate in Congress because . . . we are heavily clogged with instructions from those shamefully interested proprietary people, and this will continue until Virginia sets the example of . . . sending peremptory orders to their delegates to pursue the most effectual measures for the security of America.[1]

—RICHARD HENRY LEE TO CHARLES LEE, APRIL 22, 1776

NORTH CAROLINA was the ideal place for the beginning of the southern campaign for independence. It was of all the colonies the least exposed to British invasion. It had only three communities that might properly be called towns, and it lacked the network of deepwater ports and rivers such as the British navy needed for raids on the interior. Its people overwhelmingly supported the American cause. Governor Martin, writing at New Bern in May 1775, told of "the people of this town and county having formed themselves into companies and taken up arms, watching most narrowly every movement about my house, both day and night, while I am not supported by a single man."[2] By February, the governor had collected in the back country a force of about twelve hundred settlers who were loyal to the king. On a march down the South River they were beset by two bands of patriots. One insurgent force decisively defeated them on February 27 at Moores Creek Bridge, about twenty miles above Wilmington. The chief British officer was taken prisoner, the second in command was killed, and the troops were slain, captured, or scattered. The victory crushed the king's friends in the province and saved it from a threatened invasion.

The news of the battle reached General Lee at Baltimore. He

continued his journey southward, arriving at Williamsburg on March 28. There he established headquarters, preparatory to launching a campaign against the Tories in the southeastern tip of Virginia around Norfolk.

About eighty-five miles to the southwest of Williamsburg lay the little town of Halifax, located some twenty miles south of the Virginia border on a river, the Roanoke, which flowed down from the Old Dominion. Early in April one of Lee's staff, Brigadier General James Moore, was there. Representatives of the insurgents of North Carolina had assembled to consider issues of vast importance. They had been scheduled to convene in May, but urgent matters had prompted the leaders to summon them to meet on April 4. For their president they chose one of the strong men of the province, Samuel Johnston. On April 6 he submitted to them two letters from the North Carolina delegates in Congress. They solicited instructions from the convention with respect to the question: should the United Colonies enter into foreign alliances? By an odd coincidence, General Lee at Williamsburg was thinking about the same question. Writing to Edward Rutledge on April 3 he exclaimed: "Unless you declare yourselves independent . . . you richly deserve to be enslaved. . . . Without a more systematic intercourse with France and Holland . . . we have not the means of carrying on the war."[3]

While the delegates at Halifax were considering the momentous question a number of things happened. From the northward came the news of the evacuation of Boston. On April 6, General Lee ordered the arrest of the British governor of Maryland. Two days later he gave the signal for seizing the Tories of southeastern Virginia—only a short distance from Halifax. One of Lee's chief assistants, Brigadier General Robert Howe, arrived at the little capital to add his weight to that of General James Moore. The two generals personified the militant spirit of the south. Moore was one of the victors in the campaign that had routed the British forces at Moores Creek Bridge. That victory, so fresh in mind, animated the convention with confidence and pride. General Howe had made a name for himself by battling Lord Dunmore in the Norfolk area. An advocate of independence, he thought that reconciliation would bring only "a milder degree of slavery." [4]

In instructions to one of his brigadier generals, Lee directed that he become acquainted with the "politics and disposition of the people." [5] As soon as the Halifax convention assembled, Lee wrote to its leaders, assuring them that he expected to arrive within a few days. If the enemy should appear he would march at once. Each day reports of his coming circulated in the town. After General Howe arrived there, the convention urged him to remain. "It will be my inclination," he wrote to Lee, "to send you instant information of every circumstance of importance, and to solicit that aid you so kindly offer, and which it is probable this country may soon find so absolutely necessary." [6]

Such was the setting at Halifax when the North Carolina convention, on April 12, distinguished itself by adopting the first resolve that instructed a delegation in Congress to vote for independence. It empowered its delegates "to concur with the delegates of other colonies in declaring independence and forming alliances. . . ." [7] The convention also decreed that, should any British negotiators arrive in North Carolina, "the person or persons of such commissioners be seized, and immediately sent to Congress." [8]

General Lee voiced his satisfaction with the work of the Halifax convention. One of its leaders, Thomas Burke, replied: "We are very happy to find that the efforts of our colony in support of the defense of the common rights of mankind have been thought by you to merit those sentiments which you so warmly express." [9]

The first result of the southern campaign for independence was encouraging. But it left something to be desired. The North Carolina resolve did not direct the delegates of the province to make a motion in Congress for separation. It merely asked them "to concur with the delegates of the other colonies." The phrase showed the reluctance of an individual colony to assume, alone, the responsibility for the hanging decision.

Although General Lee was not at Halifax when the North Carolina convention acted, his presence nearby was strongly felt. It was not his influence as a person that counted, or even his status as a general. He represented the union. Congress had invested him with its dignity and prestige. It did that at a time when he advocated independence and when he urged direct action against the Tories. In placing him in a high position Congress put a stamp of approval on his views. One of his duties was to bring into the south the personalized force of the union. Thereby Congress might encourage and animate the militants and discourage the enemy. That Lee was a highly articulate man of unusual energy and courage certainly helped. But he was essentially an agent who inspired people by giving them a sense that they were not alone—by making them aware that behind them were the strength, the will, and the resources of Congress and the other colonies.

ii

South Carolina quickly felt the impact of the independence vote of its northern neighbor. To the North Carolinians General Lee wrote on April 13: ". . . there is reason to think that your example will inspire others with that vigor and decision which alone are wanting to insure victory."[10] In his original plan for the southern department Lee proposed that Charleston "should be well secured."[11] Soon after North Carolina declared for independence, he informed Congress that the danger to that province had passed. His thoughts had now turned to the southward. To President Hancock he wrote on April 19: "I confess myself in great pain for South Carolina; the force in that province seems alarmingly small."[12] He then proposed to send thither three or four battalions from North Carolina and Virginia. Since Lee was detained near Williamsburg until the Virginia convention adopted its independence resolve, he sent General Armstrong ahead to South Carolina. In his instructions to Armstrong, dated April 10 at Williamsburg, Lee advised against ceding an inch of ground to the enemy, adding that "in slave countries so much depends on opinion, and the opinion which the slaves will entertain of our superiority or inferiority will naturally keep pace with our maintaining or giving ground." Therefore, if the enemy should "show an intention of lodging themselves in that province," Armstrong was to "assure the inhabitants, as an encouragement to act with vigor, that a strong force shall be immediately marched to their assistance." [13]

A view of Lee in the south appears in the memoirs of General William Moultrie, one of South Carolina's foremost soldiers. Lee's presence, said Moultrie, "gave us great spirits, as he was known as an able, brave and experienced officer. . . . His coming among us was equal to a reinforcement of a thousand men . . . because he taught us to think lightly of the enemy, and gave a spur to all our actions." [14]

Early in the war a martial spirit had animated the South Carolinians who dwelt in the coastal area of the province. The wealthy planters had stepped forward to take the posts of leadership. After the flight of the royal governor and the dissolution of the old royal government, they had devised a makeshift provincial congress. But temporary bodies did not possess the prestige and authority that were deemed essential to effective government. As yet, the colony suffered from the lack of courts and of an accepted system of taxation. If the revolutionary agencies should collapse, ruin and anarchy might engulf the colony. In response to the pleas of the South Carolina delegates, Congress on November 4, 1775, authorized the province to set up a new government that would operate "during the continuation of the present dispute." [15] The brothers Rutledge, Edward and John — sponsors of General Lee — pressed for this authorization, since it promised to place all the weight of the union behind what otherwise might be a feeble constitution. Soon after Congress acted, John Rutledge returned to Charleston, to aid in devising the new government.

Within the province there existed the same division between the men of caution and the men of action that prevailed in most of the colonies. At Charleston, in the early weeks of 1776, the cautious party, headed by Rawlins Lowndes, objected to the plan for a new government on the ground that it would plunge the colony into independence. On the other side, a band of energetic militants, led by Christopher Gadsden and William Henry Drayton, strove to persuade the provincial congress to frame and adopt a native constitution. The balance of parties inclined toward the militants, as indicated by the fact that Drayton was the president of the provincial congress and Gadsden was the chief military officer of the colony. John Rutledge, acceptable to both parties, served as a bond of union.

Rutledge presided over the lowland aristocracy. Its plight early in 1776 was precarious, beset as it was by a host of actual or potential enemies. The leaders were unwilling to submit to the extreme claims of Britain, which would have exposed them to any levies the imperial authorities might have seen fit to demand. Within the province, a latent democracy offered a challenge to the entrenched power of the seacoast aristocracy. Beyond the settlements, the Choctaws and Cherokees were a danger. In this settled area, the Negro slaves outnumbered the whites by about ten to seven.

In the face of such menaces, John Rutledge strove to preserve the unity of the relatively small group of men who composed the lowland aristocracy. The issue of independence divided them. The militant group wished to drive ahead. The moderates preferred to avoid drastic acts and utterances that might lead Britain to retaliate by bombarding Charleston and the seacoast plantations. The moderates sought to avert such attacks by holding out to Britain the hope of a negotiated peace, short of independence.

Two strong pressures drove the lowland aristocracy to acquiesce in the necessity of separation. As a minority group within an exposed colony, they needed the support of the whole union. As it moved toward independence, they had to follow. Secondly, the strongest menace to their interests came from Britain. By proposing to tax away the profits of their plantations, for the benefit of favored groups overseas, Britain's policy threatened to reduce the Carolina planters to the status of poorly paid overseers of slaves.

The hazards of slavery were such that the system lacked attraction unless it rewarded the owner with wealth and distinction. If the planters remained masters of their estates, they could use some of their surplus to ameliorate the condition of their slaves. But if their surplus was taken from them by Britain, they would be forced to operate a grinding system of exploitation, without honor or profit to themselves. The best friends of the slaves were the strongest opponents of the British measures that provoked the revolt.

South Carolina made its *de facto* declaration of independence on April 23. Late in 1775 the leaders had undertaken to fit out armed vessels to prey on British ships. Both friends and foes of the plan regarded it as a long stride toward independence. On February 9 Christopher Gadsden arrived at Charleston from Philadelphia. In a welcoming ceremony he presented to the provincial congress or convention the flag that was to be used by the American navy. On the next day he made a strong speech in which he advocated not only a new state government but complete independence as well. On the thirteenth he assumed command of the provincial forces. Rutledge and Drayton then pressed the convention to frame a constitution. Charging that such an act would mean a final separation, the moderates insisted upon delay, pending receipt of official news from Britain of the intentions of the ministry. On March 21 a copy of the Prohibitory Act arrived at Charleston. There it had the same electrifying effect as in Congress. The moderate opposition subsided, and on March 26 the convention adopted a new constitution. "The colony of South Carolina," wrote Elbridge Gerry, "has behaved nobly in taking up government."[16]

Although the constitution asserted that the people should rule, it did not go all the way to independence. In line with the views of John Rutledge, the leaders followed the advice of the Continental Congress. Its resolve of November 4 had proposed that a government be set up to serve the colony "during the continuance of the present dispute." The constitution said that the new government should last "until an accommodation of the unhappy differences between Great Britain and America can be obtained (an event . . . we still earnestly desire)."[17] Rutledge's desire to keep South Carolina in tune with the other colonies appeared also in the rule which the convention adopted on March 23 to guide its delegates at Philadelphia. They were told to "agree to every measure which they . . . together with a majority of the Continental Congress, shall judge necessary for the . . . welfare of this colony . . . and of America."[18]

Before March 26, the South Carolinians did not know of the recent actions of Congress which denoted independence. During the four weeks that passed after the adoption of the constitution, they learned of many things. First came reports of the establishment of the southern department of the army under the command of General Lee and the appointment of a Continental general for South Carolina. Then followed the gratifying news of the evacuation of Boston. Other dispatches brought the word that Congress had authorized privateers and prize courts and had invited the Canadians to form a free government and to join the union on a permanent basis. Later reports told that General Lee was en route to South Carolina and would soon arrive; that General Armstrong was on the way. On April 12, only about two hundred and seventy miles from Charleston, the North Carolina convention voted for independence.

By April 23, the situation in Charleston was entirely different from that of March 26, when the provincial leaders had voiced their desire for concord with Britain. All recent events pointed in one direction — to independence. In an impressive ceremony on the twenty-third the authorities inaugurated the judicial system of the new order. The chief justice was the robust militant, William Henry Drayton. The two houses of the legislature, by joint ballot, had elected him and his fellow judges. By a similar vote he could be removed. In a charge to a grand jury, Drayton expounded the nature of the new government and its laws. He reviewed at length the acts of the crown that had placed the colonies outside its protection. He proclaimed that South Carolina was free. The law of the land, he said, "authorized him to declare, and . . . it was his duty boldly to declare, that George the Third . . . has abdicated the government; and that the throne was thereby vacant: that he has no authority over us, and we owe no allegiance to him . . . true reconciliation never can exist between Great Britain and America. . . . The Almighty created America to be independent of Britain."[19]

Thus spoke the chief judicial officer of the *de facto* state of South Carolina — the first of the southern colonies to proclaim a virtual independence. The two houses of the legislature did not remove Drayton from his high position. Instead, the justices of the court of general sessions, on the motion of the attorney general, directed that his address be printed. John Rutledge, the first president, sent a copy of it to the Continental Congress. There it was referred to a committee that had been appointed to draft a declaration of independence.

iii

Like a sentinel, South Carolina stood guard over its weaker, less populous neighbor, Georgia. There the Revolutionary struggle unfolded in such a way as to place the hardiest militants in the posts of leadership. Many conditions hampered the insurgents. Within the province the British government exerted an especially potent influence. Georgia alone among the thirteen colonies had been established under the supervision of the crown, with the assistance of financial grants from parliament. An active, able governor, Sir James Wright, labored skillfully to silence and defeat the insurgents. Largely by reason of his efforts they failed to send delegates to the First Continental Congress. Nor was the province officially represented when the Second Congress began its work in May 1775. Only one Georgian then appeared — and he spoke for a single parish, not for the colony as a whole.

Less than a third of the present state had been occupied by 1775.

The settled part extended a hundred miles along the coast, reaching inland about two hundred miles to the northwest, and only ten miles into the interior at the south. A half-dozen rivers traversed the coastal plain, providing many inlets and harbors, "most of them capable of receiving any frigate."[20] Rice plantations, employing about fifteen thousand slaves, overspread an area twenty miles wide along the sea. Savannah, the capital, stood on a bluff about fifteen miles up the Savannah River. At its mouth, in the Inlet of Tybee, lay a small flotilla of British warships. Like their compatriots in the other southern colonies, the insurgents of Georgia had to reckon with three groups of potential enemies at home: the Indians in the west, the partisans of the king, and the slaves. In addition, the British province of East Florida was securely in the hands of the king's forces. From its fortified stronghold, St. Augustine, they might smite the Georgians without ceremony.

It is no wonder that, in a colony so small, so isolated, so exposed, and so beset with enemies, the insurgent leaders proved to be sturdy men who did not shrink from the idea of independence. Prior to 1777, the province elected seven delegates to the Continental Congress. Six were militants. The only conciliationist, Dr. John J. Zubly, attended the session that began in September 1775. He soon left. He "was against independence, which he plainly saw the Congress was resolved on."[21]

The British officials in Georgia had the backing of a small party of the wealthy men but received little support from the generality of the people. Before January 1776 the insurgents refrained from military action against Governor Wright. They were not organized into independent companies and they were woefully short of arms and powder. However, the governor deemed it unwise to attack the insurgent leaders, in view of the popular sympathy for their cause. He reported in December 1774 that the "sanction given to rebellion" by the First Continental Congress had "greatly encouraged the spirit of political enthusiasm, which many were possessed of before, and raised it to such a height of frenzy that God knows what the consequences may be."[22]

Congress gave the impulse which led the Georgians to set up a revolutionary government and to resort to arms. On November 4, 1775, it signaled to both South Carolina and Georgia to engage in military resistance. A resolve of that date ordered "that for the defense of the colony of Georgia there be one battalion kept up there at the continental expense."[23] This assurance of support from the whole union encouraged the insurgent leaders of Savannah to act. On January 20 they established a government, replete with legislature, president, council of safety, armed forces, and courts. For president, they chose a stalwart militant, Archibald Bulloch. At this time they also seized Governor Wright and held him as a hostage to forestall bombarding attacks on the provincial towns. By the end of January, the Continental battalion had been formed and placed under the command of a rugged militant, Colonel Lachlan McIntosh. As yet it was largely a paper organization. It had not received instructions from either Washington or Congress, though its officers had pledged to respect their orders as superior to those of the provincial authorities. Recruiting was slow. McIntosh reported to Washington: "We expect very few in our own province; that of South Carolina is said to be drained of such people as will enlist. . . . Therefore, I expect we must have recourse, distant as it is, to North Carolina."[24]

Governor Wright escaped from his captors on the night of February 11–12, and fled to a warship on the river, from which post he directed the moves against the insurgents. The struggle for the moment revolved around twenty vessels at Savannah which were preparing to take cargoes of rice to Britain. The insurgents endeavored to prevent their sailing. This led to a sharp battle with the ships (March 2–3). Four were burned, ten captured, and the rest escaped. Soon after this skirmish a sizable patriot force arrived from South Carolina, whereupon the insurgents disabled the captured vessels. The weakness of Britain in Georgia was indicated by the fact that the king's forces were routed by about four hundred colonists, inadequately trained and poorly armed.

The events of March gave the insurgents control of the Savannah area. They had been encouraged by Congress and assisted by troops from South Carolina. Another impetus to militant action now came from the north. The news arrived that Congress had taken Georgia completely under its wing by including the province within the southern department of the army and by assigning a brigadier general to its defense. That valiant, dashing, inspiring general, Charles Lee, Washington's "chief of staff," would soon summon the whole southland to arms. Early in February, the insurgent leaders of Georgia had elected five delegates to the Continental Congress — militants all. Now, on April 5, the provincial congress empowered them to vote for independence. "We therefore, gentlemen," declared their instructions, "shall rely upon your patriotism, abilities, firmness and integrity, to propose, join, and concur in all such measures as you shall think calculated for the common good."[25] Soon afterward, two of the delegates, Lyman Hall and Button Gwinnett, departed for Philadelphia. They took their seats in Congress on May 20. Another colony was securely in the militant camp, ready to vote for independence.

iv

In April Richard Henry Lee explained the role of Virginia in the campaign for independence. Some of the middle colonies, he pointed out, had instructed their delegates in Congress to oppose the step. The conciliationists then asserted that they could not favor it because their constituents were opposed. Therefore, according to Lee, it became necessary for the militants to appeal directly to the people, in order to obtain new mandates. It behooved Virginia, the largest colony, to set an example that would arouse the people of the middle colonies and move them to instruct their delegates to vote for separation.

When General Lee arrived at Williamsburg on March 28 he found much to complain about. Lord Dunmore was active around Norfolk with his fleet. The British navy controlled Chesapeake Bay;

and the plantations of the coastal area lay open to its attacks. The provincial authorities had failed to erect defenses on the great rivers. Nor had they struck against the Tories who were supplying the enemy's ships. Dunmore's efforts to incite slave revolts had awakened feelings of anxiety, repulsion, and dread. Should men of property in the coastal area seek safety in submission to Britain? Or should they ally themselves with the yeomen of the interior in determined resistance, thereby exposing themselves to British vengeance? Already, the liberal ideas of the militants were causing a ferment in provincial politics. Plain people, under the leadership of Patrick Henry, had become assertive, threatening to wrest political power from the aristocracy. Many of the older men of the tidewater country, whose horizons were bounded by their plantations, seemed more disposed to yield to Britain than to endure the hazards of war and to suffer the birth pangs of a democratic society. Young, active men, whose range of vision extended to the great west, preferred to co-operate with the progressive yeomen in the fight for old rights and a better future.

General Lee had not been in Virginia a week before he was exasperated by the leaders of the cautious party. They included Edmund Pendleton, president of the provincial committee of safety, the venerable Richard Bland, another member of the committee, and Robert Carter Nicholas, provincial treasurer. They had been chosen in the preceding August, when the tide of conciliation sentiment ran high. It was said that this party sent Carter Braxton to the Continental Congress in December to oppose independence. To their hesitations General Lee attributed the inadequate defense preparations of the colony. He spoke disparagingly of the "timidity of the senatorial part," the "excess of prudence and economy in the committee of safety," and the "apathy and oblique squinting toward what the milk-and-water people call reconciliation." [26]

About the middle of April, the opposition to independence subsided. General Lee, so pessimistic in March, reported enthusiastically on May 10: "There is a noble spirit in this province, pervading all orders of men." [27] The change was marked by a statement made by

Pendleton on April 20 that independence was certain within a few months.

In addition to Dunmore's obnoxious conduct, a variety of factors worked together to strengthen the independence party. The news of the evacuation of Boston made an especially profound effect in Virginia, since it sounded so loudly the praise of the colony's foremost son, and vindicated the judgment of the leaders whose support had placed him in command. The provincial convention in the preceding August had expressed its regard for the general. "You will believe," wrote its president, Peyton Randolph, "it gives me the greatest satisfaction to convey to you the sentiments of your countrymen and at the same time to give you every testimony of my approbation and esteem."[28] The militants, headed by Richard Henry Lee, were as one with the general on the great issue of the moment. He also had the confidence of many of the cautious, conservative men, such as Landon Carter and Robert Carter Nicholas. Soon after the triumph at Boston he sent two long letters to Virginia — one to Landon Carter and one to his brother, John Augustine Washington, who was then actively co-operating with Richard Henry Lee in the independence campaign. In each letter, Washington described the evacuation of Boston and made known the tributes he had received in Massachusetts for the respect and deference he had shown to the civil authorities. One may imagine the interest with which the leaders of Virginia read the authentic report of the great victory, from the pen of the principal actor — the hero of the continent. The star of Pendleton faded as the gloom of doubt was dispersed by the rays of victory from a new sun in the political sky.

In the letter of March 31 to his brother, Washington struck at the argument of the conciliationists that peace might come from the British plan of sending commissioners to the colonies. "The device," he said, ". . . is shallow, the covering thin." It might have an effect "upon weak minds among us" — upon those who "wish for reconciliation . . . without attending to the conditions."[29] In this letter, Washington approved the plans for the southern department of the army. He gave a strong endorsement of General

Lee (who, he said, "I expect is with you before this"), and put in a good word for the chief brigadier general under Lee—Andrew Lewis. It is likely that Washington's tribute to Lee improved the latter's standing in Williamsburg and removed some of the thorns from his path.

John Augustine Washington attended the Virginia convention which voted for independence on May 15. Presumably, he went as the substitute for Richard Henry Lee. Did he take with him to Williamsburg the arresting letter from his illustrious brother? If so, how many of the delegates read therein the general's allusion to "weak minds" that were deluded by the thin, shallow device of conciliation? How many of the delegates read Washington's praise of the colorful Charles Lee, then basking at Williamsburg in the sunshine of publicity—and all the while broadcasting his urgent pleas for independence?

During April a stream of news poured into Williamsburg from Philadelphia. Congress had invited the Canadians to form a free government and to unite permanently with the thirteen colonies. It had acted as a sovereign by authorizing privateering and prize courts. It had sent an emissary to France. It had assailed Britain's authority at its most tender spot by nullifying the navigation acts and by opening American ports to foreign merchants, foreign vessels, and foreign goods. From the south came news of similar import. North Carolina had instructed its delegates to vote for independence. Georgia, in effect, had done the same thing. South Carolina had established a new government and its chief justice had pronounced separation from Britain to be an accomplished fact. Truly the torrent of independence was swelling to a flood.

At Williamsburg, the energetic, ubiquitous General Lee symbolized the will of Congress to offer full assistance to the south. He expressed the determination of the majority to advance all the way to independence. For more than six weeks he remained at or near the provincial capital. He said he thought that the British would soon invade Virginia, although the sagacious George Mason expected them to move from Boston to Halifax, Nova Scotia. Everywhere Lee went he aroused the militants and disheartened the opposition. Everything he did spelled one word—independence. Not that he acted alone. Two days after his arrival, the military officers of Virginia tendered him a welcoming address. They expressed their "high satisfaction" in his appointment, being "perfectly convinced" of his "great abilities as a commander" and of "his firm attachment to the cause."[30] By whom had the Virginia officers been thus "perfectly convinced"? Washington, in the letter to his brother, spoke of Lee as "zealously attached to the cause," lauded him as "the first officer in military knowledge and experience we have in the whole army," and congratulated the Virginians on his appointment.[31] Most significantly, the Virginia officers referred to George III as a "bloodthirsty king." Did they owe allegiance to such a character? "We shall rejoice," they assured Lee, "to unite with you in this great design, and endeavor by a strict attention to the duties of our several stations, to establish the freedom of America on a lasting and permanent basis."[32]

Lee conducted a dramatic campaign against the adherents of Dunmore. It struck the note of independence, for it imputed to them the crime of treason. In Norfolk and Princess Anne counties disaffected persons were supplying Dunmore's troops and fleet, and many of the people had taken a British loyalty oath. Lee persuaded the committee of safety, which previously had not molested the offenders, to order the removal of all inhabitants from the two counties. He then went to Suffolk and sent his aides into the disaffected area. The inhabitants were given five days for preparations to leave, but that part of the plan was dropped. The chief business of the expedition was a raid on the town of Portsmouth, the supply base for Dunmore's forces. A few Tories were arrested; three houses were burned; and some goods of the sort useful to Dunmore were seized. Lee did not attack the entrenched positions of the enemy.

The attentions he received from the Virginians satisfied his craving for recognition. At the end of his visit he reported: "I am extremely well in the opinion of the senatorial part, as well as of the people at large."[33] He was not a man to dissemble when he had been treated badly. The day after the convention convened, he sent to Patrick Henry (soon to be elected governor by the members) a long letter urging independence. He contended that the union must become a nation before it could obtain aid abroad, and argued that the interest of France would impel its government to assist a full-fledged enemy of Britain.

"The opinion for independence seems to be gaining ground; indeed most of those who have read the pamphlet *Common Sense* say it is unanswerable." [34] Thus wrote Washington's brother-in-law on March 6. The election campaign of April hinged on the great question. Many petitions in favor of separation were circulated in the counties, advising the representatives to take the fateful step. The notables of the colony assembled on May 6. The elder statesman, Richard Bland, linked the old order with the new. Patrick Henry led the militants; Edmund Pendleton represented the earlier attitude of caution that had yielded to the pressure for independence. As the members had gathered to assume a tremendous responsibility, it was appropriate that the encouragement and support of the whole union should be manifested. On May 2, General Lee returned from Suffolk and remained more than a week. With him were Brigadier Generals Andrew Lewis and Robert Howe. All the high army officers met in council on May 8 to form a military program for the convention's consideration. Lee notified Washington that every recommendation was approved. As the delegates approached the historic decision, they had the satisfaction of knowing that they were not alone. Behind them stood Washington, the army, and the Congress.

The vote was unanimous. The resolve of May 15 went nearly as far as one colony could go. It directed the delegates of Virginia to propose that Congress should declare the colonies free and independent states, "absolved from all allegiance to the crown or parliament of Great Britain." It pledged that Virginia would give its assent "to such declaration and to whatever measures may be thought proper and necessary by Congress for forming alliances and a confederation of the colonies. . . ." [35]

"In consequence of these resolutions," states a newspaper report of May 17, ". . . some gentlemen made a handsome collection for the purpose of treating the soldiery, who next day were paraded in Waller's grove, before Brigadier-General Lewis, attended by the gentlemen of the committee of safety, the members of the general convention, the inhabitants of this city, etc., etc. The resolutions being read aloud to the army, the following toasts were given, each accompanied by a discharge of artillery and small arms, and the exclamations of all present.

"1. The American Independent States.

"2. The grand Congress of the United States, and their respective legislatures.

"3. General Washington, and victory to American arms."[36]

XV. Action in the Center

> I think a change in American representation necessary; frequent appeals to the people can be attended with no bad, but may have very salutary effects.[1]
>
> —WASHINGTON TO JOSEPH REED, APRIL 1, 1776

AFTER the victory of the militants in Virginia, the center of the contest shifted to the middle area. Five colonies had not yet pledged themselves: New York, Pennsylvania, Delaware, Maryland, and New Jersey. If Pennsylvania should join Virginia in the independence camp, Maryland, squeezed in between them, would have to follow. Delaware would not then be able to stand against its stronger neighbors. New Jersey would be greatly influenced by Pennsylvania. The shift of four of the middle colonies would leave New York isolated between two solid blocks of independence territory. It would then have to fall in line. Thus the whole middle area was destined to swing with the turn of events in the pivotal colony of Pennsylvania, the stronghold of conciliation.

The resistance of the wealthy leaders of the middle colonies was now the chief obstacle to independence. The Pennsylvania assembly on November 9, 1775, had directed its delegates in Congress to oppose separation. The instructions of New York, Maryland, and Delaware so emphasized the tie with Britain as to deter the individual delegate from assuming the fateful responsibility, without a new mandate from home.

Prior to the spring of 1776 the Quaker colony had escaped with a minimum of change. It did not have a revolutionary congress. The old provincial government, based on a British charter, survived intact. It consisted of an elected assembly, now thoroughly undemocratic, plus executive and judicial officers appointed by the proprietors—heirs of William Penn. The assembly, led by John

Dickinson, chose the colony's delegates to the Continental Congress. The seeming weakness of local militants did not mean that the Pennsylvanians were pro-British. The conciliationists, a minority, voiced in part the antiwar views of the numerous Quakers. They also spoke for the German Pietists of the eastern counties who, like most of the Quakers, were apostles of peace.

Dickinson's party also represented a small group of wealthy leaders whose estates, located on or near the coast, were within easy reach of the British navy. The proprietary government suited these men of fortune, since the Penn family permitted them to exercise the essential political power. Representation was so devised that they controlled the assembly. The discontented majority (mechanics, yeomen, and squatters) strove to attain equal representation for all the freemen. The wealthy leaders clung to the old government, fearing that if it were set aside a new one of ultrademocratic cast would arise, whereupon their property and power would be swept away by the hostile majority. In *Common Sense* Tom Paine had identified independence with a leveling democracy. That widely circulated handbook of the militants proposed that each colony should adopt a type of government that would permit the majority to gain complete control of all offices and to rule without hindrance from the minority.

ii

Early in November 1775 Joseph Reed had returned to Philadelphia from the army headquarters at Cambridge, partly in order to lead Pennsylvania into the independence fold. Late in January he was elected to the provincial assembly. He then proposed that the membership of that body should be enlarged, hoping thereby to give the militants a majority that would enable them to revoke the standing instructions against independence. On March 14 the assembly voted to admit seventeen new members. The reform, however, did not go far enough. It did not enfranchise the unprivileged. In the election of the new members on May 1, the Dickinson party won three of the four new seats allotted to Philadelphia. The enlarged assembly then refused to repeal the instructions against separation, whereupon the popular party demanded that a provincial convention should be elected by all the freemen. Such a body would cast aside the old government under the royal charter and set up a new one that would give equal representation to all the freemen, rich and poor alike.

At this point the militants in Congress went to the aid of their partisans in Pennsylvania, seeking to strengthen them with the support of the union and to spur the people to action. To attain this end, Congress on May 10 recommended that any colony without an adequate government should choose representatives who would create one that would promote the welfare of its people. However, this resolve was indecisive. It called for a new government only if the old one was inadequate. Dickinson said that the Quaker colony might properly ignore the resolve because the people already had an adequate government.

While this struggle was going on, news arrived in Philadelphia that greatly aided the militants. On May 11 the local press printed reports that Britain had engaged a large number of German mercenaries for service in America. George III had entered into treaties with the Duke of Brunswick, the Landgrave of Hesse-Cassel, and the Count of Hanau. The three princes had agreed to furnish 16,968 men — all to be ready to march by April 1. A reliable letter from Massachusetts told that a fleet of sixty British transports had been sighted en route to America. They were reputed to have on board 12,000 Hessians. A second expedition was on its way to Quebec, with 4000 Hanoverians under the command of General Burgoyne.

The season of delay had ended. The reports of enemy reinforcements and the disclosure of the full intent of the foe portended a hard struggle. Now was the time to call forth the latent strength of America, to release the full energies of the people, to create conditions conducive to foreign aid, to unshackle the American governments, and to dedicate them to the tasks of war. The occasion required the solid, nourishing fare of independence. Yet, in some colonies, men in authority were still "feeding themselves upon the dainty food of reconciliation." Without the unqualified support of those colonies, all plans and exertions might prove to be unavailing.

Against the cautious men of the Quaker colony was now directed the force of the independence party. Speaking through Congress, the militant majority again called upon the Pennsylvanians to cast off their obstructing government. This time Congress acted without equivocation. On May 15 it affixed to the resolve of the tenth an antiking preamble which branded George III as an enemy and declared him guilty of "cruel depredations against the American people." It condemned the taking of oaths "for the support of any government under the crown of Great Britain." It asserted that it was now necessary to suppress, totally, "the exercise of every kind of authority under the said crown."[2]

The antiking resolve of May 15 put the force of the union behind the independence party in Pennsylvania and armed it with a potent weapon. Congress had named the king as one of the principal authors of the wrongs of America. It had called him an enemy. It had brushed aside the fiction of a guilty ministry and an innocent king. To fight against the king was to fight against the sovereign to whom the colonists had previously owed allegiance. To declare him an enemy—to fight against him as such—was to renounce that allegiance. The Pennsylvania conciliationists could no longer adhere to the king without defying the will of Congress.

iii

Washington gave timely aid to the militants in Congress in their effort to renounce the old allegiance to the king. On May 5 he sent an important letter to President Hancock. For the first time, in an official communication to Congress, he spoke of the British army as "the king's troops."[3] That letter was read to the members on May 8. A week later Congress adopted the resolve that called the king an enemy and declared that the American resistance was directed against him. In this manner Congress endorsed Washington's announcement that he was fighting against the king's troops, and therefore against the king.

Washington assisted the independence party in another way. He encouraged the leaders of Rhode Island to set the example which Congress followed when it adopted the antiking resolve of May 15. The Rhode Island assembly, on May 4, enacted a drastic law. It assailed George III for seeking to establish a "debasing and detestable tyranny," declared that the Rhode Islanders no longer owed allegiance to him, ordered the deletion of his name from legal documents, and proclaimed that the citizen's allegiance should henceforth be given to the colony alone.[4] Rhode Island asserted itself in this audacious manner at a time when its leaders were acting in concert with Washington.

The fact that a colony belonged to the union did not guarantee that it would be defended by Congress. Washington insisted that the army be held together as a large unit and kept in the presence of the main British force. He often refused to send small detachments to localities that were threatened with minor attacks. Ordinarily, each colony was expected to provide for its defense, short of an invasion by the British army. This plan was not wholly satisfactory. The people of exposed areas clamored for some protection. In consequence, Congress was obliged to expand its defensive measures. From time to time it created Continental battalions for the protection of neglected colonies. Usually it did this by taking existing colonial forces into the army, by providing them with Continental officers, and by pledging to pay their expenses. Such actions assured the people concerned that Congress was interested in their defense. It made them feel that they had the support of the union — that they could count on aid from the outside in an emergency. Such a sense of security braced the people and encouraged them to drive ahead.

In January the leaders of Rhode Island had asked Congress to guarantee its defense and to place its troops in the army on Continental pay. Unfortunately, they did not obtain Washington's approval of their plan before they submitted it to Congress. Governor Cooke merely solicited his aid, as an afterthought. Washington did not bestir himself and Congress failed to act. Nearly three months later, when he was moving the army from Boston to New York, he stopped at Providence and visited the governor. The plan was again presented to him and he now agreed to recommend it to Congress. The results of the talks were then recorded in letters. "I beg the favor of your excellency," wrote Governor Cooke on April 23, "to represent the state of the colony to Congress, and to recommend to them their taking over our brigade (which is enlisted to serve in any of the United Colonies) into continental pay, and to establish a force here for the defense of the colony."[5] Washington replied on April 28 that he would immediately write to Congress. "And if my recommendation thereof," he said, "has any weight with that august body, it will give me much pleasure to render service to your colony."[6]

The general's letter to Governor Cooke probably arrived at Providence about May 2. When the assembly passed its independence act of May 4 it must have been encouraged by Washington's promise to sponsor its defense plan. Obviously, its members trusted his promise and had confidence in his ability to get the approval of Congress. On April 30 he wrote to Philadelphia, endorsing the plan. "I have made inquiry into the situation . . . of the colony," he said, "and find it to be as stated. . . ." He emphasized the importance of Rhode Island in the union and pointed to its "extensive seacoast, affording harbors for our shipping . . . at the same time exposing . . . the inhabitants to the . . . depredations of our enemies." He praised the colony for "the zeal and attachment which it has shown, and which still animates it, toward the common cause," and acknowledged its "incapacity to pay a sufficient number of men for its defense . . . after so many engaged in other services." "What they chiefly wish for," he concluded, "is that the troops they have raised may be taken into the continental pay, and the commanding officers be appointed by Congress."[7]

The letter was read in Congress on May 2. Nine days later the members resolved that "the two battalions, directed by the assembly of Rhode Island to be raised, be taken into the continental pay."[8] What the Rhode Island leaders had failed to accomplish by themselves in more than three months they were able to accomplish, with Washington's aid, in nine days. One of the Rhode Island delegates explained how it happened. Stephen Hopkins wrote to Governor Cooke on May 15: "A letter from General Washington to Congress warmly recommending it to them to take this step respecting the Colony of Rhode Island had great influence in procuring it to be done. I could therefore wish the colony in a handsome manner to acknowledge their favor, and to return thanks to the general for his good offices in their behalf."[9]

When Governor Cooke sent a copy of the independence act of May 4 to the Rhode Island delegates in Congress, he also forwarded a newly adopted set of instructions for their guidance. Again the note of independence was sounded. The colony now recorded itself in favor of "entering into treaties with any prince, state, or potentate."[10] Copies of these independence measures reached Philadelphia shortly before Congress adopted its antiking resolve of May 15. Rhode Island had condemned the king and renounced allegiance to him. Could the whole union do less than its smallest member had done? Should Congress support Rhode Island or leave it in a state of perilous isolation? The antiking resolve of May 15 duplicated, in substance, the Rhode Island independence act of May 4. Congress now denounced George III as an enemy, disapproved of oaths given for the "support of any government under the crown of Great Britain," and urged that "the exercise of every kind of authority under the said crown be totally suppressed."

iv

At the critical point in the struggle for Pennsylvania, Washington acted as a leader of the popular party. Its backbone consisted of revolutionary companies of military associators — citizens of the democratic faith who had banded together with the object of enforcing the measures of the Continental Congress. They were the most radical opponents of John Dickinson and his friends. Their organizations were the offspring of Washington's program of 1774, which he and George Mason had incorporated into the Fairfax Resolves. Dickinson had prevented the formation of military companies in Pennsylvania until the news of Lexington and Concord moved the citizens to take up arms. General Lee then came forward to organize, drill, and inspire the associators. In Philadelphia their chief was Thomas Mifflin. In May 1776 he was an ardent militant and active aide of Washington. At that time the general made it plain that he was prepared to head a radical, popular movement, if that should become necessary for victory. If cautious men of fortune should deny the means of success (by delaying independence), he would have to depend upon the people who were willing to fight. He had endorsed the radical doctrines of *Common Sense.* Writing to Joseph Reed on April 1 he said: "I think a change in American representation necessary; frequent appeals to the people can be attended with no bad, but may have very salutary effects." [11] He warned his wealthy friends of the need for unity. "If the house is divided," he wrote, "the fabric must fall, and a few individuals perish in the ruins." [12] Obviously, he did not expect the people at large to be ruined by a collapse of the old order.

As soon as the news of the employment of foreign mercenaries by Britain arrived in Philadelphia, the military associators presented to Congress an important petition. It dealt with the defenseless state of the province. The petitioners, noting that their companies were disconnected and poorly trained, complained that their defense efforts had been thwarted by the negligence of certain leaders of the colony—by men who, "if they wished well to our cause, would have treated us in a very different manner." More specifically, they criticized some of the Pennsylvania delegates in Congress. The petition proposed that Congress should establish a few battalions in the colony and appoint General Mifflin to co-ordinate and train the troops. They also asked that Congress order a survey of the defenses of Philadelphia and the Delaware River. Such a survey should be directed by Washington. Since opposition had been made locally to their plans, they suggested that "the opinion . . . of General Washington . . . may save us the labor of further applications."[13]

Congress considered the petition at once. On May 16 it promoted Mifflin to the rank of brigadier general and summoned Washington to Philadelphia. He arrived on the twenty-third. Both Gates and Mifflin were then in the city. Washington remained until June 4. On the day of his arrival, Congress appointed a small committee to confer with him. Three of its five members—Benjamin Harrison, John Adams, and Richard Henry Lee—were independence men. At the call of Congress he attended its sessions on May 24 and 25. An enlarged committee was now appointed to assist him and Generals Gates and Mifflin in the preparation of plans for the coming campaign. Nine of its fourteen members were militants. Repeatedly the issue of independence cropped out. On May 27, the delegates of North Carolina and Virginia presented to Congress the resolves of their conventions which approved of separation. Two days later the committee that had been set up to confer with Washington recommended "that an animated address be published, to impress the minds of the people with the necessity of their now stepping forward to save their country, their freedom, and property."[14] Congress immediately accepted the proposal and appointed a committee to prepare a declaration. Jefferson and Samuel Adams were two of its four members. But the time had not come. The men of caution still had a veto power.

The presence of Washington in the city provided the occasion for a grand review of the military companies, which was held, at the request of Congress, on May 27. A Philadelphian described it: "Past two [I] took a walk on the commons to see the review of sundry battalions of militia and the recruits, which were drawn up regularly with the troop of horse and train of artillery. The generals were Washington (chief), Gates, and Mifflin, with the Congress, members of assembly, a number of clergymen, officers, &c., and a vast concourse of people, with between twenty and thirty of the Indians of the six nations." [15]

During his stay in Philadelphia Washington wrote an important letter to his brother (May 31), in which he sketched the situation in Congress. He said that representatives of "whole provinces are still feeding themselves upon the dainty food of reconciliation." Praising the independence resolve of Virginia as "noble," he dismissed the idea of British concessions as an illusion. No peace commissioners "were ever designed except Hessians and other foreigners." The plan for a negotiated peace was intended merely "to deceive and throw us off our guard." It had succeeded too well; many members of Congress had been taken in. Their hope for an amicable adjustment affected "every part of their conduct and is a clog to their proceedings." He then went to the heart of the matter. No man, he said, "that entertains the hope of seeing this dispute speedily and equitably adjusted by commissioners will go to the same expense and run the same hazards . . . as he who believes that he must conquer or submit to unconditional terms and its concomitants, such as confiscation, hanging, etc., etc." [16]

Before Washington left Philadelphia Congress adopted an ambitious program in line with the recommendations of the large committee which had conferred with him. The new plan called for the employment of 19,800 militia in Canada and New York. Of this number New England was to supply 13,500. Neither Pennsylvania nor Maryland was asked to send troops outside its territory. For the defense of those two colonies Congress authorized a flying camp of 10,000 men — 6000 from Pennsylvania, 3400 from Maryland, and 600 from Delaware. This flying camp would consist of the most zealous militants. Its purpose was to inspire the people with confidence. Its recruits would have the support of the union and serve under the direction of Washington. He endorsed the leading officers of the Philadelphia militants, Colonels John Shee and Robert Magaw, and advised that their battalions be kept in the city, alluding to "encouragements . . . to the disaffected which are circulated no one knows how." The movements of such people, he said, were "more easy to perceive than describe."[17]

The climax of Washington's stay in Philadelphia came on June 4. On that day President Hancock sent out a circular letter to all the colonies that were affected by the recently adopted legislation. Thus the letter went to the authorities of Delaware, Pennsylvania, Maryland, New Jersey, and New York. It transmitted to them the statements of their obligations under the new military plan. Each colony was requested to raise a number of troops, and to do that on the principle of independence. Hancock wrote: "Such is the unrelenting spirit which possesses the tyrant of Britain and his parliament, that they have left no measure unessayed that has a tendency to accomplish our destruction."[18] Did the colonies owe allegiance to such a tyrant? The official voice of Congress told them that they did not.

v

Immediately after Congress adopted its antiking resolve of May 15, the militants of Philadelphia intensified their campaign for independence. On the next day a committee of citizens issued a call for a provincial conference to meet at the capital in June. The conference, consisting of delegates from the revolutionary committees of the counties, would call upon the Pennsylvania delegates in Congress to vote for independence. It would also make plans for a general convention that would abolish the old government and set up a new one that would give full representation to the people. "A convention chosen by the people will consist of the most fiery independents": thus lamented a leading conciliationist.[19] A multitudinous meeting in Philadelphia on May 20 denounced the assembly on the ground that its authority was derived "from our mortal enemy, the king of Great Britain," adding that its members "were elected by such persons only as were either in real or supposed allegiance to the said king, to the exclusion of many worthy inhabitants whom . . . the resolve of Congress hath now rendered electors." [20] The defenders of the old order were assailed as enemies of Congress, of the union, and of the American cause. The people now had the highest authority for refusing to respect the old government.

The old assembly tottered to its end. Most of the members lost interest and ceased to attend. Two communications, arriving together, delivered the final blow. From Virginia came a copy of its independence resolve of May 15; from Congress arrived the letter in which President Hancock referred to George III as a tyrant. On June 8 the expiring assembly withdrew its instructions of November 9 and authorized the Pennsylvania delegates "to concur with the other delegates in Congress in forming such further compacts between the United Colonies, and concluding such treaties with foreign kingdoms and states, and in adopting such other measures as shall be judged necessary for promoting the liberty, safety, and interest of America." This last statement from the citadel of John Dickinson sounded the doom of conciliation. It cited, as the major reasons for separation, the king's contemptuous rejection of the humble petition of Congress, the branding of the "just resistance" of the colonies as rebellion, and Britain's employment of foreign mercenaries. These acts manifested such "a determined and implacable resolution to effect the utter destruction of these colonies that all hopes of reconciliation, on reasonable terms, are extinguished." [21]

Such was the swan song of the Pennsylvania assembly. Joseph Reed had attended its meetings until it pronounced the final word. He had helped to prepare the new instructions of June 8. Having finished his task of guiding the independence campaign in the Quaker colony he bade farewell to Philadelphia and rejoined Washington and the army. "When, my good sir," the general at New York had written to him on April 15, "will you be with me? I fear I shall have a difficult card to play in this government, and could wish for your assistance and advice to manage it."[22] Congress had recently strengthened the independence party in the army. In addition to Mifflin's being made a brigadier general, Gates was promoted to the rank of major general, Stephen Moylan became quartermaster general, and Reed, at Washington's insistence, replaced Gates as adjutant general.

June 14 marked the transition from the old to the new in Pennsylvania. On that day the expiring assembly admitted that, for want of a quorum, it could not raise the six thousand men requested by Congress for the flying camp. On that day, also, the insurgent committees of the counties selected their delegates to the provincial conference. They assembled on the eighteenth. First, they listened to two readings of the antiking resolve of May 15, whereupon they pronounced the demise of the old regime and directed that a provincial convention be summoned for the purpose of creating a new government. Since the old assembly had failed to provide for the flying camp, the conference undertook to recruit the men. Then came the high point of the meeting. On June 24 the delegates, after asserting that George III had forfeited the allegiance of the colonists by "an accumulation of oppressions unparalleled in history," expressed their readiness to "concur in a vote of the Congress declaring the United Colonies free and independent states."[23]

vi

The attraction of Pennsylvania quickly drew Delaware into the orbit of independence. The tie between the two neighbors was so close that, for all practical purposes, they formed one province. As in Pennsylvania, the insurgents of Delaware retained their old government, which operated through an elected assembly. Both colonies had the same governor; residents of one took part in the politics of the other. Thus Thomas McKean served as president of the Pennsylvania conference of June 18–25 while he was a delegate representing Delaware in Congress. However, the smaller colony had not gone quite so far toward conciliation as its northern neighbor. In March 1776 it instructed its delegates in Congress "to embrace every favorable opportunity to effect a reconciliation with Great Britain, on such principles as may secure to your constituents a full and lasting enjoyment of all their just rights and privileges." [24]

Three men represented Delaware in Congress prior to August 1776: Caesar Rodney, a moderate; George Read, a conciliationist; and Thomas McKean, a militant. When Rodney was absent, Read and McKean tended to cancel each other and to render the colony voteless. The outcome in Delaware was foreshadowed by a letter which Washington wrote on August 30, 1775, to Rodney and McKean. The two delegates had asked the general to provide an office for one of their friends. He notified them of his compliance and solicited their support for one of his policies. This identification of Rodney with Washington and McKean indicated the trend in Delaware. When all three delegates were present, the vote of the colony would be cast against the conciliationists.

The victory of the militants in Pennsylvania forced Delaware into the independence column. On June 14, McKean presented to the assembly of the smaller colony a copy of the antiking resolve of May 15. The members at this time approved a new set of instructions to their delegates, using the exact wording of the statement adopted by the Pennsylvania assembly on June 8. Having thus authorized its delegates to vote for independence, the Delaware assembly then renounced allegiance to the king. On June 15 it ordered that all officers should exercise authority in the name of the colony, "as they used legally to exercise it in the name of the king, until a new government shall be formed agreeable to the resolution of Congress of the 15th of May last." [25] Since two of Delaware's three delegates now belonged to the independence party, it was not necessary for the assembly to choose new ones or to adopt positive instructions in favor of separation.

In New Jersey, the flame of conciliation did not burn brightly, although the province was one of the last to embrace independence. Its hesitation arose from its location rather than from the temper of the people. It was not large enough to stand against both Pennsylvania and New York; hence the reluctance of those neighbors discouraged extreme militancy. The colony was directly under British rule, but its royal governor, William Franklin, acted a mild, passive part and did not provoke bitter resentments. He refrained from the sort of antics by which Lord Dunmore had infuriated the Virginians. British troops were not present to irritate the inhabitants. Exposure to invasion had a moderating effect. On the other hand, certain conditions fostered the militant attitude. The province lacked a group of those wealthy merchants who counseled caution. Most of the people were farmers, strong in the democratic faith, who meant to keep their rights of self-government and the benefits of home rule.

The provincial congress met at Burlington on June 10. The work of the session began with the reading of President Hancock's letter of June 4, in which he called George III a tyrant. On the next day the members received from Virginia a copy of its independence resolve. After early ballots showed that the conciliationists were a feeble minority, two of the New Jersey delegates to the Continental Congress resigned, presumably because they were unwilling to go on record for independence. In response to the Congress resolve of May 15, the assembly ordered the arrest of Governor Franklin. It voted to raise three thousand troops to serve in the general army, placed Joseph Reed (Washington's former secretary) in command of them as a brigadier general, and authorized Washington to call the provincial militia to service in New York. On June 22, the members elected five new delegates to Congress — all independence men — and empowered them to unite with the other colonies in making the anticipated declaration.

While the New Jersey congress was thus advancing step by step, it received assurances that Delaware and Pennsylvania had joined the procession. Ten colonies were then committed. New Jersey made the eleventh. The Continental Congress had provided amply for its defense and had placed the strength of the union behind the independence party there. To the south, only Maryland had failed to come forward. Across the Hudson, Washington and the army stood guard in New York, the last refuge of conciliation.

vii

As an actor in the Revolution, Maryland had some distinctive features. The provincial leaders, a cohesive group of wealthy planters, dominated the government and guided the resistance with a steady hand. They were so strongly entrenched in power that neither Britain nor their domestic foes could dislodge them, and they remained at the helm through all the storms of the tempestuous era. They had schooled themselves in the arts of political opposition. For many years they had battled against hostile influences exerted from the outside. The province was the proprietary domain of the Calvert family, and the heirs of the founders, the Lords Baltimore, enjoyed the privilege of exacting a tribute by means of various dues, rents, and fees. Since such exactions were not precisely defined, and since the proprietary lord claimed the right to determine the sums of many of them, the colonists were in a precarious financial state. Numerous agents of the proprietor formed a "court party" which, supported by these revenues, labored to augment them. Opposition was voiced in the elected assembly. The leaders of the settlers, known as the "country party," fought many a hard campaign against the proprietary forces. From this strife emerged the planter chieftains who aroused the colony against Britain's rule. The whole British government, exercising an unlimited taxing power, appeared to be far more formidable than a single family in search of revenue.

None of the colonists surpassed the Marylanders in the will to resist the British imperium. In 1775 the leaders of the country party formed a temporary government which they endowed with power sufficient for the preservation of law and order. Thereafter they did not need to create new agencies capable of providing security at home. To Philadelphia they sent some of the strongest men of the colony, among them Matthew Tilghman, Samuel Chase, William

Paca, and Thomas Johnson. The governing elite did not operate on a democratic basis. It retained the property qualifications for voting that had previously disfranchised the poorer people. However, the voteless inhabitants were not strong enough to cause serious trouble to the entrenched leaders. The "mechanics" of Baltimore were less numerous and articulate than their fellows in Boston, Philadelphia, and New York. The crowding together of the slaves and the freemen tended to unite the white people under the leadership of men of wealth and energy. Above all, Maryland differed from the other southern colonies in that it did not have a large back country. The western half of the colony was a narrow strip only twenty-five miles, on the average, in width. The seacoast planters were not vexed by a numerous body of inland settlers who clamored for full representation in the assembly and for other democratic rights.

During the first half of 1776 the men of property who governed Maryland were well satisfied. The proprietor and his agents had lost their power. The governor, Robert Eden, was a harmless neutral. No British troops stood on Maryland soil. On the other hand, no colony—with the possible exception of New York—was more exposed to the striking power of the British fleet. The wealth of the colony was concentrated within two narrow peninsulas. So dominant was the influence of the sea that the main divisions were known as the Eastern Shore and the Western Shore. British warships could come within easy range of all the large plantations.

Such conditions helped to shape the policy to which the leaders stubbornly adhered. They would resist at all costs the attempt of Britain to tax them and to rob them of their right to manage their affairs. They would cling tenaciously to their posts of leadership. They would not provoke attacks from the enemy and to that end they denied any design or ambition for independence. They set themselves against separation by sending, out of eight delegates to Congress, five who were not likely to endorse the step, and by ordering that the delegation could not commit the province unless four of them cast an affirmative vote.

In spite of its spirit of self-reliance, Maryland could not withstand the tide of opinion that had engulfed its neighbors. When the leaders met in their provincial congress late in June, they stood alone. Eleven of the colonies had moved into the independence column. The only other reluctant colony, New York, was securely in the care of Washington and the army. The two strong neighbors of Maryland had given up the illusion of conciliation. The first item the convention considered on June 20 was the "tyrant" letter from President Hancock. It accompanied a request from Congress that Maryland give military aid to the American cause. Could the provincial leaders reject the appeal and thereby withdraw from the union? If they were to continue to belong, they must help their partners to attain independence. They could hardly avow loyalty to the king while giving aid to a dozen of his onetime provinces in their struggle to free themselves from his authority. America or Britain. The choice could no longer be evaded. The Maryland leaders (one of whom, Thomas Johnson, had nominated Washington for the army command) decided not to break the union. Congress had asked Maryland to provide more than three thousand troops for the flying camp. The convention complied, and in so doing completed a circle by placing the force under a newly appointed general—Thomas Johnson. On June 28 the delegates gave their unanimous answer to the great question. They revoked their previous instructions and resolved anew, "that the deputies of this colony attending in Congress . . . or any three of them, be authorized and empowered to concur with the other United Colonies, or a majority of them, in declaring the United Colonies free and independent states." [26]

XVI. The Last Act

When, my good sir, will you be with me? I fear I shall have a difficult card to play in this government [New York], and could wish for your assistance and advice to manage it.[1]

— WASHINGTON TO JOSEPH REED, APRIL 15, 1776

ON May 18 a courier brought to army headquarters a bundle of papers from Europe. They included copies of the treaties between George III and the three German princes. Washington dispatched some of them to Congress. Others, of a confidential nature, he forwarded to Richard Henry Lee, to whom he sent also a rather cryptic letter. "In great haste I write you a few lines to cover the enclosed," he explained to Lee. "I hesitated some time in determining whether I could, with propriety, select them from the rest, considering in what manner they came to my hands; but as there are some things in each which may serve to irritate, I concluded it best to send not only the one directed to you, but the other also (to Doctor Franklin) under cover to you, as you may communicate and secrete such parts as you may like." The letter then concluded: "I have no time to add the necessity of vigorous exertions; they are too obvious to need any stimulus from me." [2]

Washington's action revealed his partnership with Richard Henry Lee, at the time when the latter was one of the chief directors of the campaign for independence.

While Washington was in Philadelphia, between May 23 and June 4, he saw much of Lee. Three days after the general left the Quaker City to return to New York, Lee presented in Congress the following resolution: "That these United Colonies are, and of right ought to be, free and independent states, that they are absolved from all allegiance to the British Crown, and that all political connection between them and the State of Great Britain is, and ought to be, totally dissolved."[3] The members then debated the motion. On June 10 they voted to postpone further consideration of it until July 1 and authorized the appointment of a committee to draft a declaration of independence. The discussion of June 8 and 10 revealed that some of the middle colonies were not yet ready to agree; hence the postponement to enable their provincial assemblies to equip their delegates with the necessary mandates.

The introduction of the Lee Resolution prompted the delegates of New York to write on June 8 for instructions from their provincial congress. "Some of us," they explained, "consider ourselves as bound by our instructions not to vote on that question, and all wish to have your sentiments thereon. The matter will admit of no delay."[4]

Under the rule of unanimity that applied to independence, New York could interpose a veto. No link in the chain of the union was more important. Heretofore the New Yorkers had held back. "It appears to me now," wrote Elbridge Gerry on June 25, "there is not even a doubt of any colony on the continent, except New York and Maryland."[5] The unfolding of the drama assigned a central part in the last act to the leaders of New York. With them, on the middle of the stage, was General Washington.

ii

Late in March and early in April the army moved from Boston to New York. Washington arrived in the city on April 13. At once it appeared that the political complexion of the colony had not changed during the few weeks that had passed since the finale of the expedition of General Charles Lee. All the troubles that had plagued him were now inherited by Washington.

After the British setback in New England, the ministry planned to conquer America through New York. Its military plan was supplemented by a campaign of political activity. The royal government, headed by Governor William Tryon, provided the chief agency for this work. He conducted his operations from a small fleet of warships stationed in the harbor. The mayor of New York, an appointee of the crown, directed the Royalist activities in the city and acted as an intermediary between the warships and Britain's partisans on land. The functionaries of King's College, an Anglican and Royalist center of learning, preached the gospel of obedience to the consecrated authority of the king. Agents of the ministry warned the people that overpowering British forces would soon arrive, that the province could not be defended by the insurgents, and that the king's enemies would soon suffer for their rebellious conduct. So, also, the royal officials strove to sharpen the animosity between New England and New York. They pictured the Yankees as a horde of uncouth fellows who were about to swarm into New York with the intent of seizing its best lands. The king's agents wooed the speculators of New York by supporting the claim of the province to present-day Vermont, then being occupied by New Englanders under grants from the government of New Hampshire. To partisans of Britain, other royal agents supplied arms from the warships in the harbor and urged the recipients to be ready to strike in conjunction with the approaching invasion. For the benefit of farmers there was an opportunity to sell produce to the king's fleet, with the promise of a vast increase in the business upon the arrival of the main British force in the near future.

In their efforts to resist the power of Britain, the New Yorkers were in a much weaker position than that occupied by the New Englanders when they had stood on the front line. Geographically, New York was not a unit, divided as it was into five areas of settlement, each separated from the others by water. No other province served as a buffer against invasion. The population of the colony was only about a fourth of that of New England, only about 30 per cent of that of the area between the Hudson and the Potomac, and only about 15 per cent of that of the four southern colonies. Exposed to attack from both the Atlantic and Canada, New York was like a nut in the jaws of a nutcracker. Its position did not afford well-to-do patriots of New York City the luxury of truculent hostility toward

Britain. There was too great a likelihood that the province would be occupied by the king's troops. The resulting caution of the patriots encouraged the king's friends to assert themselves. That in turn encouraged the British government to make special exertions in their behalf. The other middle colonies and the south constituted a large territory, much of which was remote from the enemy. The settled parts of New York, in the form of strips of accessible land, were destined by the fortunes of war to be the highways of invading armies.

The patriot party in New York contained two groups. One consisted of men of fortune who wished to preserve their place in society and their power in politics. They mistrusted democratic ideas and resisted radical change. To the other group belonged the plain people who subscribed to the democratic creed and responded to appeals for militant action against the enemy. Washington found the conservative leaders in control of the provincial government. He sought the assistance of both factions. For the moment the cautious men held back. A decisive factor was the army. If it should favor the militant democrats, they would rise to the top. Washington hinted that that might happen. He did not want to give needless offense. He took pains to assure the cautious men that his proposals were intended to achieve victory — not to aggrandize a faction. He kept the authorities informed, addressed them with politeness and respect, sought their consent for his actions, and expressed regret when disagreements arose. His method suggested the iron hand in the velvet glove.

iii

The policy of caution did not survive long after Washington's arrival. Its effect was to supply the British forces, to animate the king's friends, and to aid Britain's preparations for the coming invasion. Washington dealt at first with the provincial committee of safety. It had been elected by the second provincial congress, a group of conservative men who endorsed the policy of caution. General Lee's impetuous actions had left a legacy of mistrust of the army. Jealous of its authority, the provincial congress on March 15 had instructed its agent, the central committee of safety, to comply "with any requisition by the generals of the continental army," to such an extent as the committee should "think proper."[6]

Washington directed his first blow at the weakest point in the position of the provincial officials—the agreement which permitted the inhabitants to supply the British warships in New York harbor. On April 17 he wrote at length to the central committee of safety. The common cause, he said, would be injured by a continuance of the traffic. "We are," he pointed out, "to consider ourselves either in a state of peace or war, with Great Britain. If the former, why are our ports shut up, our trade destroyed, our property seized, our towns burnt, and our worthy and valuable citizens led into captivity and suffering the most cruel hardships?" He conceded that prudence might have justified the trade in the past, when the city was in a "weak and defenseless state." But that excuse was no longer valid, now that the main army was present to afford protection. "To tell you, gentlemen," he went on, "that the advantages of an intercourse of this kind are altogether on the side of the enemy, whilst we derive not the smallest benefit from it, would be telling what must be obvious to every one." Not only did the traffic enable the enemy's ships to remain in the harbor; it also opened "a regular channel of intelligence by which they are from time to time made acquainted with the number and extent of our works, our strength, and all our movements." The committee was then informed that the general considered it his duty to suppress the trade altogether. He expressed his hope that the committee would assist him. "It will certainly add great weight to the measures adopted when the civil authority cooperates with the military to carry them into execution." Such cooperation would "redound much to the honor . . . of your committee . . . for the world is apt to judge from appearances, and while such correspondence exists, the reputation of the whole colony will suffer in the eyes of their American brethren."[7]

The committee replied at once. "Your recommendation of yesterday," it notified the general, "we took into consideration immediately upon receipt of it. . . . We cannot sufficiently thank your excellency for your most delicate attention to the civil government of this colony, and beg leave to give you the strongest assurances that we most eagerly embrace this . . . opportunity of co-operating with you in every measure which shall come recommended to us with the argument of public utility."[8] By a resolve of April 18, the committee prohibited all inhabitants of the province from communicating with the British ships "upon pain of being dealt with in the severest manner as enemies to the rights and liberties of the united North American colonies."[9] The general incorporated this resolve into a proclamation which banned completely all intercourse with the enemy vessels in the harbor.

In order to enforce the prohibition, Washington organized a fleet of small vessels which he placed under the command of Colonel Benjamin Tupper. Writing on board the sloop *Hester,* off Amboy, the doughty colonel described his activities. He had just seized a small sloop in the act of communicating with the British ships. One of the captives, a woman, refused to talk. "It is the opinion of our friends in this town," said Tupper, "that she is able to bring out a number of rascalls & villins in sundry towns nigh here." He thought his activities were having a good effect, noting that "the Tories have begin to hang their heads like Bull rushes, and the friends of America have taken great courage and act more vigoros since my arival." To the general he sent some limes, which he had taken from a British official who was "very insolent. . . . I thought no person could be more desarving of them than your excellency. I have also kept a few to drink your excellency's health."[10]

Having succeeded in his first move against the British warships, Washington immediately took up another issue. It pertained to the status of certain Continental troops in New York that were not a part of the main army. Congress had empowered New York to raise and maintain four battalions at the expense of the union. General Schuyler, when in command of the province, had allowed the local authorities to look after these troops. Now the question arose: should they remain under the control of the central committee of safety, or should they be turned over to the commander in chief and incorporated into the main army?

Washington urgently needed the four battalions. However, he could not make known the weakness of the army. He did not address the committee of safety with an air of urgency. He merely asked for some information. How many men had been recruited? To what extent were they supplied with arms? The committee admitted that its supply of arms was wholly inadequate. It did not have satisfactory muster rolls, and its list of officers was so "mutable" that no purpose would be served by sending it to the general. The committee implied strongly that it was invested with the control of the troops. It referred to them as "our battalions" and as "under our immediate direction."[11] It implied that they had been authorized by Congress solely for the defense of New York. It reported that it had spent a large sum of Continental money, and—although it said its accounts were in an imperfect state—it asked Washington to lend it £6000 from the army's funds.

Thus the general learned that the committee had spent all its money without recruiting the required troops or obtaining the necessary arms. It claimed authority over the men and asked him to ratify the claim by supplying it with £6000.

Washington manifested neither resentment nor disappointment. In his reply he said that the army's cash was so low that he could not accommodate the committee with an advance. It was his duty, he said, to inquire whether the troops could be ordered to serve outside New York or whether they were limited to local duty. He sent the committee a recent resolve of Congress which directed him to receive arms that were collected in the province, and explained that he could not furnish arms to the four battalions if they were not under his command.

The committee surrendered. It conceded that the troops had been recruited on the condition that they could be ordered to serve outside New York, and that they were a Continental rather than a provincial force. Washington's claim to command them was no longer disputed. The reply was profuse with apologies, promises of co-operation, and expressions of esteem for the general.

The episode ended in a victory for Washington. It weakened the hold on the province of the conservative men whose inactivity had blocked decisive measures. His success arose largely from the backing of the Continental Congress. Its resolve authorizing him to receive the arms collected in New York enabled him to place the committee of safety in the position of seeking to control troops which it could not equip with weapons. He made use of George Clinton, a militant democrat, to procure the arms in question. Although the general was obliged to expose the shortcomings of the committee of safety, he went out of his way to spare the feelings of its members. If it was possible to remedy a defect and at the same time to retain the support of the persons involved, he certainly did all that he could to accomplish the difficult feat.

iv

After the middle of May the committee of safety receded into the background. The provincial congress convened on the fourteenth, and thereafter Washington dealt with a special committee which it appointed to confer with him on "all such matters relative to the execution of his office" as he should choose "to mention or communicate."[12] The congress had been elected in April, when the spirit of caution prevailed in the Manhattan area. The cautious party had chosen most of the delegates for New York City. Probably a third of all the members opposed independence. Eight were partisans of the king.

For a short time the new congress did not renounce conciliation. It was not moved to resolute action by the antiking resolve of May 15, which urged the colonies to set up new governments. The members merely arranged for a new election, in order that the voters might speak. Even the call for the election hinted at conciliation, for it said that a new government, if established, should "continue in force until a future peace with Great Britain shall render it unnecessary."[13] Similarly, the provincial congress shrank from independence. "We cannot presume," it declared on June 4, "by any instruction, to make . . . any resolutions or declarations upon so general and momentous a concern."[14]

After Washington's return from Philadelphia on June 6 the provincial policy of caution began to fade. On the fifth, the congress had received the Virginia independence resolve of May 15. Two days later the members learned of the military arrangements that Congress had made during Washington's stay in Philadelphia. The news arrived in company with the letter in which President Hancock branded George III as a tyrant. On June 7, after considering the new military plan, as set forth in Hancock's letter, the provincial congress voted its approval. On the next day it directed its president to call on Washington and present to him the following resolve: "That the thanks of the congress be presented to his excellency, General Washington, for the important services he has rendered to the United Colonies, and for the attention he has paid to the interest and civil authority of this colony, and that he be assured of the readiness of this congress to afford him all aid in their power to enable him to execute the important trust reposed in him."[15] The New York congress had moved far since March 15, when it directed its committee of safety to give such aid to the Continental generals as it should "think proper."

On June 8 the provincial congress transferred to Washington the control it had previously held over Forts Montgomery and Constitution on the Hudson. He placed them in command of Colonel James Clinton (a brother of George Clinton), a militant, at the same time removing an officer who had shown a tender regard for the feelings of the king's friends. Next, on June 9, the provincial congress appointed John Morin Scott, an outstanding militant and leader of the independence party, to command the New York militia, giving him the rank of brigadier general. Scott, a stanch supporter of Washington, now joined the general's inner circle of military advisers, while retaining his seat in the provincial congress. Two days later the congress tackled the thorny problem of independence. It then voted to submit the issue to the citizens at the impending election, in order that they might vest their representatives "with full power to deliberate and determine on every question whatsoever that may concern or affect the interest of this colony."[16]

A time of testing was near. Reliable reports made certain that at least twenty thousand British troops were en route to New York. To oppose such an armada, Washington had available for duty about seventy-five hundred men. Another large enemy force was headed for Canada, where the American army had recently suffered shattering defeats. On May 6 a force besieging Quebec had been attacked and driven off in "a most precipitate and confused retreat," with the loss of all its provisions, ammunition, and cannon.[17] The news of this disaster prompted Washington to write that "the prospect we had of possessing that country, of so much importance in the present controversy, is almost over."[18] Then, on June 7, he reported that the American force in Canada was in a desperate plight that foreshadowed the loss of Montreal. He had just received a letter from Arnold's camp telling that four hundred and fifty Americans were about to be attacked by a thousand Indians, Canadians, and British regulars. "Their drums were heard this evening at our camp. . . . The morning dawns — that morn big with the fate of a few, a handful of brave fellows."[19] To meet the gathering crisis Congress had voted to call about twenty thousand raw recruits to the colors for service in Canada and New York. What tasks of organization, training, and supply must be accomplished before the enemy would arrive! Danger and misfortune set in motion a sifting process that separated the weak from the strong. Two thirds of the members of the New York provincial congress met the test.

v

Before Washington's arrival in New York, the local authorities had not interfered with the Tories. He had not been in the province long until reports of anti-Tory activities began to trickle into headquarters. A letter from an insurgent committee in Suffolk County prompted him to act. It reported certain arrests and solicited his help. He replied: ". . . with great pleasure I will lend any aid in my power . . . to root out or secure such abominable pests of society." He promised to "set on foot a proper inquiry . . . and [to] concert some plan for defeating the designs which you think are in agitation."[20] He then conferred with John Morin Scott and Gouverneur Morris. Their inquiries satisfied them that the Tories in the Manhattan area were corresponding with the enemy and planning to join the British army upon its arrival. It was decided that the civil authorities should designate suspected persons and that the army should arrest them. The plan was being prepared when Washington left for Philadelphia on May 21. Three weeks later, observing that nothing had been done during his absence, he surmised that "we may therefore have internal as well as external enemies to contend with."[21]

On June 5 the provincial congress adopted a plan of action. It appointed a committee of seven and authorized it to summon suspects, to consider evidence, to determine innocence or guilt, to exact security from minor offenders, and to imprison the most dangerous culprits or to remove them from the vicinity of their homes. At the head of the committee the congress put Gouverneur Morris, one of the now numerous company of independence leaders in Washington's circle. The general was assigned a part in the plan, in that he was directed to provide soldiers for the purpose of locating and arresting the suspects.

On June 14 the provincial congress ordered the confinement of two Continental soldiers, Micha Lynch and Thomas Hickey, who had been arrested on the charge of attempting to pass counterfeit money. The congress also directed that statements containing the evidence against the two men should be delivered to Washington. Two days later, a report of a conference between the general and one of the brothers Clinton was submitted to the congress. Thereupon the members named Philip Livingston, Gouverneur Morris, and John Jay as a secret committee "to confer with General Washington relative to certain secret intelligence communicated to this Congress." [22]

The secret committee promptly made an extensive investigation which disclosed the details of the celebrated "Tory Plot." The official American version of the evidence told a grim story. Governor Tryon, on board the warship *Duchess of Gordon,* was directing a plan that was designed to destroy the American army. To his chief agent on land, the Royalist mayor of New York City, David Matthews, Tryon sent a large sum of money. Matthews passed it on to one Gilbert Forbes, who used it to recruit men for service in the British army. Among the Americans thus ensnared was Thomas Hickey, a soldier in Washington's guard. Tryon's company of secret operators was to strike in conjunction with the forthcoming attack of the main British army. They were to destroy ammunition, spike the cannon, and cut down the bridge that linked the city with its reinforcements in New England.

So damaging was the evidence against Mayor Matthews that Jay, Morris, and Livingston decided to arrest him. They appealed to Washington for troops and he endorsed their request with an order to General Greene, who seized the mayor at his house in Flatbush at one o'clock in the morning on June 22. When examined, he admitted that he had received a large sum of money from Governor Tryon and had relayed it to Gilbert Forbes.

The provincial congress now was in a delicate situation. It had on its hands an important official who admitted that he had received and paid money in a manner that gave aid and comfort to the enemy. Treason being a crime against a sovereign, the congress could not proceed against Matthews without proclaiming that it was the agent of an independent country—that the British king was an enemy—that to aid him was an act of treason rather than an act of allegiance. The provincial congress was not yet ready to act unequivocally on the basis of independence. On June 17 it had refused to prosecute Lynch and Hickey when they stood accused of the minor crime of attempting to pass counterfeit money. The congress had then declared that the "courts of judicature of this colony, being as yet held by authority derived from the crown of Great Britain, are for that reason incompetent to the full and impartial trial of the two said continental soldiers for the offense wherewith they stand charged." For this reason the congress concluded that they "must of necessity be tried by a court-martial only."[23]

If the New York courts lacked the power to try two obscure men who were charged with a minor offense, they obviously did not have the power to try a high British official whose assistance to the king was construed as treason.

vi

The Continental Congress met as usual on Monday, June 24. It had a weighty question to consider. The New York authorities had arrested Mayor Matthews and two American soldiers, but they had also declared that persons accused of acts against the union could not be tried in the provincial courts because they were held "by authority derived from the crown of Great Britain." At the same time, Washington had been given the custody of Hickey, with the recommendation that he be tried by court-martial. Washington could not plead lack of authority as an excuse for inaction. The probing of the Tory Plot indicated that Hickey had taken money for the purpose of giving military aid to the enemy. Congress on November 7, 1775, had authorized the army, by means of a court-martial, to impose the death penalty on a soldier who was found guilty of taking part in a mutiny or sedition. Such was Hickey's offense. Congress could hardly expect the army to execute a soldier for a crime and at the same time acquiesce in the plea of civilian authorities that they lacked the power to punish a civilian guilty of the same crime. If civil authorities should punish for treason, they would act as agents of a sovereign, independent state. If they should fail to act, they would condone activities that would imperil the army. The time had come when Congress must apply the same rule to civilians that it had applied to soldiers. It must call upon the colonies to do what the army had been authorized to do — to provide suitable punishments for treason. It must urge the provincial authorities to assume the powers of sovereignty. Thus it happened that on June 24 Congress faced the issue of independence in a way that did not permit equivocation or evasion.

The members met the issue head on. That day they enacted three momentous resolves. The first asserted that "all persons abiding within any of the United Colonies, and deriving protection from the laws of the same, owe allegiance to the said laws, and are members of such colony. . . ." The second resolve pertained to treason. It affirmed that "all persons . . . owing allegiance to any of the United Colonies . . . who shall levy war against any of the said colonies" or "be adherents to the king of Great Britain, or others the enemies of the said colonies . . . giving to him or them aid and comfort, are guilty of treason against such colony." The resolve then urged the "legislatures" of the colonies to enact "laws for punishing, in such manner as to them shall seem fit, such persons . . . as shall be proveably attainted by open deed . . . of any of the treasons before described." The third resolve urged the colonies to enact "laws" for the punishment of persons who were guilty of counterfeiting the Continental currency or of passing counterfeit bills of credit.[24]

When Congress defined the king as an enemy, it renounced his authority, repudiated the old allegiance, and proclaimed independence. When it defined acts in support of the king as treason, it took unto itself and exercised the power of a sovereign government.

On June 25 Elbridge Gerry wrote an important letter to General Gates. For the first time a member of Congress, in a semiofficial communication, used the phrase "The United States of America." Gerry said: "I think we are in a fair way to a speedy declaration of independence, confederation, and other measures that depend on secrecy for success." Congress, he pointed out, had prescribed the death penalty for spies and had recommended suitable punishments for persons who should aid the king or Great Britain, "or other enemies of the United States of America." [25]

The resolves of June 24 provided the provincial authorities of New York with the support, authority, and encouragement of the whole union for such punishment as they might inflict upon participants in future Tory plots. President Hancock wrote to Washington on June 25, enclosing copies of the three resolves. "It is sufficient to observe," he said, "that internal convulsions do always extremely weaken the force and springs of government, and must necessarily render its operations against foreign enemies less vigorous and decisive." [26]

The court-martial of Hickey, held at headquarters on June 26, found him guilty as charged. On the next day a council of general officers reviewed and confirmed the verdict and the sentence. Washington then sent the order to the provost marshal. Hickey was hanged on the twenty-eighth. The army acted under the articles of war, adopted by Congress on November 7, which authorized the death penalty for soldiers convicted of taking part in a mutiny or sedition. The resolves of June 24, recognizing in full the crime of treason, undoubtedly strengthened the army in its proceedings against Hickey.

vii

The best reports of British forces en route to New York in June estimated their strength as three times that of the main American army. Shortly before Congress voted formally for independence, on July 2, it listened to the reading of a letter from Washington, dated June 30. "When I had the honor of addressing you yesterday," he said, "I had only been informed of the arrival of forty-five of the [British] fleet in the morning. Since that time I have received authentic intelligence from sundry persons, among them General Greene, that one hundred and ten sail came in before night that were counted, and that more were seen about dusk in the offing. I have no doubt but the whole that sailed from Halifax are now at the Hook."[27]

Britain's use of foreign troops created a strong pressure for independence as a means of securing aid from France. Five days before Richard Henry Lee introduced the independence resolution he wrote: "*It is not choice . . . but necessity that calls for independence, as the only means by which foreign alliances can be obtained.* . . . Now, although we might safely venture our strength . . . against that of Great Britain only, yet we are certainly unequal to a contest with her and her allies, without any assistance from without, and this more especially as we are incapable of profiting by our exports for want of naval force."[28] The news that came into Philadelphia during June gave confidence that France would grant full aid to an independent enemy of Britain.

Congress voted twice for independence: on July 2, when it adopted the resolution which Richard Henry Lee had introduced on June 7, and on July 4, when it approved the Declaration. New York did not vote on either occasion; hence the decision was made by the affirmative votes of twelve colonies. The evidence concerning those two days is somewhat confused. The important facts, however, are known. By the end of June every provincial government, except that of New York, had authorized or encouraged its delegates to vote for separation. The four New England colonies, together with Virginia, North Carolina, and Georgia, had long been firmly committed. On June 28 the Maryland provincial convention had authorized any three of its delegates to pledge the colony to independence. A onetime moderate leader, William Paca, took the lead in bringing the Maryland delegation into line. In the proceedings between July 1 and July 4 four of the colonies figured in a special way. A new set of delegates from New Jersey—all militants—entered Congress for the first time and cast a solid vote for separation. On July 1, the Delaware delegation consisted of one militant and one conciliationist. The tie was broken by the arrival of Caesar Rodney. His vote put the colony in the independence column. The political revolution in Pennsylvania had undermined Dickinson's party. Some of the moderates of the Quaker colony delegation (including Robert Morris and Thomas Willing) abstained from voting and allowed three of the members (Franklin, James Wilson, and John Morton) to cast an affirmative ballot. Edward Rutledge of South Carolina doubted the wisdom of formal action at this time. But the policy of the leaders of his colony was that of preserving the strength of the union. Rather than defy all the other colonies, the South Carolinians, who had demurred on July 1, voted "yes" on July 2.

On the last page of the *Pennsylvania Evening Post,* in its issue of July 2, appeared a short notice, tucked in between advertisements and routine news items. It said: "This day the Continental Congress declared the United Colonies free and independent states." Such was the journalistic treatment given to the greatest event in American history.

The debate of July 3 and 4 on Jefferson's immortal Declaration did not decide the issue of independence. The adoption of the Lee Resolution on July 2 had done that. "All men are created equal." Those imperishable words aimed a mortal blow at the institution of slavery. They did not describe the political reality of 1776. They proclaimed an ideal to which the new nation dedicated itself—an aspiration to be realized in the future.

New York had a final word to say. On June 26 its provincial congress received copies of the allegiance and treason resolves which the Continental Congress had adopted on June 24. The New Yorkers accepted the resolves as a declaration of independence and acted accordingly. On June 30 their congress authorized Washington "to take such measures for apprehending and securing dangerous and disaffected persons as he shall think necessary for the security of this colony and the liberties of America." [29] By the last action of the session, on June 30, the congress declared New York to be a state.

The leaders of the province had decided that New York would

transform itself into a state by action at home rather than at Philadelphia. For this reason the New York delegates did not vote for either the Lee Resolution or the Declaration, although most of them favored separation. The provincial congress on May 31 had ordered a new election, and on June 11 it had directed the voters to express themselves through the election on the subject of independence. The outcome of the voting, late in June, was a victory for the independence party. Its opponents vanished from the provincial congress. The newly elected members met in convention at White Plains on July 9. There they resolved, unanimously, "that the reasons assigned by the Continental Congress for declaring the United Colonies free and independent States are cogent and conclusive; and that, while we lament the cruel necessity which has rendered that measure unavoidable, we approve the same, and will, at the risk of our lives and fortunes, join with the other colonies in supporting it." [30]

* * *

"When in the course of human events, it becomes necessary for one people to dissolve the political bands which have connected them with another, and to assume among the powers of the earth the separate and equal station to which the Laws of Nature and of Nature's God entitle them, a decent respect to the opinions of mankind requires that they should declare the causes which impel them to the separation.

"We hold these truths to be self-evident, that all men are created equal, that they are endowed by their Creator with certain unalienable rights, that among these are life, liberty, and the pursuit of happiness. That to secure these rights, governments are instituted among men, deriving their just powers from the consent of the governed. . . .

"Nor have we been wanting in attention to our British brethren. . . . They too have been deaf to the voice of justice and of consanguinity. We must, therefore, acquiesce in the necessity, which denounces our separation, and hold them, as we hold the rest of mankind, enemies in war, in peace friends.

"We, therefore, the Representatives of the United States of America, in General Congress assembled, appealing to the Supreme Judge of the world for the rectitude of our intentions, do, in the name, and by authority of the good people of these Colonies, solemnly publish and declare, That these United Colonies are and of right ought to be Free and Independent States: that they are absolved from all allegiance to the British Crown, and that all political connection between them and the State of Great Britain is and ought to be totally dissolved. . . .

"And for the support of this declaration, with a firm reliance on the protection of Divine Providence, we mutually pledge to each other our lives, our fortunes, and our sacred honor."

Notes

CHAPTER I

1. *The Letters of Horace Walpole* (ed. Mrs. Paget Toynbee, 16 vols., Oxford, 1904), VIII, 308. **2.** Tobias Smollett, *The Expedition of Humphrey Clinker* (2 vols., London, 1900), I, 46. **3.** Toynbee, *Walpole Letters,* IX, 15. **4.** D. A. Winstanley, *Lord Chatham and the Whig Opposition* (Cambridge, 1912), 198. **5.** Toynbee, *Walpole Letters,* IX, 15. **6.** *The Letters of Lord Chesterfield* (ed. Bonamy Dobrée, 6 vols., London, 1932), VI, 2696. **7.** David D. Wallace, *The Life of Henry Laurens* (New York, 1915), 185–186. **8.** *The Diary and Letters of Thomas Hutchinson* (ed. Peter O. Hutchinson, 2 vols., Boston, 1884, 1886), I, 379. **9.** Lord Mahon, *History of England from the Peace of Utrecht* (7 vols., London, 1851–1854), V, 497. **10.** Toynbee, *Walpole Letters,* IX, 63. **11.** Toynbee, *Walpole Letters,* IX, 86–87. **12.** Hutchinson, *Diary,* I, 423. **13.** *The Correspondence of King George the Third with Lord North* (ed. W. B. Donne, 2 vols., London, 1867), I, 34–35. **14.** *The Letters of Horace Walpole* (ed. Peter Cunningham, 9 vols., London, 1891), VI, 267 *n.* **15.** Josiah Quincy, *Memoir of the Life of Josiah Quincy, Junior* (Boston, 1825), 333. **16.** Hutchinson, *Diary,* I, 431. **17.** *The Parliamentary Register* (3 vols., London, 1775–1776), III, 441. **18.** George Bancroft, *History of the United States* (6 vols., Boston, 1879), III, 155. **19.** Hutchinson, *Diary,* I, 441. **20.** Horace Walpole, *Memoirs of the Reign of George the Third* (ed. G. F. Russell Barker, 4 vols., London, 1894), IV, 90 *n.* **21.** John Buchan, "Lord Mansfield," *Atlantic Monthly,* 88 (December 1901), 790. **22.** *Ibid.,* 786. **23.** *Ibid.,* 787–788. **24.** *Parliamentary History of England* (ed. William Cobbett, 36 vols., London, 1806–1820), XVI, 172. *Representative British Orations* (ed. Charles K. Adams, 3 vols., New York, 1890), I, 164, 165, 166. **25.** Hutchinson, *Diary,* I, 354. **26.** William E. H. Lecky, *The American Revolution* (ed. J. A. Woodburn, New York, 1932), 150. **27.** Carl Van Doren, *Benjamin Franklin* (New York, 1938), 476. **28.** *Dictionary of National Biography,* LVI, 344. **29.** Walpole, *Memoirs,* IV, 56. **30.** *The Parliamentary Register,* II, 89–90. **31.** George H. Guttridge, "Lord George Germain in Office," *American Historical Review,* XXXIII (October 1927), 34. **32.** Hutchinson, *Diary,* I, 309. **33.** Donne, *Corre-*

spondence of George III, I, 86–87. **34.** John Wade, *Junius* (2 vols., London, 1868), II, 182. **35.** Hutchinson, *Diary,* I, 412. **36.** *Ibid.,* 279.

CHAPTER II

1. Donne, *Correspondence of George III,* I, 107. **2.** *The Correspondence of King George the Third* (ed. Sir John Fortescue, 6 vols., London, 1927–1928), III, 153. **3.** *The Grenville Papers* (ed. William J. Smith, 4 vols., 1852–1854), IV, 318. **4.** *Ibid.,* 267. **5.** William S. Johnson to William Pitkin, September 18, 1769. *Trumbull Papers* (*Collections,* Massachusetts Historical Society, Boston, 1885), 358. **6.** *Ibid.,* 360. **7.** *Autobiography . . . of Augustus Henry Third Duke of Grafton* (ed. Sir William R. Anson, London, 1908), 136–137. **8.** Smith, *Grenville Papers,* IV, 128. **9.** Anson, *Grafton Autobiography,* 188. **10.** *The Correspondence of John Wilkes* (ed. John Almon, 5 vols., London, 1805), III, 273–276. **11.** Wade, *Junius,* II, 60. **12.** *Correspondence of William Pitt, Earl of Chatham* (4 vols., London, 1838–1840), II, 422. **13.** *Ibid.,* 422–423. **14.** *Ibid.,* 418, 422. **15.** William S. Johnson to William Pitkin, September 18, 1769, *Trumbull Papers,* 364. **16.** *The Works and Correspondence of Edmund Burke* (8 vols., London, 1852), I, 115. **17.** *Ibid.,* 128, 173. **18.** Donne, *Correspondence of George III,* I, 106. **19.** *Ibid.,* 107. **20.** *Ibid.,* 105–106. **21.** *Chatham Correspondence,* IV, 336. **22.** Fortescue, *Correspondence of George III,* III, 64 65. **23.** *Parliamentary History,* XVII, 1178, 1210. **24.** Hutchinson, *Diary,* I, 368. **25.** Mary Marks, *England and America, 1763 to 1783* (2 vols., New York, 1907), I, 353. **26.** Fortescue, *Correspondence of George III,* III, 154. **27.** James Boswell, *The Life of Samuel Johnson* (2 vols., London, 1904), I, 560. **28.** *Ibid.* **29.** Samuel Johnson, *Taxation no Tyranny* (3rd ed., London, 1775), 24, 50, 54. **30.** *Ibid.,* 2, 67, 66, 68, 55. **31.** *Ibid.,* 7, 80, 55. **32.** *Ibid.,* 80–82, 89, 8. **33.** *Ibid.,* 85, 89, 86, 88.

CHAPTER III

1. *The Writings of George Washington* (ed. John C. Fitzpatrick, 39 vols., Washington, 1931–1944), III, 292. Hereafter cited as *Bicentennial.* **2.** Fortescue, *Correspondence of George III,* III, 59. **3.** *Ibid.,* 116. **4.** Cunningham, *Walpole Letters,* VI, 185. **5.** Hutchinson, *Diary,* I, 368. **6.** Dartmouth to Gage, January 27, 1775, Library of Congress Transcripts, P.R.O., C.O. 5:92, 65–75. **7.** *Ibid.* **8.** *Letters of Hugh Earl Percy* (ed. Charles K. Bolton, Boston, 1902), 52. **9.** *Diary of Frederick Mackenzie* (2 vols., Cambridge, Massachusetts, 1930), I, 21–22. **10.** *Percy Letters,* 29, 38. **11.** *Ibid.,* 53. **12.** E. Dyer to Silas Deane, April 14, 1775. *The Deane Papers* (ed. Charles Isham, *Collections,* New York Historical

Society, 5 vols., New York, 1887–1890), I, 43. **13.** Silas Deane to Mrs. Deane, May 7, 1775. *Ibid.*, 43. **14.** *Ibid.*, 44–45. **15.** Silas Deane to Mrs. Deane, May 12, 1775. *Ibid.*, 46. **16.** *Ibid.*, 46–47. **17.** *Journal and Letters of Samuel Curwen* (ed. George A. Ward, New York, 1842), 28. **18.** Bancroft, *United States,* IV, 593.

CHAPTER IV

1. *Bicentennial,* II, 426. (See Note 1, Chapter III.) **2.** Washington to William Fairfax, June 7, 1755. *Ibid.*, I, 133. **3.** Washington to John Augustine Washington, June 28, 1755. *Ibid.*, 144. **4.** Washington to Governor Dinwiddie, July 18, 1755. *Ibid.*, 149. **5.** Washington to John Robinson, December 1755. *Ibid.*, 532–533. **6.** Washington to Robinson, August 5, 1756. *Ibid.*, 428. **7.** *Ibid.*, 428. **8.** Loudoun to Dinwiddie, November or December, 1756. *Ibid.*, 491–492 *n.* **9.** Washington to Robinson, December 19, 1756. *Ibid.*, 528. **10.** Washington to Robert Cary, October 12, 1761. *Ibid.*, II, 368. **11.** Washington to J. Pollard, August 22, 1766. *Ibid.*, 441. **12.** Washington to Cary, July 20, 1767. *Ibid.*, 461. **13.** Washington to Cary, June 20, 1768. *Ibid.*, 491. **14.** Washington to Cary, June 23, 1766. *Ibid.*, 437–438. **15.** Washington to Cary, September 27, 1763. *Ibid.*, 405–406. **16.** Washington to Cary, July 21, 1766. *Ibid.*, 439. **17.** Washington to Cary, August 22, 1767. *Ibid.*, 440. **18.** Washington to Cary, September 28, 1760. *Ibid.*, 350. **19.** Washington to Cary, October 12, 1761. *Ibid.*, 370. **20.** Washington to Francis Dandridge, September 20, 1765. *Ibid.*, 425–426. **21.** *Ibid.*, 426. **22.** Washington to Cary, July 25, 1769. *Ibid.*, 512. **23.** Washington to John Posey, June 24, 1767. *Ibid.*, 459. **24.** Quoted in R. C. Downes, "Dunmore's War," *Mississippi Valley Historical Review,* XXI (December 1931), 319. **25.** Grace L. Nute (ed.), "Washington and the Potomac," *American Historical Review,* XXVIII (April 1923), 510. **26.** Washington to George Mercer, November 7, 1771. *Bicentennial,* III, 68. **27.** Richard Thompson to Washington, September 30, 1775. Library of Congress, Washington Papers, XIV. **28.** Instructions for William Stevens, March 6, 1775. *Bicentennial,* III, 269. **29.** Quoted in Downes, *Mississippi Valley Historical Review,* XXI, 312.

CHAPTER V

1. Joseph Reed to Mr. Pettit, September 29, 1775. William B. Reed, *Life and Correspondence of Joseph Reed* (2 vols., Philadelphia, 1847), I, 120. **2.** Curwen, *Journal,* 29. **3.** Silas Deane to Mrs. Deane, May 12, 1775, *Deane Papers.* I, 49. **4.** *Journals of the Continental Congress* (ed. Worthington C. Ford and others, 34 vols., Washington, 1904–1937),

II, 25. **5.** Dartmouth to Gage, April 15, 1775. Library of Congress Transcripts, P.R.O., C.O. 5:92, 112. **6.** Gage to Dartmouth, January 18, 1775. *Ibid.*, 81. **7.** Reed, *Life of Reed,* I, 75. **8.** Letter of Governor Eden, December 30, 1775. *Parliamentary Register,* I, 103. **9.** Curwen, *Journal,* 28. **10.** Gage to Dartmouth, October 30, 1774. Library of Congress Transcripts, P.R.O., C.O. 5:92, 21–23. **11.** Gage to Dartmouth, March 28, 1775. *Ibid.*, 135. **12.** *The Works of John Adams* (ed. Charles Francis Adams, 10 vols., Boston, 1850–1856), II, 415. **13.** John Adams to James Warren, May 21, 1775. *Letters of Members of the Continental Congress* (ed. Edmund C. Burnett, 8 vols., Washington, 1921–1936), I, 95. **14.** *Journals of Continental Congress,* II, 79. **15.** *Passages from the Remembrancer of Christopher Marshall* (ed. William Duane, Jr., Philadelphia, 1839), 32–33. **16.** *Journals of Continental Congress,* II, 85. **17.** Samuel Adams to James Warren, June 10, 1775. Burnett, *Letters,* I, 121. **18.** *Ibid.*, 124. **19.** Washington to J. A. Washington, June 20, 1775. *Bicentennial,* III, 299. (See Note 1, Chapter III.) **20.** Statement of May 31, 1774, signed by Washington. Washington Papers, XV. **21.** Washington to Bryan Fairfax, July 20, 1774. *Bicentennial,* III, 231. **22.** Bryan Fairfax to Washington, August 5, 1774. Washington Papers, XV. **23.** John Adams, *Works,* II, 360. Diary entry for August 31, 1774. **24.** *Ibid.*, 352. Diary entry for August 23, 1774. **25.** Harrison, Randolph, and Bland to Washington, October 24, 1774. *Journals of Continental Congress,* I, 52–53. **26.** Dunmore to Dartmouth, December 24, 1774. *Bicentennial,* III, 248 *n.* **27.** G. W. Fairfax to Washington, March 2, 1775. Washington Papers, XV. **28.** Washington to B. Fairfax, August 24, 1774. *Bicentennial,* III, 240. **29.** Washington to B. Fairfax, July 20, 1774. *Ibid.*, 233. **30.** Fairfax Resolves, No. 9. Washington Papers, July 18, 1774. **31.** Washington to B. Fairfax, July 20, 1774. *Bicentennial,* III, 231. **32.** Fairfax Resolves, No. 7. Washington Papers, July 18, 1774. **33.** Washington to B. Fairfax, July 20, 1774. *Bicentennial,* III, 232–233. **34.** Washington to Mackenzie, October 9, 1774. *Ibid.*, 246. **35.** Washington to G. W. Fairfax, May 31, 1775. *Ibid.*, 292. **36.** Washington to Mackenzie, October 9, 1774. *Ibid.*, 246. **37.** *Journals of Continental Congress,* II, 64–65. **38.** *Ibid.*, 65. **39.** *Ibid.*, 161. **40.** *Ibid.*, 159–160. **41.** Dickinson to A. Lee, July [7, 1775]. Burnett, *Letters,* I, 157. **42.** Franklin to Joseph Priestley, July 7, 1775. *Ibid.*, 156. **43.** *Journals of Continental Congress,* II, 68–70.

CHAPTER VI

1. Roger Sherman to Joseph Trumbull, July 6, 1775. Burnett, *Letters,* I, 154. **2.** John Adams, *Works,* II, 360, 379, 400. Diary entries for

August 31, September 12, October 23, 1774. **3.** Quincy, *Memoir,* 192–195. **4.** Joseph Galloway, *Historical and Political Reflections on the Rise and Progress of the American Rebellion* (London, 1780), 68. **5.** John Adams, *Works,* I, 308. Diary entry for November 30, 1774. **6.** *American Archives,* 4th Series (ed. Peter Force, 6 vols., Washington, 1837–1846), II, 969. **7.** Bancroft, *United States,* IV, 582. **8.** *The Writings of Thomas Jefferson* (ed. Paul L. Ford, 10 vols., New York, 1892–1900), I, 15. **9.** Library of Congress Transcripts, P.R.O., C.O. 5:92, 331–333. **10.** Gage to Dartmouth, November 8, 1775. *Ibid.,* 325. **11.** John Adams, *Works,* II, 362–363. Diary entry for September 3, 1774; *ibid.,* III, 31 (Autobiography). **12.** *Letters of William Lee* (ed. Worthington C. Ford, 3 vols., Brooklyn, 1891), I, 87. **13.** Arthur Lee to Samuel Adams, December 22, 1773. Richard H. Lee, *The Life of Arthur Lee* (2 vols., Boston, 1829), I, 239. **14.** Arthur Lee to Samuel Adams, January 25, 1773. *Ibid.,* 228. **15.** Josiah Quincy, Jr., to Mrs. Quincy, November 24, 1774. Quincy, *Memoir,* 248. **16.** Quincy to ——, December 14, 1774. *Ibid.,* 269. **17.** *Ibid.,* 267. **18.** Quincy to ——, December 7, 1774. *Ibid.,* 256. **19.** *Ibid.,* 259. **20.** Quincy to ——, December 14, 1774. *Ibid.,* 266. **21.** Quincy to Mrs. Quincy, January 7, 1775. *Ibid.,* 295. **22.** Benjamin Rush to Arthur Lee, May 4, 1774. Lee, *Life of Arthur Lee,* I, 36. **23.** Quincy to Mrs. Quincy, November 27, 1774. Quincy, *Memoir,* 250. **24.** *The Writings of Benjamin Franklin* (ed. Albert H. Smyth, 10 vols., New York, 1905–1907), V, 311–312.

CHAPTER VII

1. *Journals of the Continental Congress,* II, 97. **2.** Washington to Jonathan Trumbull, February 19, 1776. *Bicentennial.* IV, 340. (See Note 1, Chapter III.) **3.** Washington to John Augustine Washington, March 31, 1776. *Ibid.,* 450. **4.** Robert Mackenzie to Washington, September 13, 1774. Washington Papers, XV. **5.** Washington to Mackenzie, October 9, 1774. *Bicentennial,* III, 244–246. **6.** Burnett, *Letters,* I, 132 *n.* **7.** John Adams to Mrs. Adams, June 17, 1775. *Ibid.,* 130–131. **8.** Samuel Adams to R. H. Lee. *The Writings of Samuel Adams* (ed. H. A. Cushing, 4 vols., New York, 1904–1908), III, 297. **9.** Samuel Adams to Gates, June 10, 1776. *Ibid.,* 292–293. **10.** *Ibid.* **11.** Washington to R. H. Lee, October 29, 1775. *Bicentennial,* IV, 52. **12.** R. H. Lee to Washington, August 1, 1775. *American Archives,* 4th Series, III, 1. **13.** *Letters of Richard Henry Lee* (ed. James C. Ballagh, 2 vols., New York, 1911), I, 150. **14.** Landon Carter to Washington, May 9, 1776. Washington Papers, XXVI. **15.** Silas Deane to Mrs. Deane. *Deane Papers,* I, 59. **16.** Hancock to Washington, July 10, 1775. *Bicentennial,*

III, 353 *n.* **17.** Washington to Hancock, July 21, 1775. *Ibid.,* 353. **18.** Washington to R. H. Lee, August 29, 1775. *Ibid.,* 450. **19.** Robert Morris to Joseph Reed, July 20, 1776. Reed, *Life of Reed,* I, 202. **20.** John Adams, *Works,* II, 360. Diary entry for August 31, 1774. **21.** Samuel Adams to James Warren, October 3, 1775. Burnett, *Letters,* I, 214. **22.** Lynch to Washington, December 8, 1775. Washington Papers, XXI. **23.** Lynch to Washington, November 13, 1775. *Ibid.,* XX. **24.** *Ibid.* **25.** Lynch to Washington, December 8, 1775. *Ibid.,* XXI. **26.** Lynch to Washington, January 16, 1776. *Ibid.,* XXII. **27.** Washington to Reed, January 23, 1776. *Bicentennial,* IV, 268. **28.** John Adams, *Works,* III, 31. **29.** *Ibid.,* 362–363. Diary entries for September 2, 3, 1774. **30.** Charles Lee to Benjamin Rush. *The Lee Papers* (*Collections,* New York Historical Society, 4 vols., New York, 1872–1875), I, 213–214. **31.** Washington to Josiah Quincy, March 24, 1776. *Bicentennial,* IV, 421–422. **32.** Washington to John Augustine Washington, March 31, 1776. *Ibid.,* 450. **33.** Washington to Massachusetts Legislature, March 1776. *Ibid.,* 441. **34.** Washington to Wooster, September 2, 1775. *Ibid.,* III, 466. **35.** Washington to Reed, December 15, 1775. *Ibid.,* IV, 165. **36.** Washington to Reed, March 3, 1776. *Ibid.,* 367. **37.** Gates to Washington, June 22, 1775. Washington Papers, XVI. **38.** *Journals of the Continental Congress,* III, 488, quoting John Adams, Notes of Debates. **39.** Washington to Schuyler, June 25, 1775. *Bicentennial,* III, 303. **40.** Lee to Washington, January 5, 1776. Washington Papers, XXII.

CHAPTER VIII

1. *Bicentennial,* IV, 179. (See Note 1, Chapter III.) **2.** Schuyler to Washington, January 5, 1776. Washington Papers, XXII. **3.** *Journals of the Continental Congress,* II, 16. **4.** New York Provincial Congress to Washington, June 26, 1775. Washington Papers, XVI. **5.** Schuyler to Washington, June 15, 1776. *Ibid.,* XXVIII. **6.** Schuyler to Washington, November 5, 1775. *Ibid.,* XX. **7.** Schuyler to Washington, June 15, 1776. *Ibid.,* XXVIII. 8. Francis V. Greene, *General Greene* (New York, 1893), 20. **9.** *Ibid.,* 24. **10.** William Heath, *Memoirs* (Boston, 1798), 9. **11.** Charles Martyn, *Life of Artemas Ward* (New York, 1921), 182. **12.** *Ibid.,* 83. **13.** Reed to Washington, March 15, 1776. Washington Papers, XXIV. **14.** Hutchinson, *Diary,* I, 298. **15.** Gage to Dartmouth, December 15, 1774. Library of Congress Transcripts, P.R.O., C.O. 5:92, 49. **16.** *Ibid.* **17.** Jared Sparks, *Life of Charles Lee* (Boston, 1846), 71. **18.** John Adams to Gerry, June 18, 1775. Burnett, *Letters,* I, 136. **19.** George Cuthbert to General John Dalling, *Pennsylvania Magazine of History and Biography,* LXVI (April 1942), 209. **20.** Washington to

John Augustine Washington, March 31, 1776. *Bicentennial,* IV, 451. **21.** Printed in *Lee Papers,* I, 151–166. **22.** *Ibid.*, 161. **23.** *Ibid.*, 162. **24.** *Ibid.* **25.** *Ibid.*, 157. **26.** *Ibid.*, 163. **27.** *Ibid.*, 158. **28.** *Ibid.*, 155 *n.* **29.** Gates to Charles Lee, July 1, 1774. *Ibid.*, 124. **30.** Samuel W. Patterson, *Horatio Gates* (New York, 1941), 30. **31.** Gates to Charles Lee, July 1, 1774. *Lee Papers,* I, 123. **32.** *Ibid.*, 125. **33.** *Ibid.* **34.** John Adams to Gerry, June 18, 1775. Burnett, *Letters,* I, 136. **35.** Washington to Gage, August 11, 1775. *Bicentennial,* III, 416–417. **36.** Gage to Washington, August 13, 1775. *Ibid.*, 417–418 *n.* **37.** Washington to Gage, August 19, 1775. *Ibid.*, 430–431. **38.** Gage to Dartmouth, May 15, 1775, Library of Congress Transcripts, P.R.O., C.O. 5:92, 173. **39.** Schuyler to Washington, July 18, 1775. Washington Papers, XVI. **40.** Fairfax Independent Company to Washington, July 8, 1775. *Ibid.* **41.** Lund Washington to Washington, January 31, 1776. *Bicentennial,* IV, 446 *n.* **42.** Portsmouth Committee to Washington, July 17, 1775. Washington Papers, XVI. **43.** Freeholders of Stoughtonham to Washington, March 11, 1776. *Ibid.*, XXIV. **44.** Washington to Congress, April 18, 1776. *Bicentennial,* IV, 489.

CHAPTER IX

1. *Bicentennial,* IV, 4–5. (See Note 1, Chapter III.) **2.** Reed to Pettit, August 7, 1775. Reed, *Life of Reed,* I, 118. **3.** *Bicentennial,* III, 418 *n.* **4.** Gage to Dartmouth, August 20, 1775. Library of Congress Transcripts, P.R.O., C.O. 5:92, 299. **5.** Washington to Schuyler, November 5, 1775. *Bicentennial,* IV, 65. **6.** Washington to Arnold, January 27, 1776. *Ibid.*, 282. **7.** *Journals of the Continental Congress,* II, 109–110. **8.** Schuyler to Washington, July 31, 1775. *American Archives,* 4th Series, II, 1762. **9.** *Ibid.* **10.** Schuyler to Washington, August 27, 1775. *Ibid.*, III, 447. **11.** Washington to Schuyler, August 20, 1775. *Bicentennial,* III, 282. **12.** *Ibid.* **13.** *Ibid.*, 479. **14.** Washington to Congress, September 21, 1775. *Ibid.*, 510. **15.** *Ibid.* **16.** Washington to Congress, January 19, 1776. *Ibid.*, IV, 259–260. **17.** Washington to Reed, January 23, 1776. *Ibid.*, 370. **18.** Washington to Schuyler, January 27, 1776. *Ibid.*, 279. **19.** Washington Papers, XVI, June 2, 1775. **20.** Washington to Congress, September 21, 1775. *Bicentennial,* III, 505. **21.** Lynch to Washington, November 13, 1775. Burnett, *Letters,* I, 253. **22.** *Journals of the Continental Congress,* III, 331. **23.** Proceedings of Council of War, October 4, 1775. Washington Papers, XIX. **24.** *Ibid.* **25.** Resolve of Massachusetts, November 11, 12, 1775. *Ibid.*, XX. **26.** Dartmouth to Gage, August 2, 1775. Library of Congress Transcripts, P.R.O., C.O. 5:92, 229. **27.** *American Archives,* 4th Series, III, 240–241. **28.** Dartmouth to Lords of Admiralty, August 29, 1775. Library of Congress Transcripts, P.R.O., C.O. 5:122, 5. **29.** Dartmouth to Gage, September 22, 1775. *Ibid.,* C.O. 5:92, 303. **30.** Germain to Clinton, December 6, 1775. *Ibid.,* 463–465. **31.** Washington to Gage, August 19, 1775. *Bicentennial,* III, 431. **32.** *Journals of the Continental Congress,* III, 412. **33.** *Ibid.* **34.** R. H. Lee to Washington, October 22, 1775. Washington Papers, XIX. **35.** *Bicentennial,* IV, 44. **36.** Washington to William Ramsay, November 1775. *Ibid.,* 113–114. **37.** Washington to Reed, November 20, 1775. *Ibid.,* 106. **38.** Lee to John Adams, October 5, 1775. *Lee Papers,* I, 210. **39.** Lee to Rush, October 20, 1775. *Ibid.,* 213. **40.** *Ibid.* **41.** *Ibid.,* 214. **42.** Greene, *General Greene,* 30–31. **43.** *Letters and Papers of Major-General John Sullivan* (ed. Otis G. Hammond, *Collections,* New Hampshire Historical Society, 3 vols., Concord, 1930–1934), I, 152–153. **44.** *Ibid.* **45.** Washington to Schuyler, November 5, 1775. *Bicentennial,* IV, 66. **46.** John Adams, *Works,* III, 6. **47.** *Ibid.* **48.** *Journals of the Continental Congress,* II, 96. **49.** *Ibid.,* III, 293. **50.** Minutes of Army Conference, October 23, 1775. Washington Papers, XIX. **51.** *Journals of the Continental Congress,* III, 375. **52.** Joseph Hewes to Samuel Johnston, January 6, 1776. Burnett, *Letters,* I, 301. **53.** Lynch to Washington, January 16, 1776. Washington Papers, XXII. **54.** Drummond to Robertson, February 5, 1776. *Ibid.,* XXIII. **55.** Washington to Congress, February 14, 1776. *Bicentennial,* IV, 330–331. **56.** Hancock to Washington, March 6, 1776. Washington Papers, XXIV.

CHAPTER X

1. *Bicentennial,* IV, 266. (See Note 1, Chapter III.) **2.** John Adams to Warren, April 16, 1776. Burnett, *Letters,* I, 424. **3.** *Journals of the Continental Congress,* II, 65. **4.** John Adams to Hawley, November 25, 1775. Burnett, *Letters,* I, 259–260. **5.** *Journals of the Continental Congress,* II, 77. **6.** *Ibid.,* 83–84. **7.** Mowat to the people of Falmouth, October 16, 1775. Washington Papers, XV. **8.** Howe to Dartmouth, October 18, 1775. Library of Congress Transcripts, P.R.O., C.O. 5:92, 397. **9.** Washington to Congress, October 24, 1775. *Bicentennial,* IV, 41. **10.** *Journals of the Continental Congress,* III, 319. **11.** J. Bartlett and J. Langdon to M. Thornton, November 3, 1775. Burnett, *Letters,* I, 246. **12.** Gates to Sullivan, October 23, 1775. *Sullivan Papers,* I, 113. **13.** Resolve of October 27, 1775. *Ibid.,* 116. **14.** Sullivan to Washington, October 29, 1775. Washington Papers, XX. **15.** Washington to Sullivan, November 5, 1775. *Bicentennial,* IV, 67–68. **16.** Instructions to Sullivan, November 7, 1775. *Ibid.,* 70–71. **17.** Resolve of New Hampshire Provincial Congress, November 16, 1775. Washington Papers, XX. **18.** Jeremy Belknap, *The History of New Hampshire* (2 vols., Boston, 1791), II, 402. **19.** Weare to Washington, January 20, 1775. Washington Papers, XXII. **20.** Weare to Washington, March 12, 1776. *Ibid.*, XXIV. **21.** Copy of instructions to Trumbull, November 12, 1775. *Ibid.*, XX. **22.** Washington to Trumbull, November 15, 1775. *Bicentennial,* IV, 90. **23.** Copy of act sent by Trumbull to Washington, January 1, 1776. Washington Papers, XXII. **24.** Washington to Cooke, January 6, 1776. *Bicentennial,* IV, 216–217. **25.** Trumbull to Washington, January 18, 1776. Washington Papers, XXII. **26.** *American Archives,* 4th Series, III, 231. **27.** Cooke to Washington, September 14, 1775. Washington Papers, XVIII. **28.** Greene to Cooke, October 24, 1775. *American Archives,* 4th Series, III, 1168. **29.** *Ibid.*, 1376. **30.** *Ibid.* **31.** Cooke to Washington, November 27, 1775. Washington Papers, XXI. **32.** Washington to Congress, December 25, 1775. *Bicentennial,* IV, 183. **33.** Charles Lee to Robert Morris, January 3, 1776. *Lee Papers,* I, 233. **34.** Lee to Congress, January 22, 1776. Washington Papers, XXII. **35.** Copy of oath, December 25, 1775. Washington Papers, XXII. **36.** Lee to Congress, January 22, 1776. *Ibid.* **37.** Washington to Congress, December 31, 1775. *Bicentennial,* IV, 197. **38.** Harrison to Washington, July 21, 1775. Burnett, *Letters,* I, 170. **39.** John Adams to Hawley, November 25, 1775. *Ibid.*, 260. **40.** Samuel Adams to Gerry, June 22, 1775. James T. Austin, *The Life of Elbridge Gerry* (2 vols., Boston, 1828, 1829), I, 90–91. **41.** Gerry to Samuel Adams, December 13, 1775. *Ibid.*, 123. **42.** Minutes of Cambridge Conference, October 22, 1775. Washington Papers, XIX. **43.** Gerry to Samuel Adams, October 9, 1775. Austin, *Life of Gerry,* I, 116–117. **44.** Copy of act of November 10, 1775. *Ibid.*, 506. **45.** *Ibid.*, 96. **46.** Mrs. Mercy Warren, quoted in *ibid.*, 95. **47.** *Journals of the Continental Congress,* IV, 122.

CHAPTER XI

1. *Bicentennial,* IV, 367. (See Note 1, Chapter III.) **2.** Lee to Washington, January 5, 1775. Washington Papers, XXII. **3.** *Ibid.* **4.** John Adams to Washington, January 6, 1776. *Ibid.* **5.** *Ibid.* **6.** Washington to Trumbull, January 7, 1776. *Bicentennial,* IV, 219. **7.** Washington to Lee, January 8, 1775. *Ibid.*, 222. **8.** Lee to Robert Morris, January 3, 1776. *Lee Papers,* I, 233. **9.** Washington to William Ramsay, December 1775. *Bicentennial,* IV, 201; Washington to Lee, January 8, 1776. *Ibid.*, 223. **10.** Lee to Washington, February 14, 1776. *Lee Papers,* I, 296–297. **11.** Washington to New York Committee of Safety, January 8, 1776. *Bicentennial,* IV, 221. **12.** New York Committee of Safety to Lee, January 21, 1776. Washington Papers, XXII. **13.** Lee to Congress, January 22, 1776. *Ibid.* **14.** Lee to Robert Morris, January 23, 1776. *Lee Papers,* I, 255–256. **15.** Lee to New York Committee of Safety, January 23, 1776. Washington Papers, XXIII. **16.** Lee to Washington, January 24, 1776. *Ibid.* **17.** Thomas Nelson to Jefferson, February 4, 1776. Burnett, *Letters,* I, 339. **18.** Hancock to Lee, January 26, 1776. Washington Papers, XXIII. **19.** Lee to Washington, February 5, 1776. *Ibid.* **20.** Sears to Lee, March 17, 1776. *Lee Papers,* I, 359. **21.** Lee to Washington, February 14, 1776. *Ibid.,* I, 296. **22.** Reed to Washington, March 15, 1776. Washington Papers, XXIV. **23.** Lynch to Washington, February 5, 1776. *Ibid.,* XXIII. **24.** *Journals of the Continental Congress,* IV, 195. **25.** Lee to Hancock, March 21, 1776. *Lee Papers,* I, 360–361. **26.** Washington to Lee, January 23, 1776. *Bicentennial,* IV, 266. **27.** *Ibid.* **28.** Hancock to Washington, January 29, 1776. Washington Papers, XXIII. **29.** Washington to Lee, January 30, 1776. *Bicentennial,* IV, 291–292. **30.** Lee to Washington, February 29, 1776. Washington Papers, XXIV. **31.** *Bicentennial,* IV, 367.

CHAPTER XII

1. Reed, *Life of Reed,* I, 183. **2.** Moylan to Reed, January 2, 1776. *Ibid.,* 139. **3.** Washington to Congress, January 4, 1776. *Bicentennial,* IV, 209–210. **4.** Washington to Reed, January 14, 1776. *Ibid.,* 244. **5.** Washington to Reed, January 23, 1776. *Ibid.,* 271. **6.** Moylan to Reed, January 30, 1776. Reed, *Life of Reed,* I, 160. **7.** Washington to Reed, January 31, 1776. *Bicentennial,* IV, 297. **8.** Washington to Reed, February 10, 1776. *Ibid.,* 321. **9.** *American Archives,* 4th Series, V, 1667. **10.** *Ibid.* **11.** Reed to Pettit, March 1776. Reed, *Life of Reed,* I, 182. **12.** William Hooper to Joseph Trumbull, [March] 13, 1776. Burnett, *Letters,* I, 387. **13.** Washington to Reed, March 7, 1776. *Bicentennial,* IV, 383. **14.** *Ibid.* **15.** Washington to Reed, April 1, 1776. *Ibid.,* IV, 454. **16.** Washington to J. A. Washington, March 31, 1776. *Ibid.,* 451. **17.** Reed to Washington, March 15, 1776. Washington Papers, XXIV. **18.** Washington to Congress, March 24, 1776. *Bicentennial,* IV, 427–428. **19.** Washington Papers, XXVI, May 6, 1776. **20.** John Adams to James Warren, October 7, 1775. Burnett, *Letters,* I, 219. **21.** *Journals of the Continental Congress,* III, 392. **22.** Washington to Congress, December 14, 1775. *Bicentennial,* IV, 163. **23.** Penet and Pliarne to Washington, December 1775. Washington Papers, XXII. **24.** Diary of Richard Smith, January 9, 1776. Burnett, *Letters,* I, 304. **25.** Pliarne to Washington, *ca.* January 11, 1776. Washington Papers, XXIII. **26.** Washington to Reed, January 14, 1776. *Bicen-*

tennial, IV, 243. **27.** *Journals of the Continental Congress,* IV, 96. **28.** Committee of Secret Correspondence to Deane, March 3, 1776. Burnett, *Letters,* I, 377. **29.** Moylan to Reed, January 2, 1776. Reed, *Life of Reed,* I, 139. **30.** Schuyler to Washington, March 27, 1776. Washington Papers, XXIV. **31.** Reed to Washington, March 15, 1776. *Ibid.* **32.** Washington to Congress, November 11, 1775. *Bicentennial,* IV, 82. **33.** *Journals of the Continental Congress,* IV, 258.

CHAPTER XIII

1. *Bicentennial,* IV, 167. **2.** Samuel Adams to James Warren, December [5], 1775. Burnett, *Letters,* I, 270. **3.** *Journals of the Continental Congress,* III, 430–434. **4.** Washington Papers, XV, July 18, 1774. **5.** *Journals of the Continental Congress,* IV, 229. **6.** Washington to Congress, December 14, 1775. *Bicentennial,* IV, 161. **7.** Washington to Reed, December 15, 1775. *Ibid.,* 167. **8.** Washington to Congress, December 18, 1775. *Ibid.,* 172. **9.** Washington to R. H. Lee, December 26, 1775. *Ibid.,* 186. **10.** Charles Lee to R. H. Lee, December 18, 1775. *Lee Papers,* I, 232. **11.** Charles Lee to R. H. Lee, December 12, 1775. *Ibid.,* 229. **12.** Ballagh, *Letters of Richard Henry Lee,* I, 168. **13.** Charles Lee to R. H. Lee, December 12, 1775. *Lee Papers,* I, 228. **14.** Charles Lee to Robert Morris, January 30, 1776. *Ibid.,* 267. **15.** Charles Lee to Robert Morris, February 21, 1776. *Ibid.,* 318. **16.** Reed to Washington, March 15, 1776. Washington Papers, XXIV. **17.** Washington to Reed, March 7, 1776. *Bicentennial,* IV, 381. **18.** Washington to J. A. Washington, March 31, 1776. *Ibid.,* 451–452.

CHAPTER XIV

1. Burnett, *Letters,* I, 429. **2.** Martin to Gage, May 26, 1775. Library of Congress Transcripts, P.R.O., C.O. 5:92, 247. **3.** Charles Lee to Edward Rutledge, April 3, 1776. *Lee Papers,* I, 272–273. **4.** Robert Howe to Charles Lee, April 14, 1776. *Ibid.,* 420. **5.** Charles Lee to Armstrong, April 10, 1776. *Ibid.,* 410. **6.** Robert Howe to Charles Lee, April 10, 1776. *Ibid.,* 400. **7.** *American Archives,* 4th Series, V, 1322. **8.** *Ibid.,* 1323. **9.** Burke to Charles Lee, April 22, 1776. *Lee Papers,* I, 439. **10.** Charles Lee to Committee of Secrecy of North Carolina, April 13, 1776. *Ibid.,* 418. **11.** Charles Lee to R. H. Lee, December 12, 1775. *Ibid.,* 229. **12.** Charles Lee to Congress, April 19, 1776. *Ibid.,* 433. **13.** Charles Lee to Armstrong, April 10, 1776. *Ibid.,* 410. **14.** William Moultrie, *Memoirs of the American Revolution* (2 vols., New York, 1802), I, 141. **15.** *Journals of the Continental Congress,* III, 327. **16.** Gerry to James Warren, May 1, 1776. Burnett, *Letters,* I, 438. **17.** John Drayton,

Memoirs of the American Revolution (2 vols., Charleston, 1821), II, 189. **18.** *Ibid.,* 179. **19.** *Ibid.,* 254. **20.** Lachlan McIntosh to Washington, February 16, 1776. Washington Papers, XXIII. **21.** *The Literary Diary of Ezra Stiles* (ed. Franklin B. Dexter, 3 vols., New York, 1901), II, 10. **22.** Wright to Dartmouth, December 13, 1774. *Parliamentary Register,* I, 99. **23.** *Journals of the Continental Congress,* III, 325. **24.** McIntosh to Washington, February 16, 1776. Washington Papers, XXIII. **25.** *Journals of the Continental Congress,* IV, 367 *n.* **26.** Charles Lee to Robert Howe, April 5, 1776. *Lee Papers,* I, 375; Lee to Washington, April 5, 1776. *Ibid.,* 377. **27.** Lee to Congress, May 10, 1776. *Ibid.,* II, 17. **28.** Randolph to Washington, September 6, 1775. Washington Papers, XVIII. **29.** Washington to J. A. Washington, March 31, 1776. *Bicentennial,* IV, 451. **30.** Virginia Officers to Charles Lee, March 30, 1776. *Lee Papers,* I, 364. **31.** Washington to J. A. Washington, March 31, 1776. *Bicentennial,* IV, 451. **32.** Virginia Officers to Charles Lee, March 30, 1776. *Lee Papers,* I, 364. **33.** Charles Lee to Washington, May 10, 1776. Washington Papers, XXVI. **34.** Fielding Lewis to Washington, March 6, 1776. *Ibid.,* XXIV. **35.** *American Archives,* 4th Series, VI, 1524. **36.** William Wirt, *Patrick Henry* (Philadelphia, 1818), 195.

CHAPTER XV

1. *Bicentennial,* IV, 454–455. **2.** *Journals of the Continental Congress,* IV, 357–358. **3.** Washington to Congress, May 5, 1776. *Bicentennial,* V, 20. **4.** *American Archives,* 4th Series, V, 1215–1217. **5.** Cooke to Washington, April 23, 1776. Washington Papers, XXV. **6.** Washington to Cooke, April 28, 1776. *Bicentennial,* IV, 528. **7.** Washington to Congress, April 30, 1776. *Ibid.,* 539. **8.** *Journals of the Continental Congress,* IV, 347. **9.** Stephen Hopkins to Cooke, May 15, 1776. Burnett, *Letters,* I, 447. **10.** *Journals of the Continental Congress,* IV, 353. **11.** Washington to Reed, April 1, 1776. *Bicentennial,* IV, 454–455. **12.** Washington to Reed, April 23, 1776. *Ibid.,* 507. **13.** *Pennsylvania Evening Post,* June 6, 1776, 283. **14.** *Journals of the Continental Congress,* IV, 400–401. **15.** Marshall, *Diary,* 83. **16.** Washington to J. A. Washington, May 31, 1776. *Bicentennial,* V, 92. **17.** Washington to Congress, June 10, 1776. *Ibid.,* 121. **18.** Hancock to provincial assemblies, June 4, 1776. Washington Papers, XXVIII. **19.** Diary of James Allen, May 15, 1776. Quoted in J. Paul Selsam, *The Pennsylvania Constitution of 1776* (Philadelphia, 1936), 115. **20.** *Pennsylvania Evening Post,* May 21, 1776, 255. **21.** *Ibid.,* June 8, 1776, 287–288. **22.** Washington to Reed. *Bicentennial,* IV, 483. **23.** *American Archives,* 4th Series, VI, 963. **24.** William T. Read, *Life and Correspondence of George Read* (Philadelphia, 1870), 149. **25.** *American Archives,* 4th Series, VI, 884. **26.** *Ibid.,* 1491.

CHAPTER XVI

1. *Bicentennial,* IV, 483. **2.** Washington to R. H. Lee, May 18, 1776. *Ibid.,* V, 57. **3.** Facsimile in *American Archives,* 4th Series, VI, 1699. **4.** New York Delegates to New York Convention, June 8, 1776. Burnett, *Letters,* I, 477. **5.** Gerry to Warren, June 25, 1776. *Ibid.,* 508. **6.** Resolve of April 18, 1776. Copy in Washington Papers, XXV. **7.** Washington to New York Committee of Safety, April 17, 1776. *Bicentennial,* V, 486–488. **8.** New York Committee of Safety to Washington, April 18, 1776. Washington Papers, XXV. **9.** New York Committee of Safety Resolve of April 18, 1776. *Ibid.* **10.** Tupper to Washington, May 16, 1776. *Ibid.,* XXVI. **11.** New York Committee of Safety to Washington, April 25, 1776. *Ibid.,* XXV. **12.** Resolve of May 18, 1776. Copy in Washington Papers, XXVI. **13.** *American Archives,* 4th Series, VI, 1352. **14.** *Ibid.,* 1363. **15.** Resolve of June 8, 1776. Copy in Washington Papers, XXVIII. **16.** *American Archives,* 4th Series, VI, 1395. **17.** Benedict Arnold to Schuyler, May 10, 1776. Washington Papers, XXVI. **18.** Washington to Schuyler, May 17, 1776. *Bicentennial,* V, 52. **19.** James Wilkinson to Greene, May 24, 1776. Papers of Continental Congress, 169, I, 352. **20.** Washington to Suffolk Committee, May 16, 1776. *Bicentennial,* V, 46–47. **21.** Washington to Congress, June 10, 1776. *Ibid.,* 122. **22.** *American Archives,* 4th Series, VI, 1412. **23.** *Ibid.,* 1410. **24.** *Journals of the Continental Congress,* V, 475–476. Copies in Washington Papers, XXIX, June 24, 1776. **25.** Gerry to Gates, June 25, 1776. Burnett, *Letters,* I, 506. **26.** Hancock to Washington, June 25, 1776. Washington Papers, XXIX. **27.** Washington to Congress, June 30, 1776. *Bicentennial,* V, 203. **28.** R. H. Lee to Landon Carter, June 2, 1776. Burnett, *Letters,* I, 469. **29.** Resolve of June 30, 1776. Copy in Washington Papers, XXIX. **30.** *Journals of the Continental Congress,* V, 560.

Acknowledgments and Bibliography

For the period covered by this study the essential materials available are more extensive than for any other comparable period in American history. First, there is the massive collection of the Fourth Series of the *American Archives,* edited by Peter Force (6 vols., Washington, 1837–1846). If the documents in this great work were printed today, in ordinary volumes, they would fill about twenty-five thousand pages. The series is especially useful because it brings together the proceedings of various colonial assemblies and congresses. A second major source is the thirty-four volume collection of the *Journals of the Continental Congress,* edited by Worthington C. Ford and others (Washington, 1904–1937). These volumes are made more usable than formerly by another outstanding work, Edmund C. Burnett's *Letters of Members of the Continental Congress* (8 vols., Washington, 1921–1936). This collection contains full citations to the texts used by Dr. Burnett, so that one may consult the originals in order to obtain much important information which the limits of the work required that he omit. The collection is also valuable for the data it presents concerning the members of Congress, with respect to attendance, elections, and participation. The Division of Manuscripts of the Library of Congress contains three collections that were used extensively: the Papers of the Continental Congress, the transcripts of American documents in the British Public Record Office in London, and the Washington Papers. The last collection consists of the papers received by Washington and copies of some of the most important letters he wrote. Finally, there is the monumental edition by John C. Fitzpatrick of *The Writings of George Washington* (39 vols., Washington, 1931–1944). It is the writer's belief that the present volume offers the first treatment of Washington's relation to American independence as revealed by a study of these seven great collections of original material. Only one newspaper has been used systematically—the *Pennsylvania Evening Post.* It was published by Washington's collaborators in Philadelphia at this time.

The writer wishes to acknowledge his gratitude for the privilege of using a large part of the extensive printed materials which were collected by Jared Sparks and which are now in the Cornell University

Library. Much of the early work on the book was done in the collections of the State Historical Society of Wisconsin. The New York Public Library and the Massachusetts Historical Society offered assistance in connection with one of the most essential parts of the study. To the officials of these libraries and to their assistants the writer is deeply grateful. To three scholars who have investigated Washington's career, Bernhard Knollenberg, Charles H. Ambler, and Louis M. Sears, the writer is indebted for the opportunity of discussing various aspects of the theme of this study. Three theses prepared in the Graduate School of Cornell University have been helpful: Allan J. McCurry, "The Struggle for Independence: A Study of Party Divisions within the Second Continental Congress"; Winnifred Poland Pierce, "General Washington and the Problem of Provincial New York"; and Rose Engelman, "Washington and Hamilton: A Study in the Development of Washington's Political Ideas."

The following lists do not intend to give a complete bibliography of all the writings on the period treated in this book. Citations are made only to those works which have supplied material which has been incorporated into the text.

I SOURCES

1. *General:*

William Cobbett (ed.), *Parliamentary History of England* (36 vols., T. C. Hansard, London, 1806–1820). Frank Moore (ed.), *Diary of the Revolution* (New York, 1863). Samuel E. Morison (ed.), *Sources and Documents illustrating the American Revolution* (Oxford, 1929). Hezekiah Niles (ed.), *Principles and Acts of the American Revolution* (Baltimore, 1823). Benjamin F. Stevens (ed.), *Facsimiles of Manuscripts in European Archives relating to America, 1773–1783* (24 portfolios, London, 1889–1895). H. W. V. Temperley (ed.), "Debates on the Declaratory Act," *American Historical Review,* XVII (April 1912). Francis Wharton (ed.), *The Revolutionary Diplomatic Correspondence of the United States* (6 vols., Washington, 1889). *The Parliamentary Register, 1775–1776* (3 vols., London, 1775–1776).

2. *Papers, Writings, Letters:*

Charles Francis Adams (ed.), *Familiar Letters of John Adams and His Wife Abigail Adams during the Revolution* (New York, 1876). Charles Francis Adams (ed.), *The Works of John Adams . . . with a Life of the Author* (10 vols., Boston, 1850–1856). Harry A. Cushing (ed.), *The Writings of Samuel Adams* (4 vols., New York, 1904–1908). *Warren-Adams Letters* (*Collections,* Massachusetts Historical Society, 2 vols., Boston, 1917, 1925). Edward Channing and A. C. Coolidge (eds.), *The Barrington-Bernard Correspondence* (Cambridge, Massachusetts, 1912). *Correspondence of John Fourth Duke of Bedford* (3 vols., London, 1842–1846). *The Works and Correspondence of Edmund Burke* (8 vols., London, 1852). Edmund Burke, *Thoughts on the Cause of the Present Discontents* (3rd ed., London, 1770). Bonamy Dobrée (ed.), *The Letters of Lord Chesterfield* (6 vols., London, 1932). *Public Papers of George Clinton* (10 vols., New York, 1899–1914). *The Letters and Papers of Cadwallader Colden* (*Collections,* New York Historical Society, 7 vols., New York, 1918–1923). *The Letter-Books of Cadwallader Colden* (*Collections,* New York Historical Society, 2 vols., New York, 1877–1878). *Letters of Thomas Cushing, 1767–1775* (*Collections,* Massachusetts Historical Society, Boston, 1858). Paul L. Ford (ed.), *The Writings of John Dickinson* (*Memoirs,* Historical Society of Pennsylvania, Philadelphia, 1895). J. H. Powell (ed.), "Speech of John Dickinson Opposing the Declaration of Independence," *Pennsylvania Magazine of History and Biography* (October 1941). *The Political Writings of John Dickinson* (2 vols., Wilmington, 1801). Verner W. Crane (ed.), *Benjamin Franklin's Letters to the Press, 1758–1775* (Chapel Hill, 1950). Israel Mauduit (ed.), *Franklin before the Privy Council, 1774* (Philadelphia, 1859). Albert H. Smyth (ed.), *The Writings of Benjamin Franklin* (10 vols., New York, 1905–1907). Clarence E. Carter (ed.), *The Correspondence of General Thomas Gage* (2 vols., New Haven, 1931, 1933). W. B. Donne (ed.), *The Correspondence of King George the Third with Lord North* (2 vols., London, 1867). Sir John Fortescue (ed.), *The Correspondence of King George the Third* (6 vols., London, 1927–1928). Romney Sedgwick (ed.), *Letters from George III to Lord Bute* (London, 1939). William J. Smith (ed.), *The Grenville Papers* (4 vols., 1852–1854). Stephen Hopkins, *The Grievances of the American Colonies Candidly Examined* (London, 1766). *The Letters of Governor Hutchinson and Lieut. Governor Oliver* (2nd ed., London, 1774). Henry P. Johnston (ed.), *The Correspondence and Public Papers of John Jay* (4 vols., New York, 1890–1893). Julian P. Boyd and others (eds.), *The Papers of Thomas Jefferson* (Vol. I, 1760–1776, Princeton, 1950). Paul L. Ford (ed.), *The Writings of Thomas Jefferson* (10 vols., New York, 1892–1900). Samuel Johnson, *Taxation no Tyranny* (3rd ed., London, 1775). "Letters of William Samuel Johnson," *Trumbull Papers* (*Collections,* Massachusetts Historical Society, Boston, 1885). *The Lee*

Papers (*Collections,* New York Historical Society, 4 vols., New York, 1872–1875). James C. Ballagh (ed.), *Letters of Richard Henry Lee* (2 vols., New York, 1911). Worthington C. Ford (ed.), *Letters of William Lee* (3 vols., Brooklyn, 1891). Philip Livingston, *The Other Side of the Question* (New York, 1774). S. V. Henkels, *The Confidential Correspondence of Robert Morris* (Philadelphia, 1917). Harry H. Clark (ed.), *Thomas Paine: Representative Selections* (New York, 1944). Charles K. Bolton (ed.), *Letters of Hugh Earl Percy* (Boston, 1902); *Correspondence of William Pitt, Earl of Chatham* (4 vols., London, 1838–1840). George T. Keppel, Earl of Albemarle, *Memoirs of the Marquis of Rockingham* (2 vols., London, 1852). George H. Ryden (ed.), *Letters to and from Caesar Rodney* (Philadelphia, 1913). G. R. Barnes and J. H. Owen (eds.), *The Private Papers of the Earl of Sandwich* (London, 1932). Otis G. Hammond (ed.), *Letters and Papers of Major-General John Sullivan* (*Collections,* New Hampshire Historical Society, 3 vols., Concord, 1930–1934). Peter Cunningham (ed.), *The Letters of Horace Walpole* (9 vols., London, 1891). Mrs. Paget Toynbee (ed.), *The Letters of Horace Walpole* (16 vols., Oxford, 1904). Worthington C. Ford (ed.), *The Writings of George Washington* (14 vols., New York, 1889–1893). Grace L. Nute (ed.), "Washington and the Potomac," *American Historical Review,* XXVIII (April 1923); Jared Sparks (ed.), *The Writings of George Washington* (12 vols., Boston, 1834–1837). John Almon (ed.), *The Correspondence of John Wilkes* (5 vols., London, 1805). Randolph G. Adams (ed.), *Selected Writings of James Wilson* (New York, 1930). Richard Frothingham (ed.), "Letters illustrating the Siege of Boston" (*Proceedings,* Massachusetts Historical Society, Boston, 1876). "Intercepted Letters of Virginia Tories, 1775," *American Historical Review,* XII (January 1907).

3. *Diaries, Journals, Memoirs, Autobiographies:*

George A. Ward (ed.), *Journal and Letters of Samuel Curwen* (New York, 1842). "Journal of William Ellery," *Pennsylvania Magazine of History and Biography,* XIII. Max Farrand (ed.), *The Autobiography of Benjamin Franklin* (Berkeley, 1949). Joseph Galloway, *Historical and Political Reflections on the Rise and Progress of the American Rebellion* (London, 1780). Sir William R. Anson (ed.), *Autobiography of Augustus Henry Third Duke of Grafton* (London, 1908). William Heath, *Memoirs* (Boston, 1798). Peter O. Hutchinson (ed.), *The Diary and Letters of Thomas Hutchinson* (2 vols., Boston, 1884, 1886). *Memoirs of the Life of Charles Lee* (Dublin,

1792). *Diary of Frederick Mackenzie* (2 vols., Cambridge, Massachusetts, 1930). William Duane, Jr. (ed.), *Passages from the Remembrancer of Christopher Marshall* (Philadelphia, 1839). William Moultrie, *Memoirs of the American Revolution* (2 vols., New York, 1802). Franklin B. Dexter (ed.), *The Literary Diary of Ezra Stiles* (3 vols., New York, 1901). G. F. Russell Barker (ed.), Horace Walpole, *Memoirs of the Reign of George the Third* (4 vols., London, 1894). John C. Fitzpatrick (ed.), *The Diaries of George Washington* (4 vols., New York, 1925).

4. *Works Containing Numerous Documents:*

James T. Austin, *The Life of Elbridge Gerry* (2 vols., Boston, 1828, 1829). James Boswell, *The Life of Samuel Johnson* (2 vols., London, 1904). Julian P. Boyd, *The Declaration of Independence* (Princeton, 1945). Moncure D. Conway, *The Life of Thomas Paine* (2 vols., New York, 1892). John Drayton, *Memoirs of the American Revolution* (2 vols., Charleston, 1821). Lord Fitzmaurice, *Life of William, Earl of Shelburne* (3 vols., London, 1875–1876). William Wirt Henry, *Patrick Henry: Life, Correspondence, and Speeches* (3 vols., New York, 1891). John Holliday, *The Life of Mansfield* (London, 1797). Richard Henry Lee, *The Life of Arthur Lee* (2 vols., Boston, 1829). Richard Henry Lee, *Memoir of the Life of Richard Henry Lee* (Philadelphia, 1825). Josiah Quincy, *Memoir of the Life of Josiah Quincy, Junior* (Boston, 1825). William T. Read, *Life and Correspondence of George Read* (Philadelphia, 1870). William B. Reed, *Life and Correspondence of Joseph Reed* (2 vols., Philadelphia, 1847). Kate M. Rowland, *The Life of George Mason* (2 vols., New York, 1892). William R. Staples, *Rhode Island in the Continental Congress* (ed. R. A. Guild, Providence, 1870). John Wade (ed.), *Junius* (2 vols., London, 1868).

II SECONDARY WORKS

1. *General Histories:*

George Bancroft, *History of the United States* (6 vols., Boston, 1879). Henry Belcher, *The First American Civil War* (2 vols., London, 1911). Edward Channing, *A History of the United States* (6 vols., New York, 1905–1925). Richard Frothingham, *The Rise of the Republic of the United States* (Boston, 1910). Evarts B. Greene, *The Revolutionary Generation* (New York, 1943). William E. H. Lecky, *The American Revolution* (ed. J. A. Woodburn, New York, 1932). Mary Marks,

England and America, 1763 to 1783 (2 vols., New York, 1907). John C. Miller, *Origins of the American Revolution* (Boston, 1943). Sir George O. Trevelyan, *The American Revolution* (4 vols., New York, 1899–1907). Claude H. Van Tyne, *The American Revolution* (New York, 1905). Claude H. Van Tyne, *The Causes of the War of Independence* (Boston, 1922). Claude H. Van Tyne, *The War of Independence* (Boston, 1929). Justin Winsor (ed.), *Narrative and Critical History of America* (8 vols., Boston, 1884–1889).

2. *The English Background:*

John Adolphus, *The History of England from the Accession of George III* (3 vols., London, 1817). John R. Alden, "Why the March to Concord," *American Historical Review,* XLIX (April 1944). John Almon, *Anecdotes of the Life of William Pitt* (3rd ed., 3 vols., London, 1793). George L. Beer, *British Colonial Policy, 1754–1765* (New York, 1907). Horace Bleackley, *Life of John Wilkes* (London, 1917). A. H. Basye, "The Secretary of State for the Colonies," *American Historical Review,* XXVIII (October 1922). John Buchan, "Lord Mansfield," *Atlantic Monthly,* 88 (December 1901). John Lord Campbell, *The Lives of the Chief Justices of England* (2 vols., London, 1849). Dora M. Clark, *British Opinion and the American Revolution* (New Haven, 1930). Max Farrand, "The Taxation of Tea," *American Historical Review,* III (January 1898). Keith Feiling, *The Second Tory Party* (London, 1938). George H. Guttridge, *English Whiggism and the American Revolution* (Berkeley, 1942). George H. Guttridge, "Lord George Germain in Office," *American Historical Review,* XXXIII (October 1927). Fred J. Hinkhouse, *The Preliminaries of the American Revolution as Seen in the English Press, 1763–1775* (New York, 1926). R. A. Humphreys, "Lord Shelburne and British Colonial Policy, 1766–1768," *English Historical Review,* L (April 1935). W. M. James, *The British Navy in Adversity* (London, 1926). W. T. Laprade, "The Stamp Act in British Politics," *American Historical Review,* XXXV (July 1930). Earl J. Hamilton, "Profit Inflation and the Industrial Revolution," *Quarterly Journal of Economics,* LVI (February 1942). William E. H. Lecky, *History of England in the Eighteenth Century* (7 vols., London, 1892). Reginald Lucas, *Lord North* (2 vols., London, 1913). Lord Mahon, *History of England from the Peace of Utrecht* (7 vols., London, 1851–1854). Sir Thomas E. May, *The Constitutional History of England* (2 vols., New York, 1882). L. B. Namier, *England in the Age of the American Revolution* (London, 1930). L. B. Namier, *The Structure of Politics at the Accession of*

George III (2 vols., London, 1929). T. W. Riker, *Henry Fox* (2 vols., Oxford, 1911). Arthur M. Schlesinger, *The Colonial Merchants and the American Revolution* (New York, 1918). Arthur M. Schlesinger, "The Uprising against the East India Company," *Political Science Quarterly,* XXXII (March 1917). Carl Van Doren, *Benjamin Franklin* (New York, 1938). Basil Williams, *Life of William Pitt* (2 vols., London, 1913). D. A. Winstanley, *Lord Chatham and the Whig Opposition* (Cambridge, 1912). D. A. Winstanley, *Personal and Party Government* (Cambridge, 1910). M. C. Yarborough, *John Horne Tooke* (New York, 1926).

3. *Individual Colonies:*

Edith A. Bailey, *Influences toward Radicalism in Connecticut, 1754–1775* (Northampton, 1920). Richard J. Purcell, *Connecticut in Transition* (Washington, 1918). Otto Zeichner, *Connecticut's Years of Controversy, 1750–1776* (Chapel Hill, 1949). Charles A. Barker, *The Background of the Revolution in Maryland* (New Haven, 1940). Philip A. Crowl, *Maryland during and after the Revolution* (Baltimore, 1943). Newton D. Mereness, *Maryland as a Proprietary Province* (New York, 1901). John T. Scharf, *History of Maryland* (3 vols., Baltimore, 1879). Kate M. Rowland, *The Life of Charles Carroll* (2 vols., New York, 1898). Ellen S. Smith, *Charles Carroll of Carrollton* (Cambridge, 1942). Bernard C. Steiner, *Life . . . of Sir Robert Eden* (Baltimore, 1898). James T. Adams, *Revolutionary New England* (Boston, 1923). E. Francis Brown, *Joseph Hawley* (New York, 1931). Harry A. Cushing, *History of the Transition from Provincial to Commonwealth Government in Massachusetts* (New York, 1896). James K. Hosmer, *Life of Thomas Hutchinson* (Boston, 1896). Jeremy Belknap, *The History of New Hampshire* (2 vols., Boston, 1791). L. S. Mayo, *John Wentworth* (Cambridge, 1921). Richard F. Upton, *Revolutionary New Hampshire* (Hanover, 1936). Donald L. Kemmerer, *Path to Freedom* (Princeton, 1940). Leonard Lundin, *Cockpit of the Revolution* (Princeton, 1940). W. C. Abbott, *New York in the American Revolution* (New York, 1929). Carl L. Becker, *The History of Political Parties in the Province of New York, 1760–1776* (Madison, 1909). A. C. Flick, *Loyalism in New York during the American Revolution* (New York, 1902). Dixon Ryan Fox, *Yankees and Yorkers* (New York, 1940). Virginia D. Harrington, *The New York Merchant on the Eve of the Revolution* (New York, 1935). Irving Mark, *Agrarian Conflicts in New York* (New York, 1940). Herbert M. Morais, "Sons of Liberty in New York," in *The Era of the*

American Revolution (ed. Richard B. Morris, New York, 1939). Jared Sparks, *The Life of Gouverneur Morris* (Boston, 1822). H. C. Van Schacht, *Peter Van Schacht* (New York, 1842). M. G. Walker, "Sir John Johnson, Loyalist," *Mississippi Valley Historical Review,* III (December 1916). Robert O. DeMond, *The Loyalists in North Carolina during the Revolution* (Durham, 1940). G. J. McRea, *The Life and Correspondence of James Iredell* (New York, 1857). François Xavier Martin, *The History of North Carolina* (2 vols., New Orleans, 1829). Charles L. Raper, *North Carolina* (New York, 1904). A. S. Salley, Jr., "The Mecklenburg Declaration," *American Historical Review,* XIII (October 1907). E. W. Sikes, *The Transition of North Carolina from Colony to Commonwealth* (Baltimore, 1898). Harry M. Wagstaff, *State Rights and Political Parties in North Carolina, 1776–1861* (Baltimore, 1906). Carl and Jessica Bridenbaugh, *Rebels and Gentlemen* (New York, 1942). J. E. Gibson, "The Pennsylvania Provincial Conference of 1776," *Pennsylvania Magazine of History and Biography,* LVIII (October 1934). Nathan G. Goodman, *Benjamin Rush* (Philadelphia, 1934). Burton A. Konkle, *George Bryan and the Constitution of Pennsylvania* (Philadelphia, 1922). Charles H. Lincoln, *The Revolutionary Movement in Pennsylvania* (Philadelphia, 1901). J. Paul Selsam, *The Pennsylvania Constitution of 1776* (Philadelphia, 1936). J. Paul Selsam, "The Political Revolution in Pennsylvania in 1776," *Pennsylvania History,* I (July 1934). W. R. Smith, "Sectionalism in Pennsylvania during the Revolution," *Political Science Quarterly,* XXIV (June 1909). Jared Sparks, *Life of Joseph Reed* (Boston, 1846). Edward McCrady, *The History of South Carolina in the Revolution* (New York, 1901). David Ramsay, *History of the Revolution of South Carolina* (2 vols., Trenton, 1785). William A. Schaper, "Sectionalism and Representation in South Carolina," *Report,* American Historical Association (1900), I. Leila Sellers, *Charleston Business on the Eve of the American Revolution* (Chapel Hill, 1934). W. Roy Smith, *South Carolina as a Proprietary Province* (New York, 1903). David D. Wallace, *The Life of Henry Laurens* (New York, 1915). C. W. Alvord, "Virginia and the West," *Mississippi Valley Historical Review,* III (June 1916). Charles H. Ambler, *Sectionalism in Virginia* (Chicago, 1910). J. S. Bassett, "The Relation between the Virginia Planter and the London Merchant," *Report,* American Historical Association (1901), I. H. J. Eckenrode, *The Revolution in Virginia* (Boston, 1916). Helen Hill, *George Mason* (Cambridge, 1938). Hugh B. Grigsby, *The Virginia Convention of 1776* (Richmond, 1855). Isaac S. Harrell, *Loyalism in Virginia* (Philadelphia, 1926). James M.

Leake, *The Virginia Committee System and the American Revolution* (Baltimore, 1917). Charles L. Lingley, *The Transition in Virginia from Colony to Commonwealth* (New York, 1910). Justin Winsor, "Virginia and the Quebec Bill," *American Historical Review,* I (April 1896).

4. *Members of Congress, Biographical:*

Charles Francis Adams, *The Life of John Adams* (Boston, 1856). Catherine D. Bowen, *John Adams and the American Revolution* (Boston, 1950). Mellen Chamberlain, *John Adams* (Boston, 1898). R. V. Harlow, *Samuel Adams* (New York, 1923). John C. Miller, *Sam Adams* (Boston, 1936). William V. Wells, *The Life and Public Services of Samuel Adams* (3 vols., Boston, 1865). E. W. Spaulding, *His Excellency George Clinton* (New York, 1938). George L. Clark, *Silas Deane* (New York, 1913). Charles J. Stillé, *The Life and Times of John Dickinson* (Philadelphia, 1891). Edward P. Alexander, *James Duane* (New York, 1938). George C. Groce, Jr., "Eliphalet Dyer," in *The Era of the American Revolution* (ed. Richard B. Morris, New York, 1939). Carl L. Becker, *Benjamin Franklin* (Ithaca, 1946). Paul L. Ford, *The Many-Sided Franklin* (New York, 1899). O. M. Dickerson, "John Hancock," *Mississippi Valley Historical Review,* XXXII (March 1946). Moses C. Tyler, *Patrick Henry* (Boston, 1899). William Wirt, *Patrick Henry* (Philadelphia, 1818). William E. Foster, *Stephen Hopkins* (2 parts, Providence, 1884). Frank Monaghan, *John Jay* (New York, 1935). George Pellew, *John Jay* (Boston, 1899). Claude Bowers, *The Young Jefferson* (Boston, 1945). Marie Kimball, *Jefferson, the Road to Glory, 1743 to 1776* (New York, 1943). Anthony M. Lewis, "Jefferson's Summary View," *William and Mary Quarterly,* 3rd Series, V (January 1948). Dumas Malone, *Jefferson, the Virginian* (Boston, 1948). Edward S. Delaplaine, *The Life of Thomas Johnson* (New York, 1927). Burton J. Hendrick, *The Lees of Virginia* (Boston, 1935). Theodore Sedgwick, *A Memoir of the Life of William Livingston* (New York, 1833). William Rawle, "Sketch of the Life of Thomas Mifflin," *Memoirs,* Historical Society of Pennsylvania (Philadelphia, 1830). Ellis P. Oberholtzer, *Robert Morris* (New York, 1903). William G. Sumner, *Financier . . . of the Revolution* (2 vols., New York, 1891). Robert L. Hilldrup, *The Life and Times of Edmund Pendleton* (Chapel Hill, 1939). Richard Barry, *Mr. Rutledge* (New York, 1942). Roger S. Boardman, *Roger Sherman* (Philadelphia, 1938). Burton A. Konkle, *Thomas Willing* (Philadelphia, 1937). Burton A. Konkle, *James Wilson* (Philadelphia,

1907). Charles C. Jones, Jr., *Biographical Sketches of the Delegates from Georgia to the Continental Congress* (Boston, 1891).

5. *Special Themes, Political:*

Carl L. Becker, *The Declaration of Independence* (New York, 1922). Weldon A. Brown, *Empire or Independence* (University, Louisiana, 1941). Edmund C. Burnett, *The Continental Congress* (New York, 1941). Louise B. Dunbar, "The Royal Governors in the Middle and Southern Colonies on the eve of the Revolution," in *The Era of the American Revolution* (ed. Richard B. Morris, New York, 1939). Paul L. Ford, "The Association of the First Congress," *Political Science Quarterly,* VI (December 1891). Herbert Friedenwald, *The Declaration of Independence* (New York, 1904). John H. Hazelton, *The Declaration of Independence* (New York, 1906). Edward F. Humphreys, *Nationalism and Religion in America, 1774–1789* (Boston, 1924). Merrill Jensen, *The Articles of Confederation* (Madison, 1940). Leonard W. Labaree, *Conservatism in Early American History* (New York, 1948). Albert E. McKinley, *The Suffrage Franchise in the Thirteen Colonies* (Philadelphia, 1905). Margaret B. Macmillan, *The War Governors in the American Revolution* (New York, 1943). Frank H. Miller, "Legal Qualifications for Office in America," *Report,* American Historical Association (1899), I. Allan Nevins, *The American States during and after the Revolution* (New York, 1924). Moses C. Tyler, *Literary History of the American Revolution* (2 vols., New York, 1897). Carl Van Doren, *Secret History of the American Revolution* (New York, 1941).

6. *Special Themes, Diplomatic:*

Samuel F. Bemis, *The Diplomacy of the American Revolution* (New York, 1935). E. S. Corwin, "The French Objective in the American Revolution," *American Historical Review,* XXI (October 1915). E. S. Corwin, *French Policy and the American Alliance of 1778* (Princeton, 1916). James B. Perkins, *France in the American Revolution* (Boston, 1911). C. H. Van Tyne, "French Aid before the Alliance of 1778," *American Historical Review,* XXXI (October 1925). C. H. Van Tyne, "Influences Which Determined the French Government to Make the Treaty with America, 1778," *American Historical Review,* XXI (April 1916).

7. *Special Themes, Canada and the West:*

Thomas P. Abernethy, *Western Lands and the American Revolution* (New York, 1937). John R. Alden, *John Stuart and the Southern*

Frontier (Ann Arbor, 1944). Clarence W. Alvord, *The Mississippi Valley in British Politics* (2 vols., Cleveland, 1916). Kenneth P. Bailey, *The Ohio Company* (Glendale, California, 1939). Alfred L. Burt, *The Old Province of Quebec* (Minneapolis, 1933). Victor Coffin, *The Province of Quebec and the Early American Revolution* (Madison, 1896). Reginald Coupland, *The Quebec Act* (Oxford, 1925). Max Farrand, "The Indian Boundary Line," *American Historical Review,* X (July 1905). Charles L. Mowat, *East Florida as a British Province, 1763–1784* (Berkeley, 1943). George M. Wrong, *Canada and the American Revolution* (New York, 1935).

8. *Special Themes, Military:*

John R. Alden, *General Gage in America* (Baton Rouge, 1948). C. K. Bolton, *The Private Soldier under Washington* (New York, 1902). Allen Bowman, *The Morale of the American Revolutionary Army* (Washington, 1943). C. E. Carter, "The Office of Commander in Chief" in *The Era of the American Revolution* (ed. Richard B. Morris, New York, 1939). C. E. Carter, "The Significance of the Military Office in America, 1763–1775," *American Historical Review,* XXVIII (April 1923). Edward E. Curtis, *The Organization of the British Army in America* (New Haven, 1927). Allen French, *The Day of Concord and Lexington* (Boston, 1925). Allen French, *The First Year of the American Revolution* (Boston, 1934). Louis C. Hatch, *The Administration of the American Army* (New York, 1904). R. F. Seybolt, "A Note on the Casualties of April 19, and June 17, 1775," *New England Quarterly,* VI (July 1931). Justin H. Smith, *Our Struggle for the Fourteenth Colony* (2 vols., New York, 1907). Samuel W. Patterson, *Horatio Gates* (New York, 1941). Francis V. Greene, *General Greene* (New York, 1893). George W. Greene, *The Life of Nathanael Greene* (3 vols., New York, 1871). Jared Sparks, *Life of Charles Lee* (Boston, 1846). William F. Livingston, *Israel Putnam* (New York, 1901). Oliver W. B. Peabody, *Life of Israel Putnam* (Boston, 1837). Benson J. Lossing, *The Life and Times of Philip Schuyler* (2 vols., New York, 1872, 1873). Bayard Tuckerman, *Life of General Philip Schuyler* (New York, 1905). Oliver W. B. Peabody, *Life of John Sullivan* (Boston, 1844). Charles Martyn, *The Life of Artemas Ward* (New York, 1921).

9. *Washington:*

Charles H. Ambler, *George Washington and the West* (Chapel Hill, 1936). John C. Fitzpatrick, *George Washington Himself* (Indianapolis, 1933). Paul L. Ford, *The True George Washington* (Philadelphia, 1896). Worthington C. Ford, *The Spurious Letters Attributed to Washington* (Brooklyn, 1889). Douglas S. Freeman, *Young Washington* (2 vols., New York, 1948). Thomas G. Frothingham, *Washington: Commander in Chief* (Boston, 1930). Paul L. Haworth, *George Washington, Country Gentleman* (Indianapolis, 1925). Rupert Hughes, *George Washington* (3 vols., New York, 1926–1930). Archer W. Hulbert, *Washington and the West* (New York, 1905). Bernhard Knollenberg, *Washington and the Revolution* (New York, 1940). Charles Moore, *The Family Life of George Washington* (Boston, 1926). Louis M. Sears, *George Washington* (New York, 1932). Nathaniel W. Stephenson and Waldo H. Dunn, *George Washington* (2 vols., New York, 1940).

INDEX

Index

ADAMS, JOHN, and Congress, 54–55, 220, 222; a militant, 60, 106, 108; seeks aid for Massachusetts, 86; and creation of army, 87; supports Virginia Resolves, 90; and John Dickinson, 101–102; and Sam Adams, 109; and Richard Henry Lee, 115–116; and George Washington, 122, 123, 203, 270; and John Hancock, 128; and Thomas Lynch, Sr., 129; and Robert Morris, 129; and Benjamin Harrison, 130; and Charles Lee, 148, 173; and General Sullivan, 174–175; for independence, 181; on provincialism, 181; and Thomas Cushing, 196; describes Privateering Act, 200; endorses Lee expedition, 203; his foreign policy, 227

Adams, Samuel, a leader, 49, 50, 53, 60; in Congress, 55–56, 96, 270; and the army, 88; described, 109–111; and treason charge, 112, 153; and Richard Henry Lee, 115, 240; and Arthur Lee, 117; and Josiah Quincy, Jr., 118; and George Washington, 122, 123, 197; peace plans, 123; and Thomas Lynch, Sr., 129; vote on British mail service, 135; and Artemas Ward, 144; and Thomas Cushing, 196; and Elbridge Gerry, 196–197, 199; and Lord Dunmore, 237

Almon, John, 38

Alsop, John, 55, 101

Amherst, General Jeffrey, 41, 224

Antiking resolve, terms, 265, 268; and Pennsylvania, 265, 272–273, 274; and Rhode Island, 266–268; effect, 275, 287

Armstrong, General John, 240, 242, 247, 248, 251

Army, American, created, 87–88; handicaps, 124, 164–165; reforms, 129–130; and Congress, 133; tasks, 134; Washington takes command, 142; militancy, 142–145; code, 164–168; fosters independence, 164, 173, 175, 182–183; southern department, 240; and foreign aid, 226–227, 229

Arnold, Colonel Benedict, 161–162, 289

Ascough, Captain, 130

Athol, Duke of, 5

BALTIMORE, 278

Barre, Colonel Isaac, 41

Barrington, William Wildman Shute, second Viscount, 21, 22, 34

Bedford, John, fourth Duke of, 27, 28, 29–30, 33, 34

Bernard, Sir Francis, 103, 144

Bland, Richard, 92, 256, 260

"Bloomsbury Gang," 34

Boone, Daniel, 79

Boston, "Hutchinson Letters," 17; resistance to Stamp Act, 26; British army in, 49–50, 53; as scapegoat, 83. *See also* Evacuation of Boston

Boston Port Bill, 43, 89

Boston Tea Party, 38, 39, 40, 43

Boundary line for settlement, 75

Braddock, General Edward, 61–62

Braxton, Carter, 256

Britain, society, 3–6, 44; government, 6–7, 12–13, 24–25, 32–33, 115; popular unrest, 8–10, 26–27, 29–30, 31, 33, 116–117; navy, 20, 177; finances, 24–25; party politics, 27–28, 29–30; and France, 35–36, 61–64; India trade, 36–37; commercial policy, 65, 71, 72; western land policy, 74–76; American policies (1775), 82–87; early attitude toward colonies, 103, 105; war plans (1775), 159, 164, 168, 170, 171, 179, 186, 211, 221–222, 236–237, 281–282; slavery, 238; mercenaries, 264. *See also* Proclamation of rebellion

British East India Company. *See* East India Company
Brunswick, Duke of, 264
Brunswick, Ferdinand, Prince of, 20
Bulloch, Archibald, 254
Bunker Hill, battle of, 142, 145, 159, 170
Burgoyne, General John, 48, 82, 264
Burke, Edmund, 33, 34
Burke, Thomas, 246
Burlington, New Jersey, 276
Bute, John Stuart, third Earl of, 103; 114, 130

CAMBRIDGE, MASSACHUSETTS, 142
Cambridge conference, members, 131; meets, 165–168; and navy, 177; and Rhode Island, 193; on privateering, 199; and firearms, 229
Campbell, Lord William, 236
Canada, British acquisition, 24, 75; letters of Congress to, 97, 222. *See also* Quebec expedition
Cape Breton Island, 76
Carter, Landon, 125–127, 257
Carter, Robert, 74
Cary, Robert and Company, 67–69
Catherine the Great, 23
Champlain, Lake, 161, 162
Charleston, South Carolina, opposes tea tax, 84; and plan of Charles Lee, 240, 247; politics, 248–252
Chase, Samuel, 277
Chatham, William Pitt, Earl of, illness, 5, 28–29; and party politics, 27–28, 30, 32, 41; views, 28, 38, 39; inactivity, 34, 115; and "olive branch" petition, 96, 114–115
Chaudière River, 161
Chesterfield, Philip Dormer Stanhope, fourth Earl of, 4
Church, Dr. Benjamin, 166–168
Clark, Reverend Jonas, 50
Clinton, George, 106, 287
Clinton, Sir Henry, 48, 82
Clinton, Colonel James, 288
Clive, Robert Clive, Baron, 5
Coercive Acts. *See* Punitive Acts
Colden, Cadwallader, 47–48
Committee of Secret Correspondence, 228, 231
Common Sense, 208, 218, 219, 260, 263, 269
Conciliation plan of Lord North, 88–89, 113
Conciliationists, 100–106, 115, 135, 227, 231–232
Concord, Massachusetts, 49, 50
Connecticut, and Ticonderoga, 53–54; self-rule, 109; and George Washington, 190–192; Tories, 190–192; Quebec expedition, 192; Lee expedition to New York, 202, 203, 206, 208, 209, 211, 213
Constitution, Fort, 288
Continental Association, 91–92
Continental Congress (First), and Dr. Johnson, 45; Virginia's role, 84, 89–92; measures, 84–85, 91–93; and George Washington, 122–123; and Charles Lee, 147; and Georgia, 252–253
Continental Congress (Second), convenes, 53–55; leaders, 56–67; task, 81–82; condemns Britain, 87; creates army, 87; bills of credit, 88; election of George Washington, 88, 121; rejects North plan, 88; and "olive branch" petition, 95–97; war aims, 95–96, 181, 184–185; and Canada, 96–97, 161–163, 222; conciliationists, 100–106; opinion in, 100, 112, 142, 173, 175, 197, 217, 219, 220, 221, 222; militants, 106–111; moderates, 111–114; and George Washington, 121, 132–136, 212; military strategy, 131; and New York, 137–139, 201, 242, 285–287; and evacuation of Boston, 157, 233; army code, 164–165; Cambridge Conference, 165–168; army hospital, 166; death penalties, 167, 168, 294; proclamation of rebellion, 172; creates navy, 176–178; privateering, 177, 198–199, 233–234; Drummond case, 178–180; and Massachusetts, 183–184, 196–197, 200; and New Hampshire, 187–189; and Georgia, 197, 222, 252–255; and the New England bloc, 197, 222; and

North Carolina, 222; and South Carolina, 222, 248, 251; and Virginia, 222, 238, 270; peace plans, 223–225; foreign aid, 227–232, 234; ban on slave trade, 234; grievances, 238–239; southern department of army, 240–242, 247, 255; Tories, 242–243, 286–287, 293, 294; resolve of May 10, 1776, 264; antiking resolve, 265–268; and Pennsylvania, 265, 270–273; military plans (1776), 266, 271–272, 289; and Rhode Island, 267–268; Hancock's "tyrant letter," 272, 273, 276, 279, 288; Lee resolution, 280, 295–298; Tory plot, 292–294; treason-allegiance resolves, 293–294, 296; votes for independence, 295–296. *See also* Committee of Secret Correspondence, Lee expedition to New York, Secret Committee of Congress
Cooke, Governor Nicholas, at Cambridge conference, 165, 193; views, 192–193; and George Washington, 192, 193, 194, 229, 230, 267, 268
Cooper, Dr. Myles, 149
Counterfeiting, 290, 293
Cruger, Henry, 42
Cumberland, Henry Frederick, Duke of, 6
Cumberland, Fort, 62–64
Curwen, Samuel, 85
Cushing, Thomas, 54, 111, 196, 198

DAGWORTHY, CAPTAIN JOHN, 62–63
Dartmouth, William Legge, Earl of, character, 20; policies, 48–49, 50, 83, 86, 170; and West, 80; on New England, 83
Deane, Silas, and Ticonderoga, 54; in Congress, 96; moderate, 111, 112, 135; and George Washington, 127–128; mission to France, 231, 232, 234
Declaration of Independence, moderates signed, 112, 113; indictment of slave trade, 238; and South Carolina, 252; preliminaries, 270; committee, 281; adopted, 295–297; debated, 296; quoted, 297–298
Delaware, favored by Britain, 87; opposes independence, 262; and independence, 274–275, 295–296
Delaware River, 85, 270
Dickinson, John, and Congress, 56–57; as writer, 60; "olive branch" petition, 96–97, 113; conciliationist, 100; described, 101–103; and George Washington, 124; and foreign affairs, 231; leader in Pennsylvania, 262–264, 269–270, 273
Dinwiddie, Governor Robert, 59, 62–64, 74
Drayton, William Henry, 249–252
Drummond, Thomas (James), Lord, 178–180
Duane, James, 55, 100, 135
Dunmore, John Murray, Earl of Ballendine, as informant, 47; quoted, 73; and George Washington, 78, 235, 239; on resistance in Virginia, 93; takes refuge, 236; proclamation of November, 1775, 237–238; plan of Charles Lee, 240–241; activities, 246, 255–256, 259, 276
Dunmore's War, 80
Duquesne, Fort, 61, 64
Dyer, Eliphalet, 54, 135

EAST INDIA COMPANY, 36–38
Eden, Sir (Governor) Robert, 85, 245, 278
Election of 1774 (Britain), 43
England. *See* Britain
Espionage, 166–168, 193
Evacuation of Boston, 157–158, 233, 257

FAIRFAX, BRYAN, 90
Fairfax, Thomas, sixth Baron, 59
Fairfax Independent Company, 57, 155–156
Fairfax Resolves, 89–93, 238, 269
Falmouth, Maine, 186–188, 193
Florida, 24, 75, 76, 253
Floyd, John, 77
Floyd, William, 55
Flying camps, 240, 271–272, 274
Forbes, Gilbert, 291
Fox, Charles James, 3, 41

France, and Britain, 35–36, 61–64, 232–233; in Ohio Valley, 61–64, 74; American views of France's interest in granting aid, 107, 150, 174, 226–227; American views of need of aid, 199, 241, 295; proposals to seek aid, 218, 232–233, 241, 268; issue of aid to colonies, 226; Deane mission, 231, 232, 234; aid received, 232
Franklin, Benjamin, and "Hutchinson Letters," 17–18, 41; at Second Continental Congress, 56–57; as writer, 60; "olive branch" petition, 96; militancy, 108; agent of Massachusetts, 117; returns to America, 119; and independence, 119–120; and George Washington, 131, 280; Cambridge conference, 165–168; and foreign affairs, 229, 231; independence vote, 296
Franklin, Governor William, 276
French and Indian War. *See* Seven Years' War

Gadsden, Christopher, 106, 141, 242, 249, 250
Gage, General Thomas, as informant, 47–48; begins the war, 49; and Dartmouth, 48–49, 50, 83, 86; urges use of force, 83; on American opinion, 85–86, 154; proclamation against Massachusetts, 112, 153; comment on letter of Thomas Johnson, 114; comment of Gates, 151–152; condemns George Washington, 153, 154, 159–160, 172; complains of independence plot, 160; and Dr. Church, 166; recall, 170–171
Galloway, Joseph, 57; quoted, 109
Gates, General Horatio, and Thomas Johnson, 113–114; and George Washington, 134, 152; and Charles Lee, 151–152; early career, 151; qualifications, 152–153; and independence, 174; in Philadelphia, 270, 271; promoted, 274
George I, 10
George II, 10
George III, brothers, 5–6; character, 10–12; and New England, 24, 44; policies, 24, 41, 42; Stamp Act, 25–26; and Chatham, 28, 96; influence, 34; forecasts war, 35; and France, 35–36; Punitive Acts, 40; and Dr. Johnson, 44; and Gage, 48; and Hutchinson, 48; and George Washington, 169; speech (1775), 217; mercenaries, 264
Georgia, favored by Britain, 87; and Congress, 222; early resistance, 236; described, 252–253; and independence, 252, 255
Germain, Lord George, 20–21, 34, 170
Germans, 263, 264
Gerry, Elbridge, and George Washington, 123, 197, 198; and Congress, 196, 197, 222; and Sam Adams, 196, 197, 199; and Privateering Act, 199–200; and South Carolina, 250; and independence, 281, 293
Gibbon, Edward, 44
Gloucester, Duke of, 5–6
Government (American), transition from colony to state, in Massachusetts, 183–184; in New Hampshire, 187–189; in Virginia, 238; in South Carolina, 248–252
Gower, Lord, 30, 34, 42–43
Grafton, Augustus Henry, third Duke of, 4, 29–30, 32
Graves, Admiral Samuel, 130
Great Britain. *See* Britain
Greene, General Nathanael, early career, 143; quoted, 174, 193; and George Washington, 291, 295
Grenville, George, Whig leader, 27, 28, 34; and Stamp Act, 26; death, 33; and George III, 41
Gwinnett, Button, 255

Halifax, North Carolina, 245–246
Hall, Lyman, 255
Hanau, Count of, 264
Hancock, John, in Massachusetts, 49, 50, 53, 82; and Congress, 55–56, 87; on American army, 88; moderate, 111, 112, 196; treason charge, 112, 153; and George Washington, 128, 180, 214, 239, 294; and John Adams, 128; and Harrison, 196; and Charles Lee, 210; and Joseph Reed, 217; joins mili-

tants, 222; "tyrant letter," 272, 273, 276, 279, 288
Hanoverians, 264
Harrison, Benjamin, and George Washington, 85, 92, 130–131, 210, 270; views, 85, 130; moderate, 111, 112–113, 174; Cambridge conference, 165–168; and Hancock, 196; mission to New York, 210; and Joseph Reed, 217; joins militants, 222; and foreign affairs, 231
Heath, General William, 143, 144
Henry, Patrick, as orator, 60, 69; and George Washington, 92, 242; militant, 106; military command, 141, 142; opposes slavery, 238; and Charles Lee, 260
Hesse-Cassel, Landgrave of, 264
Hessians, 264, 269
Hewes, Joseph, 111
Hickey, Thomas, 290, 291, 292, 294
Holland, 36, 37, 232, 245
Hooper, William, 111
Hopkins, Stephen, 268
Horne, Reverend John, 42
Howe, Richard, Viscount, 224
Howe, General Robert, 240, 245–246, 260
Howe, Sir William, comes to Boston, 48, 82; assumes command, 170–171; and Falmouth, 186–187; measures, 189
Hutchinson, Thomas, on English society, 4, 5; and Benjamin Franklin, 17–18; as informant, 47–48; and George III, 48; influence, 103; on British opinion, 164
"Hutchinson Letters," 17–18

INDEPENDENCE, sentiment for, 98–99, 106–108, 114, 159–160, 223; and parties, 101–114; reasons for delay, 102–104 (bond with England), 104–106, 125–127, 262–263 (fear of democracy), 104, 237, 249, 256, 271, 278 (fear of retaliation), 181–183, 235 (difficulty of securing united action), 223 (British peace moves), 226 (uncertainty of foreign aid); views on independence, 113 (Thomas Johnson), 119–120 (Franklin), 125–127 (Landon Carter), 128–129 (Robert Morris), 173–174, 194–195, 204, 207 (Charles Lee), 174 (Gates), 174 (Greene), 174 (Sullivan), 199 (Gerry), 218, 219, 232 (Stephen Moylan), 218–219 (George Washington), 295 (Richard Henry Lee); issues bearing on, 135, 185–186; role of army, 142, 164, 173, 175, 182–183; Washington proclaims popular sovereignty, 154; Washington's address to Canadians, 162; death penalty authorized, 167–168; Proclamation of Rebellion, 172; creation of navy, 177–178; new governments, 183–184, 187–189, 238, 248; allegiance and loyalty, 185–186, 189–192, 194–195, 204, 211, 293; action towards, 186–190 (New Hampshire), 190–192 (Connecticut), 192–195 (Rhode Island), 196–200 (Massachusetts), 244 (North Carolina), 247 (South Carolina), 252 (Georgia), 255 (Virginia), 265 (Pennsylvania), 274 (Delaware), 275 (New Jersey), 278 (Maryland), 281 (New York); privateering, 198–200, 233–234; Prohibitory Act, 221; Congress invites Canada to join union, 222; foreign aid, 226–227, 231–234; foreign trade, 226, 229–234; campaign in the South, 235–236, 239, 247–248, 255–261; campaign in middle colonies, 262; effect of Hessians, 264–265. *See also Common Sense,* Declaration of Independence, Lee expedition, Lee resolution
India. *See* East India Company
Industrial Revolution, 10
Ireland, 20
Iroquois, 145, 149, 169, 271

JAY, JOHN, at Second Continental Congress, 56, 96; conciliationist, 100; on foreign affairs, 231; and George Washington, 291
Jefferson, Thomas, at Second Continental Congress, 56; as writer, 60; militancy, 106; comment on Harrison, 113; absence from Congress, 220; opposes slave trade, 238; and Declara-

tion of Independence, 270, 296; and Thomas Nelson, 209
Jenkinson, Charles, 14, 34
Johnson, Dr. Samuel, 44–46, 238
Johnson, Thomas, moderate, 111; and George Washington, 113, 129, 279; letter on "olive branch" petition, 113–114; as general, 279
Johnson, William S., quoted, 26–27, 32–33
Johnston, Samuel, 245
Junius, 32, 42, 117

Kanawha River, 77–80
Kennebec River, 161, 162
King's College, 282
King's Friends, and George III, 11; influence, 27, 32–33, 34, 43, 118–120; and Wilkes, 31; attitude toward colonies, 34, 47–48, 105; policies, 35, 37, 40–41, 47–49, 83–86, 88–89

Langdon, John, 106, 135
Laurens, Henry, quoted, 4
Lebanon, Connecticut, 190, 191, 192
Lee, Arthur, Dr., career, 116–118; and Sam Adams, 117, 118; and William Temple, 223; agent of Congress, 228
Lee, General Charles, and Benjamin Harrison, 130; on powers of George Washington, 136; early career, 145–147; and George Washington, 147–148, 257, 259; appointed major general, 148; qualifications, 148–149; views of the conflict, 149–150; and Gates, 151–152; and John Adams, 173; and Richard Henry Lee, 173; and Robert Morris, 173; and Benjamin Rush, 173; and Edward Rutledge, 173; urges independence, 173; Rhode Island expedition, 194–195; plans for New York, 207, 210–211, 216, 242; on *Common Sense,* 208; ordered to Canada, 212; plan for the South, 239–240; given Southern command, 240; and France, 241, 245, 260; and the Tories, 241; in Philadelphia, 242; and Governor Eden, 245; and North Carolina, 245–247; and Virginia, 245, 255–260; and South Carolina, 247–248; and General Moultrie, 248; and John Rutledge, 248; and Patrick Henry, 260. *See also* Lee expedition to New York
Lee, Richard Henry, and George Washington, 85, 92, 115, 122, 124, 131, 173, 239, 270, 280; militancy, 106, 108, 135, 197; described, 115–116; and Charles Lee, 173, 240; and Congress, 173, 220, 222; and Joseph Reed, 217; opposes slavery, 238; independence campaign, 240, 244, 255, 257, 258; and Sam Adams, 240; and J. A. Washington, 257, 258; introduces Lee Resolution, 280; on need of foreign aid, 295
Lee, William, 116, 117
Lee expedition to New York, genesis, 202; and independence, 203–204, 207–209, 218; preparations, 203–204; Tories, 204–205, 208, 211, 241; and Congress, 205–207, 210, 212–215; and New York authorities, 205–207; Lee's dilemma, 206; role of George Washington, 206, 208–216; defense plans, 210–211; Lee's acts, 211; Lee rebuked, 212–213; outcome, 212–213, 214–216
Lee Resolution, text, 280–281, 298; adopted, 295, 296; and New York, 297
Letters from a Farmer in Pennsylvania, 56, 102
"Letters of Junius," 32, 42
Lewis, General Andrew, appointed, 240; and George Washington, 242, 258; at Williamsburg, 260, 261
Lewis, Fielding, quoted, 260
Lexington, battle of, events, 50–53; influence, 81–82, 269
Lexington, Kentucky, 53
Livingston, Philip, 55, 111, 291
Livingston, Robert R., 100, 135
Livingston, William, 111
Long Island, 211, 213, 216
Loudoun, Lord, 63
Louisiana, 75
Lowndes, Rawlins, 249
Lynch, Micha, 290, 292
Lynch, Thomas, Sr., and George Wash-

ington, 90, 129–130, 131, 166, 178–179; moderate, 111, 174; character, 129; Cambridge conference, 165–168; and Drummond case, 178–179; mission to New York, 210; on opinion in New York, 212; and Joseph Reed, 217

McIntosh, Colonel Lachlan, 254
McKean, Thomas, 274, 275
Mackenzie, Frederick, quoted, 52
Mackenzie, Captain Robert, 122–123
Magaw, Colonel Robert, 272
Mansfield, William Murray, Baron, libel cases, 9, 16–17, 32; career, 14–17; party politics, 29–30; position, 34, 103, 130; influence, 114
Marshall, Christopher, quoted, 88, 271
Martin, Governor Josiah, 236, 244
Maryland, public opinion, 85; British Trade Act, 87; conciliation, 101, 262; military measures, 147; described, 277–278; independence, 278–279, 281, 295
Mason, George, and Ohio Company, 74; Fairfax Resolves, 90–93, 269; and George Washington, 92; independent companies, 92–93; opposes slave trade, 238; views, 258
Massachusetts, and "Hutchinson Letters," 17–18; Punitive Acts, 40–41, 84; declared to be in rebellion, 48–49, 112; provincial congress, 49; brands Britain as aggressor, 81; army, 82; seeks aid, 82, 86; as scapegoat, 83–86, 108; accused of seeking independence, 98; agents in England, 117; and George Washington, 122–123, 198–199; case of Dr. Church, 166–168; and independence, 167–168, 181, 196–200; new government, 183; and Congress, 196–197, 200, 222; Privateering Act, 198–200
"Massacre of St. George's Fields," 22, 30–31
Matthews, David, 291–292
Middle colonies, oppose independence, 223, 244; independence campaign, 262
Middleton, Henry, 111
Mifflin, Thomas, and George Washington, 128; in Pennsylvania politics, 269, 270, 271; promoted, 274
Militants, leaders and views, 106–111, 135; sources of information in England, 115–120; and George Washington, 121–124, 219; and France, 174; strength, 197; gain control in Congress, 221; campaign for independence, 235–236; and the South, 240–248, 255–261; and middle colonies, 244, 262–265, 272–279
Milnor, William, 93
Moderates, leaders and views, 111–114, 115, 127, 135; influence, 112; join militants, 113; and George Washington, 127–131, 219
Montgomery, Fort, 288
Montgomery, General Richard, 163
Montreal, 161, 162, 205, 289
Moore, General James, 240, 245
Moores Creek Bridge, battle of, 244, 245
Morris, Gouverneur, 290, 291
Morris, Robert, moderate, 111, 128; and George Washington, 129; and John Adams, 129; and Charles Lee, 173, 204, 207, 212, 241; and Joseph Reed, 217; and foreign affairs, 227, 229, 231; independence vote, 296
Morton, John, 296
Moultrie, General William, 248
Moylan, Stephen, and George Washington, 176, 218, 232; supervises fleet, 176; and Charles Lee, 204; urges independence, 218; on foreign aid, 232; promoted, 274

Navigation Acts, 226, 228, 234
Navy, American, origins, 131, 175–178, 198; operations, 176
Negotiated peace, and Sam Adams, 123; role of Howe, 170–171; Drummond case, 178–180; Prohibitory Act, 223; Temple case, 223–224; and George Washington, 271
Nelson, Thomas (Ohio Company), 74
Nelson, Thomas, delegate, 209
New Bern, North Carolina, 236, 244
New England, charges against, 49;

British Trade Act, 82, 84; militancy, 108; self-government, 109, 112; and George Washington, 123; and New York, 140, 282; and independence, 186, 295; political unit, 186; and Congress, 197. *See also* Cambridge conference
New Hampshire, early resistance, 143; Quebec expedition, 161–162, 190; and George Washington, 186–190; new government, 187–189
New Hampshire Grants. *See* Vermont
New Jersey, British Trade Act, 87; independence, 275–276, 295
New York (province), favored by Britain, 87; defenses, 88, 242; conciliation, 101, 104–105, 138–139, 262; politics, 104–105, 137–138, 281–284; military importance, 137–138, 169, 203; described, 139–140, 282–283; and New England, 140, 282; Quebec expedition, 160–163; open to attack, 201, 216, 282–283; opposition to Lee oath, 212–213; public opinion, 216; and independence, 281, 288–297; British warships, 284–285; Continental battalions, 285–287; provincial congress (1776), 287–289, 290–291, 296; election (June 1776), 287–288, 297; Tories, 290–291, 294, 296; arrival of British army, 294–295. *See also* Lee expedition to New York
New York (town), and Lexington-Concord, 53; in May 1775, 54; opposes tea tax, 84; open to attack, 104; public opinion, 211–212
Newport, Rhode Island, 193–195
Nicholas, Robert Carter, 256, 257
North, Frederick, second Earl of Guilford, attack on, 4; and George III, 6, 35, 42, 43–44; character, 13–14; offices, 30, 34; and tea tax, 38; motion declaring Massachusetts in rebellion, 48; conciliation plan, 88–89, 113
North Carolina, favored by Britain, 87; and Congress, 222; early resistance, 236; and the army, 240; described, 244; independence, 244–247, 251, 270
Nova Scotia, 76

OATH OF LOYALTY, in Connecticut, 191; in Rhode Island, 194–195, 204; in New York, 211; resolve of Congress, 212, 213, 242
Ohio Company, 74
Ohio River, 73–80
"Olive branch" petition, adopted, 95–97; Harrison's comment, 113; described by Thomas Johnson, 113–114; rejected, 170
Oliver, Andrew, 17
Otis, James, 60

PACA, WILLIAM, 278, 295
Paine, Robert Treat, 54, 55, 196
Paine, Thomas, 208, 263
Parliament, 6–8, 31, 43
Parsons, Nancy, 4
Pendleton, Edmund, 124, 256, 257, 260
Penet, Pierre, 229
Pennsylvania, British Trade Act, 87; conciliation, 101, 104–105, 262, 264, 270; politics, 104–105, 128, 262–264; and George Washington, 128, 269–272; and independence, 265, 269–274, 296; and Delaware, 274–275
Pennsylvania Evening Post, 241, 296
Percy, Hugh, Earl, 50 51
Philadelphia, in May 1775, 55; public opinion, 82; opposes tea tax, 84; military reviews, 87–88, 270–271; open to attack, 104; politics, 105, 264, 269–270, 272–273; Drummond case, 178–180; and Charles Lee, 269; military associators, 269–272; visit of George Washington, 270–272
Pitt, Fort, 64
Pitt, William. *See* Chatham
Pliarne, Emanuel de, 229, 230
Point Pleasant, battle of, 80
Pontiac's Conspiracy, 24
Portsmouth, New Hampshire, 156, 188
Portsmouth, Virginia, 259
Prince Edward Island, 76
Privateering, 176, 177, 198–200, 233
Privy Council, 17–18, 74
Proclamation of Rebellion, provisions, 169; and Britain's war plans, 171; reply of Congress, 172; effects, 174, 228

Prohibitory Act, terms of, 221; effects, 221, 240, 250
Providence, Rhode Island, 193, 194, 267
Punitive Acts, 40, 43, 84
Putnam, General Israel, 53, 143–145

QUAKERS, 102, 263
Quebec Act, 78, 80
Quebec expedition, origins, 160–163; reinforcements, 190, 192; effect in New York, 205; defeats, 289
Quincy, Edmund, 156
Quincy, Josiah, Jr., 118–119

RALEIGH TAVERN, 89
Randolph, Peyton, 92, 128, 257
Read, George, 275
Rebellion. *See* Treason
Reed, Joseph, on treason, 81; on Congress, 84, 217; and George Washington, 128, 163, 217–218, 230, 239, 273, 274, 280; and Greene, 143; and Putnam, 144; on British opinion, 159; on Lee expedition, 215; and Congress leaders, 217; and Moylan, 218; and Tom Paine, 218; on peace plan, 225; evacuation of Boston, 233; on the South, 241; in politics, 263, 269, 273; and New Jersey, 276
Revolution of 1688, 10, 102
Rhode Island, self-rule, 109; military plans, 143; and George Washington, 192–195, 266–268; and independence, 192–195, 266, 268; Tories, 192–195; Lee expedition to, 194–195
Richmond, Duke of, 7
Rigby, Richard, 34
Robertson, General James, 179–180
Rockingham, Marquis of, and Stamp Act, 25–26; as Whig leader, 27, 28, 34; resigns, 41
Rodney, Caesar, 275, 296
Rush, Benjamin, 173
Russia, 23
Rutledge, Edward, moderate, 111; and Charles Lee, 173, 240, 241, 245, 248; and independence, 296
Rutledge, John, 111, 248–250

SACKVILLE, SIR GEORGE. *See* Germain
St. Augustine, Florida, 253
St. George's Fields, 22, 30–31
St. John, Fort, 161
Sandwich, Earl of, 19–20
Savannah, Georgia, 236, 253–255
Schuyler, Philip, moderate, 111; and George Washington, 137–138, 140–141; commands in New York, 137–141, 201, 212; views, 138, 155; and New England, 140–141; Quebec expedition, 160–163; on foreign aid, 233
Scotland, 15, 17
Scott, John Morin, 288, 290
Sears, Captain Isaac, 204–205, 211
Secret Committee of Congress, 228, 230, 231
Seven Years' War, effect on England 3, 24; service of George Washington, 59, 61–64; and Virginia politics, 116; service of Charles Lee, 146
Sharpe, Governor Horatio, 62
Shawnee Indians, 79–80
Shee, Captain John, 272
Shelburne, William, Earl of, 7–8, 41
Sherman, Roger, 54, 100, 106, 108
Shippen, Dr. William, 122, 124
Shirley, Governor William, 62
Slave revolts, 46, 237, 238, 239, 241, 248, 256
Slave trade, 19, 234, 238
Slavery, 238–239, 296
Smith, Lieutenant Colonel Francis, 50
South, the, militancy, 222; as a political unit, 236; British war plans, 236–237; Dunmore's policy, 237–238; social divisions, 237, 242, 248–249, 253, 256, 257, 260; plan of Charles Lee, 239; and the army, 240; independence campaign, 240–243, 244–248, 255–261
South Carolina, British Trade Act, 87; moderates, 111; and Congress, 222, 240, 248; early resistance, 236; and independence, 247–252, 296; politics, 248–249; and Georgia, 252, 254
Spain, 232
Stamford, Connecticut, 54, 209
Stamp Act, views of British leaders, 14,

15–16, 19, 23, 28, 34; history of, 24–26, 34, 84; and George Washington, 70
Stormont, Lord, 36
Strictures on a Pamphlet . . . (by Charles Lee), 149–150
Suffolk, Earl of, 22–23, 34
Suffolk County, New York, 290
Sullivan, General John, militancy, 106; leaves Philadelphia, 141; early career, 143; Cambridge conference, 165; urges independence, 174–175; mission to Portsmouth, 188–189

Taxation no Tyranny, 44–46, 238
Tea Act (1773), 36–38
Temple, William, 223–224
Thurlow, Edward, 18–19, 34, 98
Ticonderoga, 53–54, 161, 163
Tilghman, Matthew, 277
Tobacco trade, 65–70
Tories, a small group, 154; George Washington's first action, 154, 188–189; and independence, 185–186; in New Hampshire, 188; Connecticut laws, 190–192; in Rhode Island, 192, 193–195; and plan of Charles Lee, 240; policy of Congress, 242–243; in Virginia, 245, 256–259; in Pennsylvania, 272; and George Washington, 290–294, 296. *See also* Lee expedition to New York; Tory Plot
Tory Plot, 291–294
Townshend duties, 26, 36–38, 70
Treason (against America), Church case, 166–168; Connecticut laws, 190–192; Rhode Island laws, 192–193, 266–268; loyalty oath, 194–195, 211; Congress and Tories, 242–243; Tory Plot, 291–292; treason-allegiance resolves, 293–294
Treason (against Britain), Massachusetts declared to be in rebellion, 48–49, 153; American leaders aware of exposure to punishment, 54, 81, 112–113, 174–175, 188, 271; British charges against colonial leaders, 83, 85, 97–98, 110, 169–170; British law, 97–98; Prohibitory Act, 98, 221–222; punishment for, 99; Gage-Washington letters, 153–154; Proclamation of Rebellion, 169–170; as deterrent to independence, 182–183, 271; speech of George III, 217; Dunmore's policy, 238
Trumbull, Governor Jonathan, 53–54, 190–192, 203
Tryon, Governor William, and George Washington, 136, 214; visits New York, 138; activities, 201, 211, 281–282; influence, 214–215; and Tory Plot, 291
Tupper, Colonel Benjamin, 285
"Tyrant letter" of Hancock, 272, 273, 276, 279, 288

UNITED STATES, first use of term, 232; second, 261; third, 293–294

VAN, CHARLES, 42
Vergennes, Comte de, 231
Vermont, 140, 282
Virginia, in Seven Years' War, 61–64, 116; tobacco trade, 65–71; and the West, 73–80; and Congress, 83, 92, 222, 240; opposes Britain, 84, 89–94, 236; British Trade Act, 87; independence movement, 125–127, 255–261; Dunmore's policy, 237–238; plan of Charles Lee, 240; and George Washington, 257–261; independence resolves, 270, 273, 276, 288

WALDEGRAVE, LADY, 5–6
Walpole, Horace, 3, 4, 5, 14, 48
Walpole, Sir Robert, 27
Ward, General Artemas, 142–144
Ward, Samuel, 174
Warren, Mrs. Mercy, quoted, 200
Washington, George, relations with contemporaries, 47, 93–94 (G. W. Fairfax), 61–62 (Braddock), 62–63 (Dagworthy), 62–64 (Dinwiddie), 63 (Loudoun), 78, 235, 239 (Dunmore), 90 (Bryan Fairfax), 92 (Bland), 92, 128, 257 (Randolph), 124 (Pendleton), 125–127 (Landon Carter), 165 (Sullivan), 166–167 (Church), 178–180 (Drummond), 190–192, 203 (Trumbull), 204 (Sears), 224, 257–259, 271 (J. A. Washington), 254

(McIntosh), 272 (Magaw), 272 (Shee), 275 (McKean), 275 (Rodney), 285 (Tupper), 287 (George Clinton), 288 (James Clinton), 288 (Scott), 290 (Gouverneur Morris), 291 (Philip Livingston). (*See also* entries under John Adams, Sam Adams, Cooke, Dickinson, Deane, Benjamin Franklin, Gage, Gates, George III, Gerry, Greene, Hancock, Harrison, Henry, Jay, Thomas Johnson, Charles Lee, R. H. Lee, Thomas Lynch, Sr., Andrew Lewis, Mason, Mifflin, Robert Morris, Moylan, Reed, Schuyler.)

appearance, 57; arrives at Second Continental Congress, 57; uniform, 57, 94; character, 58–59, 156–157; early life, 58–59; nativism, 58, 61; militancy, 60–61, 85, 108; trade with Britain, 60, 65–70; early troubles with British officials, 61–64; trip to Boston, 62; as a tobacco planter, 65–70; manufactures goods at Mount Vernon, 70–71; Stamp Act, 70, 94; Townshend duties, 70; develops fishing industry, 71–72; produces wheat, 72; western projects, 72–80; Ohio Company, 74; elected to army command, 88, 121, 123; Fairfax Resolves, 89–93; views of the conflict, 89, 94–95, 107, 122–123, 171–172, 173; organizes independent military companies, 92–94; reputation in England, 93–94; and militants in Congress, 121–124, 131, 269–271; supported by Congress, 121, 131, 219; military strategy, 122–123, 131, 138, 160–161, 163–164, 175–176, 266; relations with the colonies, 122–123, 198–199 (Massachusetts), 128, 269–272 (Pennsylvania), 138–139, 202, 281, 283–296 (New York), 186, 215–216 (New England), 186–190 (New Hampshire), 190–192 (Connecticut), 192–195, 266–268 (Rhode Island), 224–225, 257–261 (Virginia), 254 (Georgia), 276 (New Jersey), 279 (Maryland); army affairs, 124, 137, 142–143, 164–165; and conciliationists, 125–127, 271; and moderates, 127–131; aims, 132–133, 157–158, 242; powers, 133–136, 176, 202–203, 215; respect for Congress, 133, 214; working agreement with Congress, 134; emergency actions, 135; first New York visit, 138, 201–202; condemned by Gage, 153–154, 157, 159–160; views on popular sovereignty, 154, 157, 172, 188; and the Tories, 154, 181, 185–186, 188–189, 190–191, 192, 194–195, 272, 290–294, 296; popular leader, 155–158, 269, 283; evacuation of Boston, 157, 233; acts on basis of independence, 159; influenced by news from England, 159, 164, 168, 169, 217, 218; Quebec expedition, 159–164; relations with Canada, 159–164, 289; address to Canadians, 162, 163, 222; Cambridge conference, 165–168; approves death penalties, 167–168; opposes peace plan, 171–172, 224–225, 257, 271; leadership for independence, 173, 175, 182–183, 185–186, 217–219; starts navy, 175–178; Drummond case, 178–180; and new governments, 184; loyalty oath, 191, 192, 194–195, 204; and privateering, 198–199, 233–234; favors foreign trade, 229–234; Penet and Pliarne, 229, 230; Deane mission, 232–233; opposes slave trade, 238; southern campaign for independence, 257–261; favors frequent elections, 262, 269; antiking resolve, 265–268; *Common Sense,* 269; trip to Philadelphia, 270–272, 280, 288, 290; political methods, 283, 287; reports British forces at New York, 294–295. *See also* Lee expedition to New York

Washington, John Augustine, 224, 257–259, 271

Washington, Lawrence, 64

Washington, Lund, 156

Waterbury, Colonel David, 213

Weare, Meshech, 189–190

Wedderburn, Alexander, 17–18, 34, 41

Wentworth, Governor John, 143

West, the, land and settlement, 72–80; and independence, 107–108

West Indies, trade, 72
Weymouth, Lord, 4, 30–31, 34
Wheatley, Phillis, 156
Whigs, before 1763, 11, 27; factions, 27–28; leaders, 33–34
White Plains, New York, 297
Wilkes, John, early career, 8–9, 32; and Sandwich, 19; "Massacre of St. George's Fields," 22, 30, 31; Middlesex election, 31; decline of influence, 33; and Arthur Lee, 117
Williamsburg, Virginia, 236, 245, 247, 255, 258, 260–261
Willing, Thomas, 128, 135, 296
Wilson, James, 56, 111, 296
Winchester, Virginia, 63, 64, 77
Woodfall, Henry S., 32, 42
Wordsworth, William, 103
Wright, Sir (Governor) James, 236, 252–254

Zubly, Dr. John J., 101, 253